THE MAKING OF URBAN SCOTLAND

CROOM HELM HISTORICAL GEOGRAPHY SERIES
Edited by R.A. Butlin

THE DEVELOPMENT OF THE IRISH TOWN
Edited by R.A. Butlin

THE MAKING OF URBAN SCOTLAND
I.H. Adams

THE MAKING OF URBAN SCOTLAND

Ian H. Adams

CROOM HELM LONDON

McGILL-QUEEN'S UNIVERSITY PRESS
Montreal 1978

© 1978 Ian H. Adams
Croom Helm Ltd, 2—10 St John's Road, London SW11

British Library Cataloguing in Publication Data

Adams, Ian Hugh
   The making of urban Scotland.
   1. Cities and towns — Scotland — History
   I. Title
   941.1'00973'2   HT133

   ISBN 0-85664-518-4

McGill-Queen's University Press
1020 Pine Avenue West, Montreal H3A 1A2

ISBN 0-7735-0329-3

Legal deposit 2nd quarter 1978

Bibliotheque Nationale du Quebec

Printed and bound in Great Britain by
REDWOOD BURN LIMITED
Trowbridge & Esher

CONTENTS

'. . . a city is more than a place in space, it is a drama in time.
Though the claim of geography be fundamental, our interest in the
history of the city is supremely greater . . .

Patrick Geddes 1905

To Judy and Christopher

ACKNOWLEDGEMENTS

This book could not have been written without help from several institutions and many individuals. The Keeper of the Records of Scotland, and his staff in the Scottish Record Office, have my heartfelt appreciation for their constant support, as do Professors Wreford Watson and Terry Coppock for the encouragement in the long task of unearthing from the archives the hidden story of Scotland's historical geography.

I have had the pleasure of discussing the work with many individuals, including George Barbour, Sheila Coppock, B. Y. Dodd, Colin Johnston, Charles Somerville, Geoffrey Stell, Liz Thoms and Ian Wyhte. I thank them all for giving me their time and knowledge.

Above all others I must thank Meredyth Somerville and Mary Young for giving unstinting labour and steadfast encouragement in the production of this book. Meredyth has again turned her bibliographic skills to a major task and provided the stimulus to bring the work to fruition, while Mary's cheerfulness lightened many a day of correcting rough drafts.

The illustrations from the Scottish Record Office are published with the approval of the Keeper of the Records of Scotland. I would also like to thank the owners of plans also in the custody of the Scottish Record Office: the Marquis of Zetland, the Earl of Eglinton and Winton and Messers. Shepherd and Wedderburn, WS, Edinburgh. Other items are published by permission of the Controller of HM Stationery Office. G. B. Arrington's photographs are but a few of a splendid portfolio taken by this American town planner. The numerous diagrams were so skilfully drawn by Ray Harris and his team of cartographers in the Department of Geography, University of Edinburgh. Permission for photographs was kindly given by: Aerofilms Ltd; John Bartholomew (dust jacket); John Dewar Studio; East Kilbride Development Corporation; New Lanark Conservation Trust; *The Scotsman*; Scottish Record Office; C. Somerville.

Lastly to my wife - my thanks for her patience.

Ian Adams, 1977

Edinburgh Corporation accepts no responsibility . . . (Photo: G.B. Arrington.)

PREFACE

On a grey November evening as a fresher at Edinburgh, tired by the grind at standard texts in the stuffy and rather decrepit vastness of the Upper Library in the Old Quad, I idly lifted a volume entitled *The Making of the English Landscape*, to have revealed from the pen of W.G. Hoskins a language of landscape. The closing bell came all too soon — down stone stairs, across the dimly lit quad and out on to the deserted Bridges — for me landscape had taken on a new meaning.

Two of the themes of Hoskins' great work are taken up in a Scottish context. First, that the landscape is a living document on which past ages have made a virtually indelible impression. Our life today and tomorrow cannot be isolated from the past; rather we have to carry both the material and cultural baggage of the past into the future. Secondly, I have tried, like Hoskins, to redress prevalent distortions: in this case the historical preoccupation with Mary Queen of Scots and Bonnie Prince Charlie, and the geographical preoccupation with the Highlands. The story of where and how ordinary people lived has been largely ignored. As for the Highlands, it is hard to find a rational explanation for the continued emphasis on this marginal region. Just over four-fifths of Scotland's population live in the Lowlands. Within that area, more people live in Airdrie than in the whole of the Highlands! If Scotland really wants to establish her social priorities, she should look no further than the living conditions of her city dwellers, particularly in the West Central Belt. The Scots are an urban people, whose rural links have been severed for almost two hundred years. In the rapid progress of agricultural revolution a large part of the population was released from rural existence. Freed from their fermtouns, Scots migrated to towns and cities to man the factories springing up in the industrial revolution and, indeed, it was the very speed and success of this transformation that led to the unhappy problems of Scottish city life. Yet we need no longer think these problems are insoluble: technical and administrative solutions exist which, if properly applied, could transform the urban situation. Some have had a certain amount of success — the new towns, overspill agreements and the swinging back of the centre of economic activity to the east coast — but others, such as the huge housing estates and the mania for high-rise flats, have not been successful and have produced new problems. At a time when we are becoming more conscious of the blunders of the past 150 years as well as of the possibilities for the future it behoves us to understand how urban Scotland came into being.

Department of Geography   Ian H. Adams
University of Edinburgh
High School Yards

For anyone bred and brought up to town life, the noise and bustle, cobble and pavement, tall building, and dark corner are part and parcel of daily life, as familiar as Brer Rabbit's briar patch. But the town is a place of ideas where every day one rubs shoulders with strangers; it is not a closed world of set-piece opinions like those found around the table of a village pub. The very existence of towns has led men to question the ideas of the origin, causes and consequences of their development. This is not a parochial question, but one of worldwide consequence.

The original components of a city, according to Lewis Mumford, consisted of a citadel, a shrine, a spring and a market. Urban civilisation, he suggests, is pervaded by that peculiar combination of creativity and control, of expression and repression, of tension and release, whose outward manifestation has been the historic city. Early cities did not grow beyond walking distance or hearing distance, for it was necessary to hear the gossip at the well, the proclamations at the tron, to engage in the business of the market, both farming and commerce, and to hear the church bells calling people to arms or to worship. The distinction between village and town was made not only by the increase in the built-up area and population but also by the numbers that could be brought under unified control to form a highly differentiated community.[1] At its widest, no medieval town extended more than half a mile from the centre. It was limited by water and food supplies, by municipal and guild ordinances which prevented the uncontrolled settlement of outsiders, and by the limitations of transport and communications.

United Nations population studies say that today there is no clear-cut dichotomy between town and country: ' . . . the distribution is not really a twofold one, in which one part of the population is wholly rural and the other wholly urban, but a graduated distribution along a continuum from the least urban to the most urban, or from the least rural to the most rural. Consequently, the line that is drawn between urban and rural for statistical or census purposes is necessarily arbitrary.'[2] Nevertheless the distinction between town and country is necessary, especially in Scotland whose urban history is so different from that of England. This distinction can be seen immediately in the need for political and administrative control wherever even rudimentary economic organisation is required. In pre-industrial times, burgesses continually tried to exclude foreigners from their towns, and at a higher level, the royal burghs objected to the development of non-royal burghs because of the threat to their monopoly.

It has been said that 'towns are agglomerations of dwellings, a majority of whose inhabitants are not engaged in producing food',[3] but this definition would fit a two-rowed mining village as well as the city of Glasgow. The definition of a town is so complex that it cannot be accomplished in one definitive sentence. Four main aspects must be considered: the physical structure and use of space; the legal identity, derived from charters and laws, giving it a separate and often privileged position in society; the economic structure that gives it a function in society; and lastly the relationship with the surrounding countryside or trading zone. An examination of any town over a long period will reveal a continuously changing balance and emphasis of these factors, making it virtually impossible to cover it with a single definition. In broad terms, one can recognize two major periods of town development in Scotland. The medieval town, which was essentially a trading centre in a largely rural society, is quite easily identified. After the profound changes that began in the second half of the eighteenth century the distinction became less clear. From then on it is probably better to relinquish the idea of the town and adopt the concept of the urban centre, defined as any place in which most people are employed in non-rural pursuits.

Which was the first Scottish town? This is a matter of speculation, for archaeologists have long sought evidence of proto-urban centres. From prehistoric times we have been bequeathed Scara Brae in Orkney, a cluster of seven self-contained huts connected by covered alleys. This splendid site is not unique, for similar settlements have been discovered at Rinyo on Rousay and Jarlshof at the southern tip of Shetland. The lack of wood forced the occupants to use stone for building, leaving to posterity a perfect picture of their material culture. One cannot find urban origins therein: their existence was one of bare rural subsistence in a northern clime.

The Romans came to Scotland but they too failed to found towns. Their occupation of Caledonia was never deep rooted nor did it last long. Southern Scotland was left in the hands of the native Celts so that the villas and farms common in southern Britain are absent. Archaeological investigations are far from complete so that large-scale settlements may yet be found. Tribal centres (*oppida*) are known to have been in existence by the time of the Roman occupation. Traprain Law, the tribal centre of the Votadini situated on top of a basaltic hill in East Lothian, was permitted to continue its existence under the Romans. Partial excavation of Traprain Law has unearthed a hoard of Roman silver and a great mass of native material indicating that the site was occupied for about a thousand years from the middle of the first millenium B.C., with a possible break in occupation some time after the end of the first century A.D. and a final desertion in the mid-fifth century.

It has been suggested that there were three or four sets of defensive works surrounding an area of 16 hectares. The inhabitants were agriculturalists, stock breeders and metal workers who traded with the south by the east coast route. Traprain was probably a very important place in Scotland and north-east England for if the Votadini had a pact with the Romans it has a unique place as a 'free' British town in Roman times[4] when no native centre of power was tolerated which seemed likely to become a focus of trouble. For example it appears that the *oppidum* of the Selgovae on Eildon Hill North (Roman *Trimontium*) was dismantled. North of Hadrian's Wall lay a buffer zone which was too insecure to support urban life. The occupation forces built a series of forts along the Antonine Wall, signal stations in Strathmore, ports at Cramond and Inveresk and some isolated forts in the Borders, but none emerged later as a significant urban centre. Only at Carriden where the Antonine Wall reached the Firth of Forth is there direct proof of a small settlement, a *vicus,* of a civil nature outside the fort.[5]

In a pastoral society meeting places were frequently on the remote borders of territories. K. A. Steer has suggested from evidence in the Roman road-books that there were seven such meeting places for the administration of justice and the holding of markets; but only four can be tentatively identified. *Taba* or *Tava* for the Tay, *Selgoes* and *Damnonii* presumably lay respectively within the territories of the Selgovae and Damnonii. There are good etymological grounds for connecting *Maponi* with the Clochmabenstane, a large boulder which once formed part of a megalithic monument on the Solway shore, south of Gretna, and which was a recognized place of assembly in medieval times. Similarly, since well-known megalithic monuments would obviously provide convenient focal points for tribal gatherings, it is tempting to suggest that *Manavi,* which is linked with Manau, the district at the head of the Firth of Forth, was located in the vicinity of the Clack Mannan, or stone of Mannan, which originally stood not far from its present position in the centre of Clackmannan burgh.[6]

At the end of the Roman period the tribes of southern Scotland slowly began to evolve into primitive states and a series of strongholds was established from the fifth century. Stirling and Edinburgh were strongholds of the Gododdin kingdom and Dumbarton was the capital of Strathclyde. The volcanic plug of Dumbarton was well situated to become the chief defensive position of the kingdom of Strathclyde during the fourth century. Although little is known of the inhabitants of this stronghold, the place (known as Alcuith or Clyde Rock) is frequently mentioned in Dark Age chronicles, and it is known to have been besieged in 756, sacked in 780, and besieged again in 870 when it yielded up to the Vikings from Ireland, after four months siege, 'great riches and countless captives'.

Although the Vikings have been regarded as destroyers, they

were basically colonists who came to find farmland in the familiar environment of the islands — Orkney, Shetland, the Hebrides and Ireland. At Jarlshof they built long two-roomed houses, with a barn, smithy, byre and stables. Evidence from place-names for the geographical distribution of the Old Norse element *bȳr* (a farmstead, a village) shows that many Scandinavians settled on the Scottish mainland, especially in the Annan valley in Dumfriesshire.[7] However, no evidence has yet been discovered of a Viking town in Scotland such as at Stamford, Jorvik (York), Dublin or Hedeby in north Germany. The archaeological record suggests that Scotland's was an agrarian society with little need for larger settlements. Anglian colonization and its village settlements were restricted to the south-east and took place essentially in the valleys and only in limited numbers. Throughout the rest of the country there was basically a cattle culture which created small-scale settlements dependent for survival on summer grazings away from the permanent dwellings.

In Europe, the church provided many an urban nucleus around which a town could grow. Yet the picture in Scotland is by no means clear for the few remaining historical and archaeological records leave many questions unanswered. The earliest Christian settlement in Scotland appears to have been Whithorn which arose from a partially Romanized settlement. The inhabitants embraced Christianity during the fourth century, when they petitioned for a bishop, St Ninian. In the latter part of the sixth century St Mungo (Kentigern) established an episcopal church associated with the kingdom of Strathclyde, although the precise location of the church itself, whether on the traditional site in Glasgow or on one in Govan, remains in doubt. The sites of other episcopal centres are equally uncertain, but Old Melrose, Stobo and Abercorn probably qualify and indeed had long ecclesiatical histories even if they did not become urban centres. With the introduction of monasticism, in which a communal life remote from worldliness was adopted, the town had little relevance. By the end of the eighth century, on the eve of the first Norse raids, the church in Pictland began to return to regular episcopal foci from which bishops controlled defined ecclesiastical regions from fixed urban sees, and Abernethy, St Andrews and perhaps Dunkeld joined Glasgow as pre-urban centres.

Clearly identified urbanization began during the Norman settlement and colonization of Scotland. In the twelfth century the kings were trying to bring the government of lowland Scotland into line with practice in England, France or Germany. In this process the monarchs from David I onwards encouraged the settlement of barons from England and even some directly from France and Flanders. Most of these settlers were established in small fiefs of one knight's fee, but great feudal estates were created in areas

Fig.1.1 Dunkeld: An
abbey for the monks
from Iona was founded
here in 315. The
present ruins date from
twelfth to fifteenth
centuries. It was a burgh
of barony in 1511 and
was erected as a royal
burgh in 1704, but
this charter remained
inoperative
(Photo: John Dewar.)

15

which were not ruled directly by the king. This twelfth-century revolution was accompanied by many innovations. One of these imports was the scarped earthen mound known as the motte. The Bayeux Tapestry shows a timber tower erected on the motte and enclosed by a palisade. A flying bridge of timber crossed the ditch from the outer bank, and a more extensive enclosure, also protected by ditch and bank, was sometimes added at a lower level. The Scottish distribution of mottes shows none at all in Lothian, a fair spread in Fife, Angus, the north-east and Moray, and the greatest concentrations in Menteith, Perthshire, the Clyde and, above all, in Ayrshire and Galloway (Fig 1.2). Mottes were common where the Crown depended for much of its authority on feudal control exercised by a great magnate.[8] The question arises as to what part mottes played as pre-urban nuclei. In the earlier stages it appears to have been very little: for example, Galloway with its numerous mottes developed very little urban life. Only later does one find burghs of barony being erected in the lee of these by then derelict structures. In contrast, the castles at Annan, Lochmaben and Dumfries acted as regional centres in Annandale and Nithsdale, where each developed a burgh. In eastern Scotland the castle was the symbol of strong royal control. In the Tweed valley sheriffs controlled the shires of Berwick, Roxburgh, Selkirk and Peebles, each shire with a castle at its centre and a burgh attached. It is clear that the provision of a castle or motte was a key factor in the establishment of stable government and society. Often, in the shadow of these structures, trading towns or burghs were planted, religious houses and hospitals built, and parish churches founded and endowed. These new burghs gradually superseded the castles in importance and it was here in the Tweed Valley that urban life took shape in the Scottish countryside (Fig. 1.3).

The evolution of a burgh was not a matter of chance, but required the active co-operation of many people: there had to be a supreme governing body to enforce law and order so that merchants and craftsmen might ply their trades. Without such social stability towns could not prosper, but in Scotland, as in much of Western Europe, these conditions did not prevail until the early Middle Ages, when, throughout Europe towns re-emerged after the Dark Ages to play an important role in economic and cultural life. Many questions arise out of this movement. What was the initial cause of their creation? Did burgesses seek royal protection and security for which they agreed to pay taxes? Did the Crown find it more convenient to administer society through towns rather than baronial estates? Was defence the main criterion in the choice of sites or was the command of a rich agricultural hinterland or commercial foreland more important? Did the existence of fords or bridge-points play a part? Again, did new burghs spring from pre-existing settlements or were they erected *de novo*?

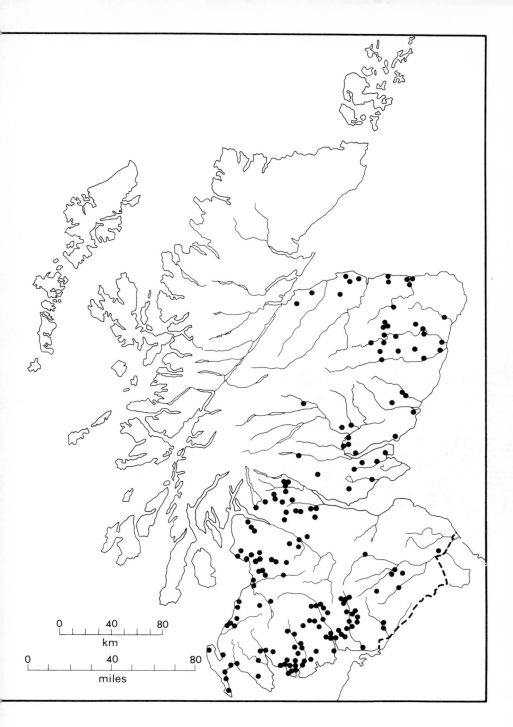

Fig. 1.2 Distribution
map of Norman mottes

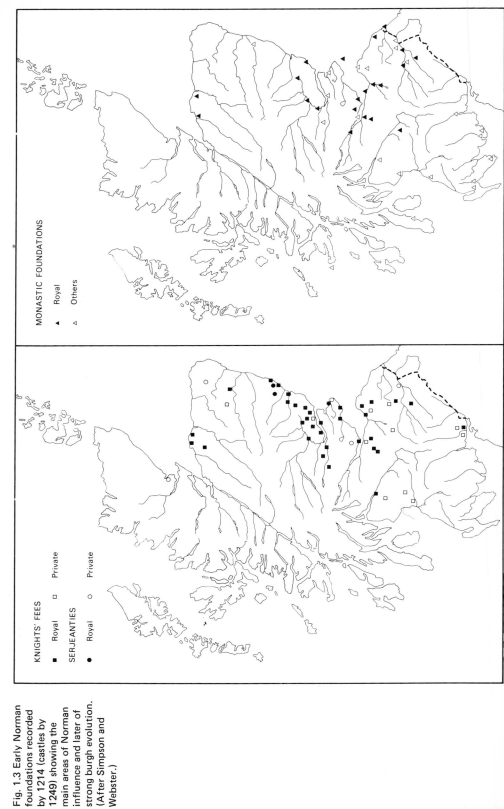

Fig. 1.3 Early Norman foundations recorded by 1214 (castles by 1249) showing the main areas of Norman influence and later of strong burgh evolution. (After Simpson and Webster.)

KNIGHTS' FEES
■ Royal   □ Private

SERJEANTIES
● Royal   ○ Private

MONASTIC FOUNDATIONS
▲ Royal
△ Others

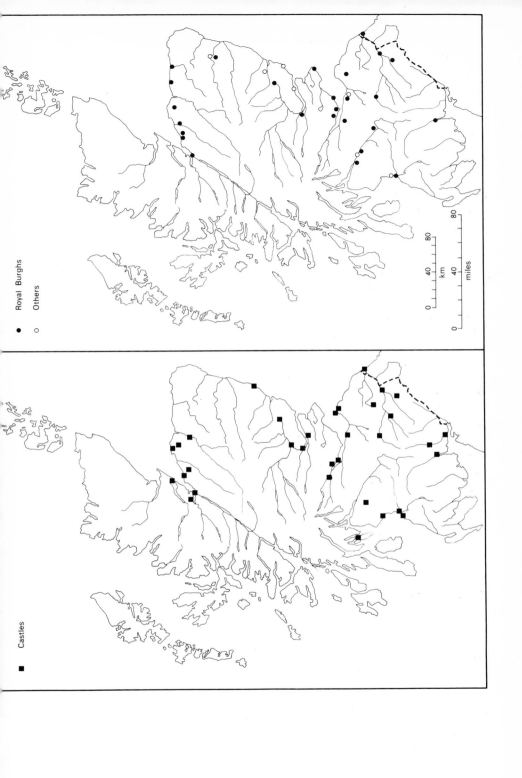

The answers to these questions cannot be given with any certainty. Information regarding the earliest burghs does not come from charters of foundation, but from many casual and incidental references such as the grant of a toft or tenement in a particular burgh. It was an age of sparse documentation, and the records have suffered considerably both from neglect and from two great dispersals at the hands of Edward I of England and of Oliver Cromwell. As a result, the earliest surviving Scottish public record is a letter, dated 1189, from Richard I of England restoring Scottish independence. The earliest surviving burgh charter is that of Ayr, dated 1205; the records of the Great Seal survive only from 1315; the earliest extant Exchequer Roll is dated 1326; and, apart from a few early rolls dating from 1292, the official records of Parliament begin in 1466. Anyone attempting to explain the actual origin and function of the early burgh is thus faced by a tantalizing lack of evidence from the earliest period. Owing to this paucity of documentary evidence scholars have been tempted to fill the vacuum with theoretical discussion.

The debate was opened in 1902 by George Neilson who put forward the *garrison theory*. He concluded that the burgh was essentially a military and administrative institution which, in close co-operation with castle and sheriffdom, was used by the Crown for the pacification and government of the country — 'castle-ward is the tie of town with country'.[9] Neilson related the rise of burghs to the spread of castles by the Anglo-Normans and quoted the pacification of Moray as an example of feudal colonizing in which burghs played a role. Most of the argument revolved around the coincidence that of the thirty-one royal burghs founded before 1286 only seven did not have a royal castle (Haddington, Selkirk, Wigtown, Montrose, Cupar, Aberdeen and Banff). Moreover, all but four (Inverkeithing, Kinghorn, Dundee and Montrose) of the thirty-one early royal burghs were the head burghs of sheriffdoms at one time or another. By 1286 the burghs had passed beyond this primitive phase of their evolution and the close connection between castle, sheriffdom and burgh was fading.

The *commercial theory* was put forward by Adolphus Ballard in 1902, in whose view Edward the Elder's law, 'let no man bargain out of port', supplied 'the principle which can be shown to be the foundation of all Scottish municipal theory'. He concluded that, 'we are therefore able to define the early Scottish burgh as the only place in which trade could lawfully be carried on or a market might be lawfully held'.[10] He tended to give retrospective strength to later evidence thus implying a strong code of mercantile law from the very beginning. It can be claimed, however, that the distinctively Scottish system of clearly defined and rigidly graded economic privileges of burghs was evolved slowly. It did not reach full maturity until David II's general charter of 1364 gave the royal burghs their exclusive rights. The trading rights of the earliest non-royal burghs were sometimes equal to those of royal burghs: as late as 1175-7 the Crown permitted the erection of the bishop's burgh of Glasgow with a weekly market and this concession was defended against Rutherglen and Dumbarton, neighbouring royal burghs. George Pryde in 1935 rejected Ballard's argument: 'The statement that the market was the germ of the burgh is therefore not universally true, and is no adequate explanation of its creation'.[11]

According to David Murray in 1924, 'the foundation of the burgh was its common property in which the burgesses had certain determinate rights, the possession of which made them a fellowship or community, in which they were united by a common oath'; the burgh itself was therefore 'a community of self-governing freemen, founded on a community of property'.[12] Murray's *communal or territorial theory* was later dismissed as a 'legalistic rationalisation of later days'.[13] Common property and the oath-fellowship had little to do with the founding of burghs, for in David II's time burgesses were still only the king's immediate tenants, holding tofts in the lands round a castle, owing rent to the king, with defined duties of watching and warding, and protected by privileges, especially in regard to buying and selling.[14] Government and self-regulation of the burgh evolved much later.

In the 1945 Rhind lectures W. Mackay Mackenzie discussed the various theories that had been promulgated about the origins of Scottish burghs and introduced the *creation theory* in an effort to rationalize the apparently sudden appearance of burghs in the reign of David I.[15] It had been suggested that burghs grew up around and under the protection of the church or castle, but, as Mackenzie pointed out, the earliest religious houses were founded by Alexander I (1107-24) at Scone and Inchcolm (although in the latter's case it could not be regarded as even a possibility). Kelso Abbey had only a special privilege of buying and selling for its men in the adjoining hamlet. Holyrood Abbey had an early burgh in Canongate which was founded by charter of King David on unoccupied land. Other religious orders, such as the Cistercians, tended to destroy rather than build up any nearby settlement when they founded a monastery. Similarly, castles did not necessarily lead to the creation of burghs. The burghs of Ayr and Dumbarton and their castles were deliberately and newly founded, although there was already a villa in the neighbourhood of Ayr which in fact had no part in the burgh. Nairn castle and burgh were built together on a new site acquired for the purpose.

Mackenzie suggested that the foundation of a burgh was a creative act, formally conferring upon a place a legal status unlike that of any other political unit. 'The key word to the burgh is creation, not growth'. He cited the provision of *kirset,* a period usually of five years during which time a newcomer could build his tenement and be free from rent, as being highly significant in that it could have no relevance to those already living in a town but only to newcomers coming to a chosen site to houses yet to be built by burgesses yet to come, and 'so marks definitely the beginning of a burgh'. These burgesses 'yet to come' were mainly of foreign origin, as their names show; and if the burghs were inhabited largely by foreigners, privileged burgesses, it would be necessary to throw defences round the burgh against possible molestation from the native settlers. It has been shown with certainty in England and Wales, and probably also in Scotland, that, as a result of diffusion by the Normans, some towns were granted the same customs and franchise as those of the Norman town of Breteuil.[16] By creating castles and free towns the Norman barons colonized and subjected regions far from the centre of government where the pressure of royal power was comparatively weak. The castle was generally constructed near an existing village; the village was converted into a free town, or even in some cases a new town was built beside the village. The creation of the market, the assured custom of the garrison, the bait of the franchises of Breteuil, all attracted settlers.

None of the theories can be exclusive and one is tempted to suggest another which may be termed the *emulation theory*. Its premise is simple: towns were seen to be desirable objects in their own right, fulfilling several functions simultaneously. Thus to rule effectively the king used the most modern tools of the time, be they feudal principles, castles or law. The burgh was but a ripple in a whirl of innovation. As far as Scotland is concerned the town was such a well-tried feature throughout the Anglo-Norman world that it would have been unthinkable not to erect them within the areas of royal control. Peer group pressures and fashions reign in royal circles as anywhere else and are persuasive in any age.

When David I became King of Scots in 1124 he had already granted charters to the burghs of Berwick and Roxburgh. Thereafter he established eleven more royal burghs — Haddington, Edinburgh, Linlithgow, Stirling, Rutherglen, Renfrew, Inverkeithing, Dunfermline, Crail, Perth and Elgin — before he died in 1153 (Fig. 1.4). Each of these burghs, except perhaps Haddington, had a royal castle and nearly all were the *caput* of a sheriffdom (Fig. 1.3). The system was designed to facilitate the keeping of the peace and to make the fiscal system more efficient.[17]

The essential criteria of a royal burgh were the erection of burgesses into communities or municipal corporations and the granting of property to the individuals and to the community under a permanent feudal tenure; in return the Crown received fixed rents and the performance of personal services for the security of the public peace. Grants or recognitions by the Crown of valuable rights and privileges to be enjoyed by the burgesses were guaranteed in early charters. The constitutions of all burghs were similar. The

Fig. 1.4 Burgh foundations 1100-1900

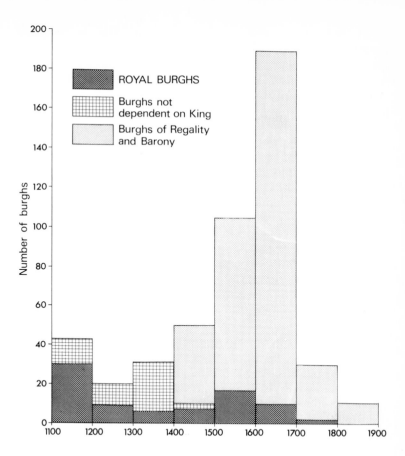

charter did not necessarily create the burgh, it conferred privileges or franchises on the burgesses beyond those implied in the existence of a burgh. The charter granted by William the Lion to the burgesses of Ayr in 1205 gave them all the liberties and free customs throughout the kingdom enjoyed by his other burghs and resident burgesses, together with a weekly market.

A royal burgh was granted the king's peace which freed the travelling burgess from tolls, pontages and similar imposts and was in some respects more valuable than the grant of a market or fair. Further, it provided the impress of royal protection, as can be seen when David I granted the burgh of Glasgow to the bishop about 1175, 'And I strictly prohibit anyone from unjustly disturbing or molesting them [the burgesses] or their chattels, or subjecting them to any injury or affront, under pain of the highest penalty.' The king's highway ran from burgh to burgh, and there was later a transference of peace from the users to the road itself. Again, from the same charter, 'who shall be resident in the said burgh, shall of

23

right have my firm peace throughout all my land in going and returning'. Manbote or payment to the king for breach of his peace, or for crime committed in his precinct, was 180 cows, a considerable fine at any period. As royal burghs were established partly for trading purposes, it was to the advantage of the burgesses to keep the peace.

Other burghs were created by the Church (Fig. 1.5). The ecclesiastical burghs of Glasgow, Aberdeen, Dunfermline and Arbroath probably preceded the foundation of their abbeys. The royal burgh of Dumfermline was granted to the abbey in 1303 and three more, Arbroath, Kirkcaldy and Whithorn, were raised to royal burgh status, as were Brechin, Glasgow, Queensferry and St Andrews after the Reformation. The remaining few, Canongate, Crawford, Kelso and Musselburgh, were erected burghs of barony. Other burghs such as Newburgh and Earlsferry in Fife and Rosemarkie and Fortrose in Ross-shire may have had ecclesiastical associations.[18] On the other hand there were eleven Cistercian abbeys in the country, but of them only Melrose and Cupar developed burghs. The burghs of Paisley, Culross, Pittenweem and Jedburgh developed later. Kelso and Holyrood abbeys created their burghs. The Church and her foundations had many scattered holdings in burghs throughout the country, granted by the king, big landowners, or burgesses or unfreemen. The Abbey of Arbroath had some of the richest endowments of land within the towns, possessing at one time holdings in seventeen burghs.[19] Originally, ecclesiastical burghs did not enjoy the same rights as those holding directly of the king but these rights were gradually acquired during the late fifteenth and early sixteenth centuries in spite of considerable opposition from neighbouring royal burghs. Some Church burghs were granted trons and customs, as at Inverness. Those burghs with rights of import and export came to rank as free burghs with the same privileges as royal burghs, were represented at the Convention of Royal Burghs in the sixteenth century and paid their share of the taxation assessed by the convention. St Andrews' burgesses could buy skins, wool and hides everywhere within the lands of the bishop, including the burgh of Cupar; the bishop had the right to have his own coquet and the great custom of all goods coming to the burgh and port of St Andrews. Dunfermline, Kirkcaldy, Musselburgh, Queensferry, Brechin and Arbroath were granted similar privileges.

Beyond the royal and ecclesiastical burghs and their areas of political and economic control the great barons ruled. A barony was a territorial unit conferred on a baron by royal charter which gave him the right to hold his own court with justice of ordeal and justice of life and limb. A barony was bound to include a *caput,* built not so much for habitation as for defensive purposes. The economic aspect of the Scottish barony served as the nucleus for a potential burgh, with its own mill, smithy and brewery, fixing its

own prices of bread and ale and 'keeping good neighbourhood' (keeping the peace, especially in agricultural terms as conflicts arose over communal lands and grazing). If the baron wished to create a burgh he petitioned the Crown for a charter of erection. From this arose a settlement which was known originally as a burgh in barony, later as burgh of barony. Between 1451 and 1484 a group of charters erecting burghs of barony conveyed four basic rights: (1) that of buying and selling any goods within the burgh; (2) that of having craftsmen and bakers, brewers, fleshers, vendors of flesh, fish, etc.; (3) that of having a market cross and weekly markets on a stated day; (4) that of holding an annual fair on a fixed day and for the week following. By 1474 the first clause was becoming more specific and two new rights were added: (5) that of having burgesses; and (6) the right to elect bailies and other necessary officers (in some burghs the burgesses could elect their own officers, in others they were nominated by the superior or elected with his consent). By 1509 the superior could feu to the burgesses and others the crofts, tofts and gardens of the burgh. The burgh of barony had no outside area of monopoly and no part in the import and export trade but within the burgh commerce was virtually open to all. Because a few burghs of barony gained trading privileges they were promoted into free burghs and were then able to carry on both internal and foreign trade but had to share the public burdens and taxes with the royal burghs. The burgh of barony's government was at the discretion of the superior and was usually under his control. The burgh held no common good property and had no inherent claim to representation in Parliament or in the Convention of Royal Burghs. Because they were included in the shires, burghs of barony had no direct liability for taxes as had the royal burghs. The older royal burghs sought to prevent the erection of any new royal burghs for fear of competition; they preferred the creation of burghs of barony which could be erected within the jurisdiction of a royal burgh.

Yet another form of subordinate burgh was the burgh of regality. A regality had even fuller rights of jurisdiction and administration than a barony, indeed the only right which a full regality did not possess was the right to try treason; but the lord of regality might have his own chancery for the issue of breves, which were served in his own name and not in the name of the king; his own mint; his own rights of admiralty. To such an extent was the regality a petty kingdom within itself that the lands of the realm were divided into royalty and regality — almost one might say into those lands in which the king's writ ran and those in which it did not.[20]

It was implicit in the erection of a burgh that trade and travelling should be fostered, not merely for the benefit of the baron but for the general welfare of the nation, and to that end a number of burghs were erected. For example, Rayne (1492) between Aberdeen and Elgin; Torry (1495) for travellers from the hills who wished to cross the River Dee; Merton (1504) for pilgrims to Whithorn; Pencaitland (1505) for travellers to the south and to Peeblesshire; Findhorn (1532) as a port and Fraserburgh (1546) as a haven; Clackmannan (1550/1) to provide accommodation for those attending sheriff courts; Fordoun (1554) for travellers from the north. Other burghs such as Kirriemuir, Abernethy and Douglas, were founded as a result of rivalry between local landlords. Other reasons for founding could be: the importance of the village as a fishing harbour (Kilrenny and Garmouth); as a port (Peterhead, Innerwick); as a market (Ardgowan, Blairgowrie); because the nearest burgh was too far away (Stranraer); for court purposes (Galashiels); as a new *caput* (Inverbrora); or for pacific purposes in a remote region (Stornoway, Cromdale).[21]

The granting of a charter was not in itself a guarantee of the success of a settlement. Failure took many forms. No action seems to have been taken even to start a settlement at Dalnagairn, Kirkmichael, Balnakilly, Balnald or Corshill-over-Inchgall. There are at least twelve others of which little or nothing is known: Spynie, Kingussie (the modern town is based on an eighteenth-century planned village), Myreton, Dunglass, Auchterhouse, Merton, Auchinleck, Scrabster, Dryburgh, Pitlessie, Durris and Newbigging. For others failure meant little growth so that they are now represented by a mere hamlet or farm as at Madderty. Some failed because they were near an older prosperous burgh and were in due course incorporated into that burgh; for instance, Linktown was absorbed into Kirkcaldy. About 50 per cent of burghs of barony and regality could be regarded as failed. On the other hand only three royal burghs — Auldearn, Fyvie and Roxburgh — failed. Roxburgh suffered from its frontier position and was burned down three times between 1377 and 1460. Furthermore it was in English hands for a total of 178 years between 1174 and 1550. But this formerly thriving trading community, that had even built a new burgh beside the old twelfth century, had already decayed by the time peace with England was established.

The main sources for the study of urban history are the archives of the burghs themselves, seventy-two of which have deposited their records in the Scottish Record Office in Edinburgh. Certain types of material are common to most collections, such as the burgh register of sasines (property register of royal burghs), register of deeds (legal transactions involving the corporation itself and individual burgesses), court books, burgh charters, town council minutes, records of specialized committees and, in the case of the older burghs, the records of the merchant guilds and craft corporations. Apart from the burghs' own archives information is to be found in the records of the Scottish Parliament and privy council who made laws affecting burgh life. Exchequer records contain the books of the customs and excise which reveal many aspects of seaport life. Later source material which often throws light on the social problems of growing urban communities in a period of industrialization includes church records. Eighteenth-century taxation schedules, particularly those of the shop tax and inhabited house tax, offer scope for analysis, as do the valuation rolls which began in 1855. Census records, particularly enumeration schedules giving details down to households, are now available to 1891. The early history of a town which began as a burgh of barony or as a planned village is often to be found in collections of family muniments, and the same source often reveals much of the murky world of burgh politics. Printed sources depend heavily on the work of Sir James D. Marwick and the Scottish Burgh Records Society which was founded in 1868. Twenty-two volumes were published up to the dissolution of the society in 1908. Further works have been published uniform but not part of the society's series.[22] Specific volumes published by the Scottish History Society and Scottish Record Society also provide useful sources. Lastly, the

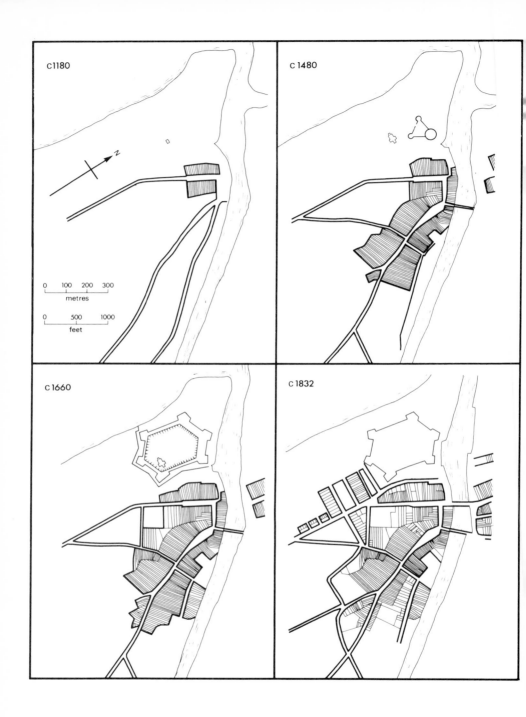

c 1180

N

| 0 | 100 | 200 | 300 |
metres

| 0 | 500 | 1000 |
feet

c 1480

c 1660

c 1832

Fig. 1.6 Ayr: the
growth of a burgh

28

numerous Parliamentary reports and commissions of the nineteenth century contain a vast quantity of evidence.

Although most of our knowledge of burgh origins has come from painstaking work by historians, the historical geographer and archaeologist have begun to make a contribution to this field. The landscape and the study of man's material culture provide further sources of evidence to be explored in the search for Scottish urban origins. Recently M.R.G. Conzen has used the town plan as an analytical tool and has provided a method to strip the burgh back to its original site. He used Alnwick for his classic example of this technique and it has since been adopted to show the evolution of Ayr (Fig. 1.6).[23] Our knowledge of material culture is being extended through the work of a small band of urban archaeologists who have recently begun to practise their craft in Scottish towns. Remarkable digs have been completed in Aberdeen, Edinburgh and St Andrews which have provided a great deal of information on such matters as trade in medieval pottery.[24]

Whatever the origins of the medieval burgh its importance lay with the people who dwelt within its walls. Their mode of living stood apart from the agricultural rhythms of the surrounding community. Their numbers were small, yet eventually their urban way of life was to embrace the bulk of society.

Notes

1. L. Mumford, *The City in History* (Secker and Warburg, London, 1961) (Pelican ed., 1966), pp 77-80.

2. *United Nations Population Studies,* No. 8, 1950, p. 2.

3. P. Bagby, *Culture and History. Prolegomena to the Comparative Study of Civilisations* (London, 1958), p. 163.

4. E. Burley, 'Metal-work from Traprain Law', *Proceedings of the Society of Antiquaries of Scotland,* Edinburgh, vol. 89 (1955-6), 118-227; R.W. Feachem, 'The Fortifications on Traprain Law', *Proceedings of the Society of Antiquaries of Scotland,* Edinburgh, vol. 89 (1955-6), 282-9; R.W. Feachem, *A Guide to Prehistoric Scotland* (Batsford, London, 1963), p. 121.

5. J. Clarke, 'Roman and Native, A.D. 80-122', in J.A. Richmond (ed.), *Roman and Native in North Britain* (Nelson, Edinburgh, 1958), p. 56; P. Salway, *The Frontier People of Roman Britain* (Cambridge University Press, 1965), p. 162.

6. K.A. Steer, 'Roman and Native in the Fourth Century A.D. and After', in Richmond, *Roman and Native,* p. 107.

7. W.F.H. Nicolaisen, 'Scottish Place-Names, No. 23, The Distribution of Old Norse Byr and Fjall', *Scottish Studies,* vol. 8 (1964), part 2, pp. 208-10.

8. G.G. Simpson and B. Webster 'Charter Evidence and the Distribution of Mottes in Scotland', *Chateau Gaillard,* V, Caen, 1972.

9. G. Neilson, 'On Some Scottish Burghal Origins', *Juridical Review,* vol. 14 (1902), pp. 129-40.

10. A. Ballard, 'The Theory of the Scottish Burgh', *Scottish History Review,* vol. 13 (1915), pp. 16-29.

11. G.S. Pryde, 'The Origin of the Burgh in Scotland', *Juridical Review,* vol. 47 (1935), p. 275.

12. D. Murray, *Early Burgh Organisation in Scotland* (Maclehose, Jackson, Glasgow, 1924), I, pp. 8, 23.

13. Pryde, 'The Origin of the Burgh', p. 273.

14. Sir Archibald C. Lawrie, *Early Scottish Charters Prior to A.D. 1153* (Maclehose, Jackson, Glasgow, 1905).

15. W. Mackay Mackenzie, *The Scottish Burghs* (Oliver and Boyd, Edinburgh, 1949).

16. For a discussion of the customs of Breteuil see M. Bateson, 'The Laws of Breteuil', *English Historical Review,* vol. 15 (1900), pp. 73-8, 302-18, 496-523, 754-7 and vol. 16 (1901), pp. 92-110, 332-45.

17. T. Keith, 'The Trading Privileges of the Royal Burghs of Scotland', *English Historical Review,* vol. 28 (1913), pp. 454-71, 678-90.

18. G.S. Pryde, *The Burghs of Scotland: A Critical List* (henceforth Pryde's List) (Oxford University Press, 1965).

19. J.M. Houston, 'The Scottish Burgh', *Town Planning Review,* July 1954, pp. 115-18.

20. W. Croft Dickinson, *The Courtbook of the Barony of Carnwath* (Scottish History Society, Edinburgh, 1937), pp. xl-xliii.

21. G.S. Pryde, *The Courtbook of the Burgh of Kirkintilloch 1658-95* (Scottish History Society, Edinburgh, 1963), p. xlix.

22. Charles Sandford Terry, *A catalogue of the publications of Scottish historical and kindred clubs and societies,* Glasgow, 1909, pp. 140-5.

23. M.R.G. Conzen, 'Alnwick, Northumberland: A Study in Town-Plan Analysis', *Transactions of the Institute of British Geographers,* no. 27, 1960, revised 1969, and W. Dodd, 'Ayr: A Study of Urban Growth', *Ayrshire Archaeological and Natural History Society Collections,* vol. 10 (1972), pp. 302-82. See also R.G. Cant, 'The development of the burgh of St Andrews in the Middle Ages', *Annual Report of the St Andrews Preservation Trust for 1970,* 1971, pp. 12-16; A.A.M. Duncan, 'Perth: the first century of the burgh', *Transactions of the Perthshire Society of Natural Science,* vol. II, pp. 30-50; and N.P. Brooks and G. Whittington, 'Planning and growth in a medieval Scottish burgh: the example of St Andrews', *Transactions of the Institute of British Geographers,* new series, vol. 2 pt. 3, pp. 278-98.

24. J.S. Dent, 'Building materials and methods of construction, the evidence from the archaeological excavations at Broad Street, Aberdeen, *in* A. Fenton, B. Walker and G. Stell, *Building Construction in Scotland. Some Historical and Regional Aspects* (Edinburgh and Dundee, Scottish Vernacular Building work group, 1976), pp. 65-71; and N.P. Brooks, 'Urban archaeology in Scotland, *in* M.W. Barley, *The Archaeology and History of the European Town,* Council for British Archaeology, London, 1977.

The fact that burghs in Scotland were plantations without significant antecedents is reflected in the uniformity of their layout. When making one's way through old burghs, medieval times can often be conjured up by such landmarks as street names. Auchtermuchty's High Street, Bow Road, Back Dykes and Middle Flatt lead one from the bustle of the town through the gate and into the burgh fields. In his work on medieval town plantation in Western Europe, Maurice Beresford omitted Scotland; yet the Scottish experience seems to be similar to that of the Anglo-Normans.[1] Most Scottish burghs appear to have been laid out on green-field sites, often using a fortification as a pre-urban nucleus. The fact that the situation may have some geographical significance, perhaps at the lowest bridging point or ford, is simply a by-product of military necessity.

The plan of a town is an historical document in its own right. What do we mean by the town plan? In essence the town plan is the composite pattern of streets, individual plots of land in distinct patterns within street-blocks, and the ground plans of the buildings themselves.[2] Most towns are composite in another sense, for each age has added streets, plots and buildings that reflect the current needs of the age. It is therefore possible to take any town plan and strip away each age's accretions till one stands at the very cornerstone of its foundation.

Analysis of a town plan can be very rewarding. To undertake this task one needs accurate large-scale plans, which are available in the form of the Ordnance Survey 25-inch series (scale 1:2,500) (Fig. 2.1). Two further series are available, namely a town atlas by John Wood, surveyed in the 1820s, and the plans produced for the Parliamentary Boundary Commission of 1832. Manuscript copies of some earlier, privately produced plans survive in collections in the National Library of Scotland, the Scottish Record Office and elsewhere. Thus for most Scottish towns it is possible to trace the key elements of the medieval layout without leaving the map room; only rarely are towns renewed on such a scale as to remove all vestiges of a previous age. Much of Glasgow's old town was destroyed by the railway; more recently Dundee has modified its medieval core to build shopping precincts. Obviously the extent of bomb damage during World War II gave an opportunity to start afresh, as in Coventry or Rotterdam. However, Clydebank, Greenock and Glasgow were the only Scottish towns to sustain much damage.[3]

The street pattern is the element in a town plan which persists longest. Almost as durable are the plot boundaries, whilst the

32

buildings themselves are most vulnerable to change. Urban durability is in direct proportion to the number of people involved. If a street pattern is changed, many people are affected; the amalgamation of plots usually concerns more than one person; but the fate of a building can lie in the hands of an individual.

With rare exceptions, the street pattern adopted in Scottish burghs consisted of a single street, which tended to be wider at one end, usually flanked by strip-like burgages (plots).[4] Over half of the single-street plans were bounded partly or entirely by back lanes, which are especially characteristic of the plans of towns granted burgh status before 1250. Twelve burghs have a parallel-street system, nearly all on the east coast with a striking concentration around the firths of Forth and Tay; these burghs had a flourishing trade with the Continent and their street pattern may be no more than a tribute to the prosperity of Scotland before the Union. In Crail no less than three market streets can be identified (Fig. 2.2). The original high street is the Nethergate lying north of the castle; then the more successful merchants moved to the new High Street; and later a further expansion was necessary and the Marketgate was built. At this stage trade ebbed away and early success became fossilized so that it could be said in 1832, 'the principal street is spacious and regular; several of the houses are good, and still exhibit indications of its former importance'.[5] Another group of burghs has a convergent-street system: a number of streets meet at a focal point, usually the market-place. Irregularity is the characteristic feature, and seems to indicate no overall planning. Strathaven, Cumnock and Coupar Angus fall into this category and date from the sixteenth and seventeenth centuries: as we shall see, they originated in the changing economy of those times.

The lands within the burgh were divided into the tofts of the burgesses. The burgage was the normal unit of ownership and was a long strip plot with a narrow frontage to the street. According to the Laws of the Four Burghs, which have much in common with the English seigneurial boroughs, the frontage was one 'burgh perch' wide (said to be 3 m),[6] though other widths are found. At first these plots would have had only a single building facing the main street, backed by a substantial though narrow garden. As time went on and pressure for land grew, men took advantage of building on the open land at the rear. This process, called repletion, can be seen clearly in Gordon of Rothiemay's plan of Edinburgh in the mid-seventeenth century. Much of the pressure for these sites came from craftsmen needing workshops or storage buildings. The close, that dark unsavoury passage into the jumble of buildings, became the symbol of the old Scots town. Other towns, such as Haddington, have extensive burgages which have not been built on to this day.

Buildings form the third element in a town plan but are rarely

Fig. 2.2 Streets and
burgages of Crail, Fife:
A relic of its prosperous
years before the Union

as old as the other elements. Burgh houses were constantly replaced through the ages, but each generation incorporated styles borrowed from elsewhere.[7] It is clear from early sources that houses throughout Scotland were very poor. It was 1175 before any houses other than mere huts were built in Glasgow, and then they were chiefly of wood. When Richard II burned Edinburgh in 1385 the townsfolk needed only three days to rebuild their houses. Stone houses were still sufficiently unusual in Ayr for them to figure in deeds and as landmarks in 1340; they became more numerous as building timber became scarce during the fifteenth century. Glasgow town council ordained in 1677 that houses should be built of stone, and in 1681 houses in Edinburgh, Glasgow, Aberdeen and Stirling were to be roofed with lead, slate, scailzie (blue slate) or tile. In the principal towns in the later seventeenth century it was still customary to face the house fronts with fir boards. Even in the best houses windows were glazed only in the upper part, the lower half having shutters. Many houses had timber balconies, boarded up to increase the chamber and shop accommodation, encroaching on the width of the street. Houses in Edinburgh were restricted to 'five storeys above the causeway' in 1698. This upward building of houses is characteristic of older towns, such as Ayr, that were confined within their defensive walls. Very few early burgh houses have survived, and even sixteenth-century houses are rare.

Ecclesiastical buildings from the Middle Ages are poorly represented in the Scottish burgh, though occasionally the shell of an abbey rears above a Border town. Early churches were built, like houses, of local material such as timber, wattle, clay and turf, and frequently thatched with heather, and it is assumed that many lie buried under later foundations. Though numerous churches and monasteries were built during the Middle Ages in town and country, few have survived the rigours of age, war or Reformation.

Public open space was at a premium in the medieval town. Thus when public buildings were required, such as a town house or tron, the burgesses were forced to occupy the only extensive space in the town, the high street. The merchants and craftsmen, too, began to erode this area by replacing their booths by permanent structures. Little room was left at street level and the overhanging storeys nearly touched above the customers' heads. This process, called market colonization, often divided the widest market-place into two separate streets (Fig. 2.3). At times the authorities' patience was exhausted and the offending structures were swept away as happened to the Luckenbooths of Edinburgh.

As important as the church in the life of the burgh, though perhaps not so physically imposing, was the tolbooth; it was used for meetings of the burgh court and council, served as the town's jail and sometimes as a schoolroom. However, tolbooths frequently fell into disrepair and council meetings might be held at a member's

home and prisoners locked up in the church steeple. The market cross was the legal *caput*, the place of proclamations, executions and display of bodies, and the place where a transgressor might sit with a paper crown on his head. The early crosses were doubtless of timber, but all surviving crosses are of stone except Kilwinning's, which has a wooden cross head. Where there were two crosses, as in Glasgow, Aberdeen and Dumfries, one was called the fish cross; certainly in Aberdeen this was regarded as the lesser cross, and the same may have been true of other burghs.

It has been suggested that one of the main functions of the burgh was to provide security for its inhabitants. This idea of security has often been interpreted as the physical barriers behind which people could live in peace; throughout Western Europe the bastide has been regarded as typical of the walled settlement, but there are grounds for questioning this in a Scottish context. Security may be gained from a military fortification, a city wall or the sheer power

Fig. 2.3 Haddington from the air showing the long burgages, market street and market colonization. (Photo: Aerofilms.)

of authority. Although Scottish society had a turbulent history, arising from both internal and external forces, few formal town walls were built. The walled towns of Scotland included St Andrews, Kirkcudbright and Edinburgh; Dundee, Dumfries, Glasgow, Elgin, Peebles and Perth have insubstantial remains of later walls.[8]

However, each indweller in the burgh was responsible for the dyke at the heidroom or tail of his toft, so that as each adjoining heidroom was carefully built up and all was 'steikit and fast shut' an additional back dyke was gained.[9] Haddington relied on this method until English forces captured the town and strengthened the defences in 1548. During the seventeenth century the gaps in the heidrooms were filled in by a common stone wall which linked the walls of churches and other stone buildings. The present walls of St Andrews Cathedral illustrate this practice. In the time of William the Lion the king agreed to build an earthen rampart round the burgh of Inverness, to be crowned with a palisade and maintained by the burgesses. Dunfermline was fortified by a ditch built by Edward I. Perth had at one time a ditch and palisade, and at another time a clay wall. Stirling, Peebles and Edinburgh had substantial stone walls by the middle of the fifteenth century, and there are traces of an earlier wall in Edinburgh (Fig. 2.4). The townspeople did not rely merely on walls for their protection but took advantage of natural features. Fourteenth-century Dumfries' defences included a wall of stone and earth, and a ditch, which encompassed the town (Fig. 2.5). There were three gates, the North Port near the moat, the East Port adjoining the chapel and the South Port near the church; the bridge was also fortified with a port, and later the Vennel Port, the Lochmaben Gate and the Southern Gate were built. Swampy ground between The Moat and Loreburn, which was used for the wapinschaws, and the more extensive Lochar Moss gave added protection.[10] Walls may not always have been effective in keeping off the enemy, but appearances were kept up by closing the gates at sundown. The only town gateway still in reasonable condition is the West Port of St Andrews, built in 1589; most have fallen victim to road-widening schemes.

Once the burgh was established under the charter of erection, the duty of the burgesses was to establish trade, undertaken during markets and fairs. Two weekly markets and an annual fair were usually granted. Stallengers set up their open stalls or booths and the dues were an important item of burgh revenue. Trading restrictions were often removed for the period of the market, and other community restraints were also lifted so that no one could be arrested unless he broke the peace of the fair. Special courts similar to the courts of piepowder in England were set up to deal immediate justice to any wrongdoer.

A market town used its tron or great beam for weighing and

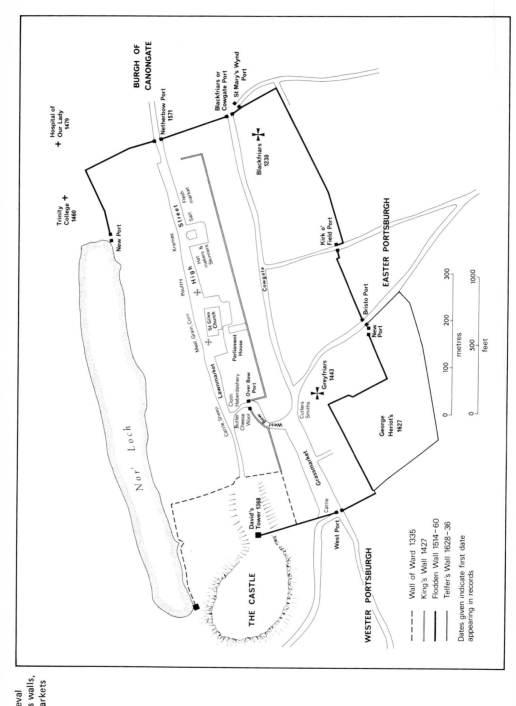

Fig. 2.4 Medieval
Edinburgh, its walls,
streets and markets

BURGH OF
CANONGATE

Hospital of
Our Lady
1479

Trinity
College
1460

New Port

Netherbow Port
1571

Blackfriars or
Cowgate Port

St Mary's Wynd
Port

Blackfriars
1230

Kirk o'
Field Port

EASTER PORTSBURGH

Bristo Port

New
Port

Greyfriars
1443

George
Heriot's
1627

Nor' Loch

Krames

Flesh
market

Salt

High Street

Poultry

Meal Grain, Corn

St Giles
Church

Parliament
House

Hat
makers &
Skinners

Cowgate

Cattle, Sheep

Lawnmarket

Cloth
Haberdashery

Butter
Cheese
Wool

Over Bow
Port

Cutlers
Smiths

West Bow

Grassmarket

Cattle

David's
Tower 1368

West Port

THE CASTLE

WESTER PORTSBURGH

0   100   200   300
metres
0   500   1000
feet

- - - - Wall of Ward 1335
‧‧‧‧‧ King's Wall 1427
────── Flodden Wall 1514–60
────── Telfer's Wall 1628–36

Dates given indicate first date
appearing in records

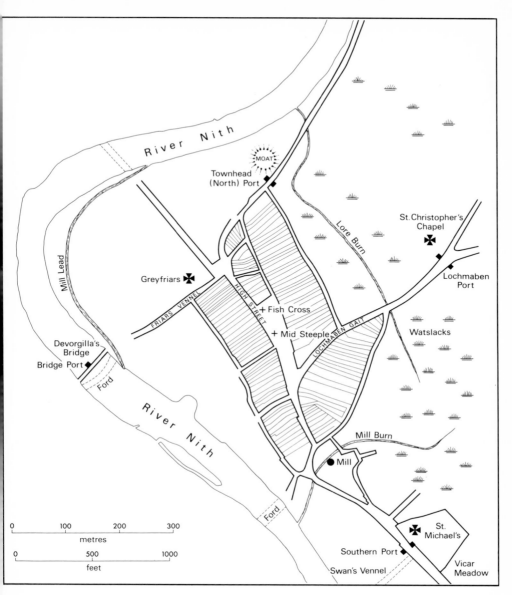

Fig. 2.5 Medieval
Dumfries

measuring all commodities from outside the burgh.

In Dumfries the leather market was held in the Cowgate, probably in Friars Vennel where a number of cordwainers still worked
in the late nineteenth century. The cattle market was held from the
seventeenth century on the White Sands, which were enlarged and
paved in the nineteenth century. In the eighteenth century a salt
market was built in Calvert's Vennel (now Bank Street) and the

butcher market and slaughterhouse, which had previously been in the narrow market square, were moved to the area between Loreburn and East Barnrows. The fruit and vegetable market was held in the High Street by the mid steeple; when the old flesh market was rebuilt to house this market, the bailies abolished the old dues called trone and three-port customs, which had been levied at the town gate on all eggs, butter and cheese.

Fairs were often closely connected with the early Church and held on the local saint's day, usually outside the burgh. About eighty fairs throughout Scotland date from before 1500; mainly agricultural and domestic tools, wool and woollen goods were exchanged. With the growing number of places erected into burghs of barony or regality, the number of fairs increased, until by 1890 nearly 900 places were known to have had fairs or markets at some time, including fifty in Aberdeenshire alone.[11]

When William the Lion granted a charter to Perth in the sheriffdom of Perth, strict rules were laid down about the conduct of trade throughout the sheriffdom, with the general intention of encouraging the growth of the market at Perth but restricting trade outside the burgh. There were even restrictions on the setting up of taverns in other towns in the sheriffdom. The Perth charter was used as a model for those of many other royal burghs.

There is some confusion about the differences in the types of trade that could be carried on in royal burghs and burghs of barony. Certainly royal burghs felt they had been given greater privileges than burghs of barony and fought hard to keep their monopoly, but George Pryde suggested that in fact the trading differences must have been slight because of the ease with which the one class of burgh passed to the other.[12] Royal burghs were given exclusive rights of trade over a specified area within the sheriffdom. Inland burghs which had boundaries reaching to the sea were granted the right to have a port within their territory, for example Edinburgh and Leith, Linlithgow and Blackness, Elgin and Lossie and Spey, Cupar with a landing place in the Motray Water, and Haddington and Aberlady. Foreign trade was concentrated in the royal burghs, making easier the collection of the Crown's great customs or export duties on staple wares. Burgh customs' returns show a wide range of imported goods: iron, timber, pitch and tar, tackle, flax, groceries, dye-stuffs, velvets, ornaments, copper and brass, cards for cloth-making, soap, beer and hops, paper, glass and tinware, playing cards and racket balls. The inhabitants of burghs of barony, however, could buy and sell only wine, wax, corn and cloth within the burgh. At the end of the sixteenth and beginning of the seventeenth centuries a few burghs of barony seem to have been granted a share in foreign trade, though little was made of this opportunity. As trade and industry increased the monopoly of the burgesses was gradually broken by strangers and unfreemen, who had the financial advantage of not paying burgh taxes. Efforts were made to limit this indiscipline by fines or the offer of burgess-ship, but it was a losing battle.[13]

The rise of trade and of burgh foundation led to a need for new standards to facilitate daily business. From the twelfth century standard weights and measures made their appearance, bearing the names of the towns with which they were associated: the Lanark pound troy, the Linlithgow firlot, the Stirling pint, the Edinburgh ell. Local standards such as these were only superseded by imperial or statute measures in 1827.

Minting of coins after the fashion of contemporary English coinage began in David I's reign some time after 1135. The name of the moneyer and the place of minting are found on these and later coins (Fig. 2.6). Edinburgh's pre-eminence over other burghs was marked, for coins minted there have survived for fifteen of the eighteen reigns of the Scottish monarchy since David I. One has to beware of placing too much stress on the location of Scottish mints,

Fig. 2.6 Medieval mints. The figures refer to the number of reigns for which coins have survived.

for a massive hoard found in 1877 contained a cross-section of the currency in Scotland in the mid-fourteenth century, but English coins outnumbered the native issues by about twenty to one.[14] Yet the number and location of mints reflect the growing need for a system of coinage to sustain the increasing commercial traffic between burghs.

Membership of a burgh community in medieval Scotland was limited to a very small proportion of the population and depended on the possession of a rood of land within the burgh and the ability to do the service pertaining to it. The inhabitants were very jealous of the burgh's privileges and had a deep distrust of all strangers; for example, an indweller had to stand pledge for any stranger guest who stayed for more than one night in his house.[15] The main duties of the burgess were the repair of bridges, maintenance of fortifications and service in war. Watch and ward duties were also obligatory. At the stroke of a staff on his door the burgess had to turn out and keep armed watch from 'coure feu till day down'.[16] Fear of fire was ever-present in the timber and thatched towns and the watch started by seeing that all fires were covered. Long weapons had to be kept in the booths, ready for any hue and cry through the burgh. Warding involved the guarding of prisoners in the tolbooth, though they were honour bound not to attempt to escape. The burgess had to defend his burgage, build a house on it within a year, and maintain it thereafter; he had to attend three head courts yearly, keep his weights and measures sealed with the burgh seal, pay his part of the civic burdens and take his turn as a burgh official.

The burgess had legal advantages as well as trading privileges. He could claim the king's peace, decline jurisdiction of any court outside his own burgh and dispose of his lands within the burgh as he pleased, provided it was not to the prejudice of his heir. He was also immune from the burdens imposed on villeins. Admittance to burgess-ship was recorded in the burgh records after payment of the burgess fee or burgess-silver and the swearing of the burgess, and was a prerequisite for membership of a merchant guild.

For many centuries the merchant guild enjoyed the exclusive privilege of dealing in merchandise and in all burghs members of the craft incorporations possessed a monopoly in respect of their own occupations. Strict division was maintained between the craftsmen who made the goods and the merchants who sold them.

The medieval world was self-sufficient in most articles of daily life, and manufacturing was limited to a few specialized crafts. Small craft shops which used organic raw materials like leather, wood and wool were scattered throughout the burgh, relying basically on muscle power augmented by the waterwheel. Little is known of the early craftsmen but by the fifteenth century they were organizing themselves into guilds or incorporations and regulating conditions of work. The records of the hammermen and weavers of Glasgow have survived from the early sixteenth century. The hammermen, usually the largest and richest guild in the burgh, included all those craftsmen who produced articles of metal and the tools needed by other craftsmen — goldsmith, silversmith, blacksmith, armourer, cutler, swordmaker, gunmaker, saddler, bucklemaker, clockmaker, pewterer, nailmaker, hookmaker and founder.[17] Inevitably the question of demarcation of work arose. Thus it was ordained in 1621 that no member of the 'brass smith craft' should set 'iron feit upon brasyn pollis', and saddlers complained that beltmakers were mending saddles. It was agreed that a member could carry on any of the trades within the craft if he could turn out good work from beginning to end without assistance.

A master weaver in 1621 had 'to teache, lerne and instruct in thir four poyntis of his weifer craft, viz. the wormd loome, sea bombacie loome, the playd loome, and playding'. An apprentice was to be indentured for five years with obligations on both parties, and then serve a further two years working for 'meat and fee'; on completion of his service and the making of his essay he could become a burgess. He might then remain a journeyman or set up in business, though he could not employ an apprentice or workman for a further two years; the master craftsman could become a guild brother after four years, with all the privileges and duties of the craft, such as setting up his booth in the burgh, attending meetings, paying his poor money and attending a fellow craftsman's funeral.[18]

Tanning and leather-working were typical burgh crafts; hides were taken from the local slaughter house to the skinners' green to be soaked in lime in order to remove hair and blood; after scraping they were again soaked for months in a mixture of tanbark, water and various noxious substances before being sent to shoe and harness makers. Glasgow and Edinburgh were important leather-working centres, as were Kilmarnock, Maybole, Ayr, Lanark, Falkirk and Linlithgow.

The remainder of the burgh population were the unfreemen including advocates, writers and notaries, journeymen craftsmen or servants of burgesses, some of whom were substantial householders. Women, often widows, kept lodging houses or became domestic servants. The unfreemen also included many tradesmen unqualified to become burgesses, a large number of unskilled men and finally, the unemployed and unemployable. Little is known of the lives of these people, unless crime or poverty brought a mention in the burgh records.

On the outskirts were many functions which contributed to the life of a medieval burgh. Just within the walls or back lane stood the friaries which gave spiritual, medical and educational care. Further out lay the butts, hospitals, chapels, inns, mills and gallows. Butts were used for archery practice and for the holding of wapinschaws. Fear led to the banishing of the infectious, especially those suffering from plague, to the burgh muir.

Suburbs grew up beyond the burgh walls, and prospered for a time before being incorporated into a more powerful nieghbour. Examples of this abound: the Nungate of Haddington, the Citadel of Leith, Portsburgh (outside Edinburgh), Newton upon Ayr and Bridgend (now Maxwelltown). Although an Act of 1593 forbade the practice of crafts in suburbs adjacent to royal burghs, it did not apply to suburbs in a barony. Portsburgh was part of the barony of Inverleith and by 1582 craftsmen who settled there included hammermen, bakers, weavers, wrights and masons. The authorities in Edinburgh, sensitive to this upstart, purchased the superiority and obtained in 1649 a royal charter erecting it into a burgh of barony. The control was thus firmly in the city's hands and Portsburgh, as a separate entity, withered away. For a period it had its share of residences of the wealthy, but these were abandoned with the development of the New Town.

Water mills played a two-fold role in town life for they provided a significant proportion of the burgh revenues and were the most powerful source of primary energy in medieval society. The annual rouping of Glasgow's mills must have been an attractive commercial proposition, for all townspeople were obliged to have their bread corn ground in them. The compulsion extended to all brewers and makers of aquavita, and the use of hand mills was prohibited. Even then good salesmanship was not ignored if this reference in the burgh records of 1576 can be taken at face value: 'for als gud service and als easie price and chaip in all respectis'.[19] But it was not easy to maintain the monopoly for there was barely enough plant to serve the numerous captive customers, dry summers slowed down the work and burgesses frequently petitioned to be allowed to grind wherever they wished. The inadequate facilities, the need to raise revenue and a desire for better service created constant friction. The system broke down during the seventeenth century and only the maltsters remained effectively thirled to the mills until the eighteenth century.

The parish church was at the core of everyday life in the medieval burgh for the spiritual and the mundane were inseparable in many aspects of life. As a sacred place, the church was a sanctuary for criminals, and business transactions carried out in the church were regarded as particularly binding. Proclamations, both local and national, were read out at high mass. The church bell regulated not only the services of the clergy, but the working hours of the burgh craftsmen; it sounded day-dawn and curfew, and warned of fire and the enemy. The churchyard was not only used for burials. Fairs were held there and frivolous pastimes indulged in until stopped by Act of Parliament in 1503, and even then trading was allowed in the church porch except during divine service.[20]

In the medieval burgh there was a high proportion of priests to people, as many as one in forty in Aberdeen, one in seventy in Dysart and one in eighty in Linlithgow. In these circumstances it is not surprising that they were so active in burgh life, particularly where some education was needed. The priest in the fourteenth century might be a custumar (excise man) as in Cupar or Hadding-ton. The schoolmaster/priest might also be the reader, precentor or session clerk, notary public or registrar, or the burgh's common clerk. By the sixteenth century the councils were taking control of the schools and tried to stop this pluralism, but the priest needed to augment his very low stipend which was usually paid out of the common good. Many small hospitals, founded by the Church, were controlled by the religious orders as staging posts for wayfarers, homes for the aged sick or infirmaries. In the fifteenth century it was laid upon the church to find lepers and put them into the care of the civil or ecclesiastical authorities. Under the Statute of Perth 1424, an adult who could earn his living in no other way was given a beggar's badge; anyone begging without a badge could be branded and banished. Even this harsh legislation failed to keep down the number of vagrants.

Throughout society, everyday matters were settled within a legal framework. In the countryside, farmers and craftsmen were regulated by baronial courts; in the burgh, the court was made up of all heritors and burgesses. The court assessed the cess or land tax and other local taxes. There were usually three head or burgh courts of which the Michaelmas one was the most important, for then were elected the aldermen, bailies and other burgh officers such as the liners (who inspected boundaries), ale-tasters, apprisers of flesh, kirkmaster and treasurer. Its criminal jurisdiction was strictly limited. The origins of the dean of guild court, like many medieval institutions, are obscure, but the statute of 1593 enacted that the dean of guild and his court should be elected by the burgh council. The court had charge of weights and measures and dealt with all internal trade disputes and the interests of the incorporated trades. The same types of business came before the town council, the burgh court and the dean of guild court and, as the same men might hold office in all three, it was not uncommon for the distinction between the different bodies to become blurred.

The Convention of Royal Burghs was a forum for the common interests of towns which, more than any other body, maintained Scotland's unique burgh monopoly. It has been suggested that the Convention was a development from the Court of the Four Burghs (Edinburgh, Berwick, Roxburgh and Stirling) or from the meetings of burgesses summoned to Parliament, or was an independent institution of merchants; whatever its origins, the Convention was of great importance by the sixteenth century. From the beginning there was a close connection between liability to taxation and membership of the Convention. In 1535 forty-one burghs were on the stent-roll, but later applicants for admission had to produce their charter of erection to royal burgh status. Occasionally burghs resigned because they were too poor to pay taxes. Although the Convention never had statutory power it could exert considerable influence and increase uniformity among the royal burghs by enforcing regulations of Parliament, Privy Council and Convention. The Convention discussed any change in burgh constitution or any dispute between burghs; it decided the proportion of tax each burgh should pay to Parliament and to the Convention; and it could grant a loan and ask members to contribute to a burgh in need of financial help.

The Convention organized and regulated foreign trade, such as the staple port for Scottish merchants in the Low Countries. The first permanent treaty between the Scottish burgh commissioners and a town in the Low Countries was contracted with Veere (Campvere) in 1578. A considerable number of Scots merchants and factors lived in this Dutch town with a conservator and a minister, and they were given commercial and other privileges relating to jurisdiction, worship and medicine. In return staple goods could be taken only to a staple port; in 1602 these goods were defined as all goods which paid custom but by 1669 they were skins, hides, plaiding and woollen manufactures, salmon, tallow and beef. The natives of Campvere were forbidden to trade in these goods. The Scottish staple remained at Campvere until the trade there withered away in the early eighteenth century.[21]

After the Union, the Convention was the principal body in Scotland to represent trading and industrial interests. An attempt was made to develop the manufacture of cloth by encouraging Flemish wool manufacturers to settle in the burghs and, at the same time, stopping exports of wool and imports of English cloth. The import of raw materials for industry was encouraged by waiving duties or granting bounties, and by levying heavy duties on imported manufactures. The Convention ensured that the Equivalent (the compensation paid to Scotland after the Union) was spent for the development of fisheries, flax growing and linen and woollen manufacture. Scotland's towns have been able to retain a single voice through the Convention of Royal Burghs and it is to this body that we owe much of the unique character of Scottish burgh life.

Notes

1. M. Beresford, *New Towns of the Middle Ages. Town plantation in England, Wales and Gascony* (Lutterworth Press, London, 1967).

2. For the terminology and methodology of this subject the reader must refer to the classic work in this field by Professor M.R.G. Conzen, 'Alnwick, Northumberland: A Study in Town-Plan Analysis', *Transactions of the Institute of British Geographers*, No. 27, 1960 (revised 1969), and his other works,

'Historical Townscapes in Britain: A Problem in Applied Geography', in J.W. House (ed.), *Northern Geographical Essays* (Newcastle-upon-Tyne, 1966); 'The Use of Town Plans in the Study of Urban History', in H.J. Dyos (ed.), *The Study of Urban History* (Edward Arnold, London, 1968) pp. 113-30.

3. Home and Health Department records. Air raids on Clydeside (SRO HH50/91-103).

4. J.W.R. Whitehand and K. Alauddin, 'The Town Plans of Scotland: Some Preliminary Considerations', *Scottish Geographical Magazine,* vol. 85, no. 2 (Sept. 1969), pp. 109-21.

5. *Report of the Parliamentary Boundary Commission* (London, 1884-5), p. xx.

6. M. Bateson, 'The Laws of Breteuil', *English Historical Review,* vol. 16 (1901), p. 110.

7. J.G. Dunbar, *The Historic Architecture of Scotland* (Batsford, London, 1966); H. Petzsch, *Architecture in Scotland* (Longman, London, 1971).

8. C.M. Heighway, (ed.), *The Erosion of History: Archaeology and Planning* (Council for British Archaeology, London, 1972).

9. W. Croft Dickinson, *The Early Records of the Burgh of Aberdeen 1398-1407* (Scottish History Society, Edinburgh, 1957), p. xxviii.

10. W. McDowall, *History of Dumfries,* 3rd ed. 1906 (reprinted by E.P. Publishing, 1972), p. 534.

11. A.R.B. Haldane, 'Old Scottish Fairs and Markets', *Transactions of the Royal Highland and Agricultural Society of Scotland,* series vi, 1961, pp. 1-12.

12. G.S. Pryde, *The Courtbook of the Burgh of Kirkintilloch 1658-94* (Scottish History Society, Edinburgh, 1963), p. xxv.

13. D.B. Thoms, *The Guildry of Brechin* (Brechin, 1968), pp. 22, 40.

14. I.H. Stewart, *The Scottish Coinage* (Spink, London, 1955), p. 34.

15. W. Croft Dickinson, 'Burgh Life from Burgh Records', *Aberdeen University Review,* XXXI, 95 (1946), pp. 214-26.

16. J.D. Marwick, *Edinburgh Guilds and Crafts* (Scottish Burgh Records Society, Edinburgh, 1909), pp. 4-10.

17. H. Lumsden and P.H. Aitken, *History of the Hammermen of Glasgow* (Paisley, 1912).

18. R.D. McEwan, *Old Glasgow Weavers* (Glasgow, 1933), pp. 21-4.

19. *Extracts from the Records of the Burgh of Glasgow 1573-1640,* (Scottish Burgh Records Society, Glasgow, 1876), p. 56.

20. D. McKay, 'Parish Life in Scotland in 1500-1560', in D. McRoberts (ed.), *Essays on the Scottish Reformation 1513-1625* (J.S. Burns, Glasgow, 1962), p. 113.

21. T. Pagan, *The Convention of the Royal Burghs of Scotland* (Glasgow University Press, 1926).

The distinction between town and country in late medieval Scotland was considerable, yet for all that, burghs remained partly rural with their gardens, pigs, poultry and surrounding arable land. A number of by-laws in seventeenth-century Peebles enjoined the inhabitants to keep their pigs in cruives or houses, or they would 'go loose up and down the town' and might be confiscated. Similarly, hens were to be kept in houses between 29 April and the end of harvest, and to wear wooden 'cloiges' to prevent them flying.[1] Up to the middle of the eighteenth century the townsfolk of Falkirk still put out their cows when the town's herd blew his horn in the High Street. Outside the built-up area lay arable land in strips (rigs) known as croft lands, burgh roods or burgh acres. Beyond the arable and linked to the town by the loan lay the common where beasts were grazed under the watchful eye of the common herd. This often barren muir was also an important source of wood, peat and stone.

Up to 1600 the estates of the nobility and gentry were closed, largely self-supporting communities. Most of the estate's agricultural produce was reabsorbed by the tenants, and indeed in the fairly frequent bad seasons all the rents in kind could be redistributed in this way. Such burghs of barony as existed were little more than villages reflecting the self-sufficiency of their parental estate. This economic insularity broke down during the seventeenth century and by 1650 the quantity of grain sold at regional and national markets had increased greatly. In his classic paper on the London food market, F.J. Fisher argued that an increase in the size of markets is one of the outstanding processes which mark the transition from a medieval to a modern economic system.[2] Much of the evidence for the rise of these city markets relates to the grain trade. Grain, particularly oats and barley, was the staple foodstuff of lowland Scotland at this time, and was the principal source of profit for many estates. The agrarian economy of much of lowland Scotland was geared to its production and changes in the supply to urban centres had a profound effect on Scotland's economy. All this was reflected in the crops which were grown, the type and quantity of fertilizers used and the services demanded from tenants, and possibly affected the basic structure of rural society by encouraging the trend towards the large single-tenant farm with its cluster of cot-houses and servants' quarters.

Most market centres were concentrated in eastern and coastal sites around the estuaries of the Forth and Tay, extending north-wards into Angus and the lowlands of the Moray Firth. Assuming

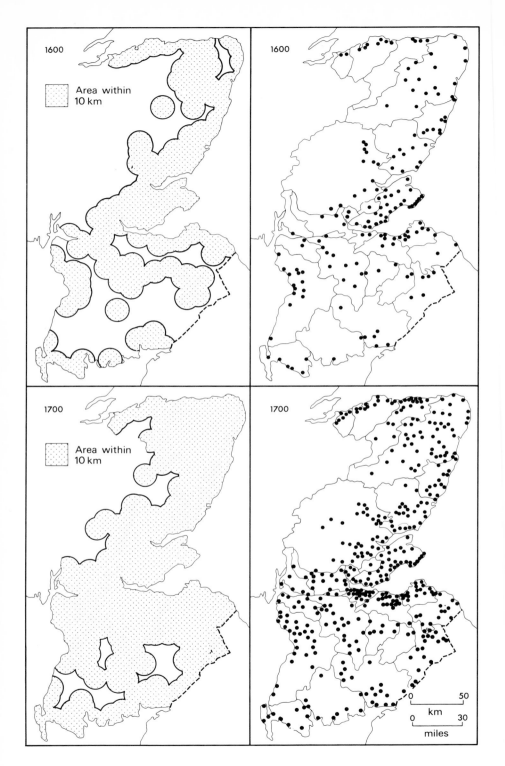

a market hinterland of 10 km, it can be seen that around 1600 lowland Scotland was fairly well served with markets (Fig. 3.1). The size of market areas was limited by the difficulties of overland transport and access to navigable water. Few land journeys could be more than 20 km a day, and most were probably nearer 10 km. This meant that the hinterland of effective coastal grain trade in Scotland lay within 20 km of the coastline. For example it was not economic to carry grain 30 km from Torphichen to Edinburgh, but the Earl of Seafield, whose estates lay along the Moray coast, found the Edinburgh market so lucrative that he maintained an agent there to receive his grain ships. Between 1600 and 1660 the local hinterland was able to meet the needs of the Edinburgh market for grain, except during years of poor harvest when the merchants had to look further afield. From the late 1660s, however, the pattern changed with the development of a regular trade by sea from the east coast ports to Edinburgh, disrupted only by the 'Seven Ill Years' (1695-70).[3]

The growth of the capital city alone does not provide adequate reason for extensive economic development. After the Restoration, English economic policy towards Scotland was marked by substantial tariff walls against Scottish goods. The Scots retaliated by restricting imports from England, and thereby encouraged the growth of home industry.[4] The great increase in urban population in the latter part of the seventeenth century was one of the most significant features recorded by Sir Robert Sibbald in 1698: 'Not only all the towns that were built in that last age are very much increased in buildings by what they were then, but several were built wher ther wer non in the last age . . . Ther was a gentleman died since the year 1660 who remembered that ther was bot one house wher now ther is the town of Borrostoness'[5] (Fig. 3.2). Sibbald concluded that this urban expansion was supported by a twofold change in the Scottish economy. First, industry was expanding and creating a substantial market for local produce. Secondly, there was an increase in arable production due to the adoption of liming and the expansion of the cultivable area.

The founding of new burghs was taken up vigorously by landowners. Between 1600 and 1650, sixty-four new burghs of barony were established throughout the lowlands, notably in east Stirlingshire and West Lothian where the coal and salt industries were expanding, with others in Renfrewshire and the south-west. The trend was reinforced by the emergence of a new type of market centre which was not accorded burgh status but had a market or fair licensed by Parliament. Up to 1661 there were only eleven markets or fairs not in burghs, including those at Brechin, Crieff, Foulis, Ruthven, Clackmannan and Bowden, but between then and the Union in 1707 about 150 non-burgh market centres were founded (Fig. 3.3). Designed to serve areas which were inconveniently

Fig. 3.1 Market centres in lowland Scotland, 1600 and 1700. (After Whyte.)

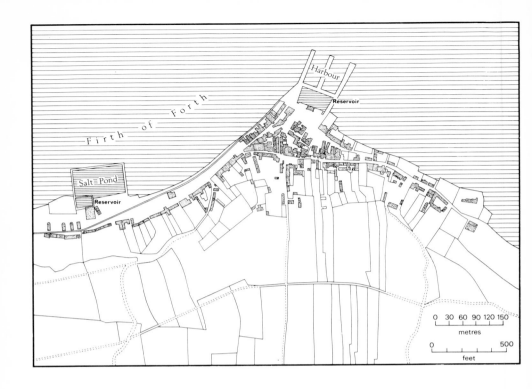

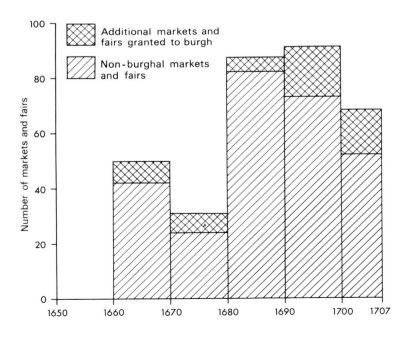

distant from existing burghs, many were set up in desolate locations, though central to a sizeable hinterland; for example in 1681 a market was set up on the moor of Whithills near Portsoy, Banffshire. The Act approving the establishment of a weekly market and an annual fair at the Kirktoun of Tarland, in Aberdeenshire, noted that 'there is no burgh or mercat toun in the paroche of Tarlan . . . whereby the inhabitants of that part of the cuntrie are much prejudged by goeing a great way to fairs and mercats . . .'[6] Thus by the time of the Union most of lowland Scotland was within 10 km of a market centre (see Fig. 3.1).

As the nature of trading burghs changed in the second half of the seventeenth century, a new type of industrial settlement grew up. These settlements were small nuclei, somewhat aloof from the surrounding agricultural communities. Usually they had one main industrial function, such as coalmining, salt manufacture or the provision of harbour facilities. They rarely developed into larger centres, and might indeed be described as industrial villages. The coal and salt industries underwent rapid expansion in the seventeenth century.[7] Both figured prominently in Scottish exports, though Scotland also imported high quality preserving salt from France, and dislocations in the French salt industry towards the end of the sixteenth century had reinforced the need to expand domestic production. The Dutch had become substantial customers for Scots coal in the early 1600s and direct exports to the Baltic rose rapidly after 1622. Continued dependence on water-borne transport confined large-scale mining to the shores of the Forth and, as salt manufacture was based on the use of waste from the mines, the expansion of the coal industry was reflected in the number of salt pans in operation there (Fig. 3.4).

The royal burgh of Culross reached the height of its prosperity during this period, guided by Sir George Bruce. In his time the burgh became an important centre of coal mining, salt manufacture, the making of iron baking girdles, cruive fishing and handloom weaving. Today, Culross is the finest surviving seventeenth-century burgh thanks to the efforts of the National Trust for Scotland. At Bonhardpans, near Bo'ness, Sir George Bruce built twenty-three pans in addition to the forty-four he owned at Culross. In 1630 the Earl of Winton built twelve pans at Cockenzie. Indeed, there were so many pans around the Forth that they were described by Brereton in the 1630s as 'infinite' and 'innumerable'.[8] The mining and saltmaking settlements had a peculiar social structure which hindered their development into towns. The estate owners, in whose hands the works lay, secured legal sanction in 1606 to bind the workers for life. This serfdom created an hereditary caste which lived apart from the rest of the population for nearly two hundred years, until colliers and salters were freed by the Dundas Act of 1799.

Lead mining gave rise to two unusual settlements high in the

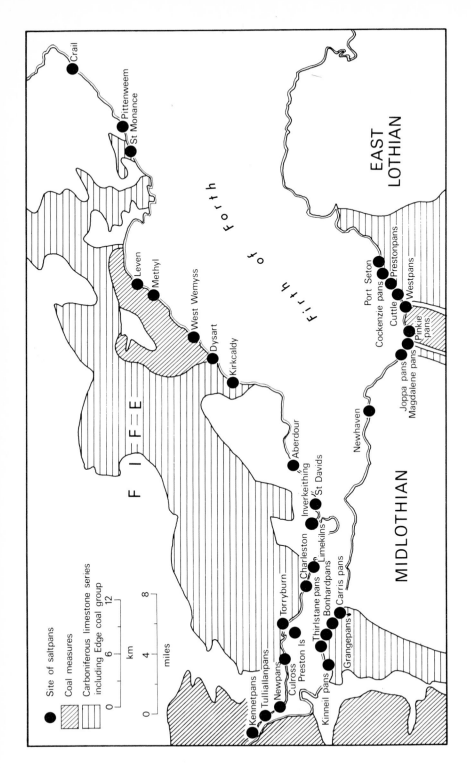

Site of saltpans

Coal measures

Carboniferous limestone series including Edge coal group

km
0 · · · 4 · · · 6 · · · 12

miles
0 · · · 4 · · · 8

Crail

Pittenweem
St Monance

EAST LOTHIAN

Leven
Methyl
West Wemyss
Dysart
Kirkcaldy

Firth of Forth

Port Seton
Cockenzie pans
Cuttle
Prestonpans
Westpans
Pinkie pans
Magdalene pans
Joppa pans

Newhaven

Aberdour

Inverkeithing
St Davids

FIFE

MIDLOTHIAN

Kennetpans
Tulliallanpans
Newpans
Culross
Preston Is
Torryburn
Charleston
Thirlstane pans
Limekilns
Bonhardpans
Carris pans
Grangepans
Kinneil pans

54

Fig. 3.4 The distribution of saltpans in the Fort Basin gives a clear indication of the main areas of industrial activity during the late seventeenth and early eighteenth centuries

Southern Uplands. Mining began in Leadhills in 1590 and though at first unprofitable, by the 1640s the mines employed fifty men and produced 300-400 tons of ore a year. Operations were started in Wanlockhead in 1675 and these two villages subsequently produced 80 per cent of Scottish lead. James Stirling became manager at Leadhills in 1734 and made many innovations, which included a reduction in the number of ale-sellers (there had been twenty-one in the village in 1739) and a ban on spirits, the appointment of a schoolmaster and a surgeon, and the establishment in 1741 of the first circulating library in Scotland, as well as a fund for sickness and old age to which the miners, the company and the landowners contributed. All this was in sharp contrast to the miserable conditions prevailing in coalmining villages. With the establishment of more permanent settlements in the early eighteenth century, lead mining companies built houses for the workforce, though the miners themselves also built houses and it became customary for any person 'in want of an house or byre, that they have a privilege of building on any spot in any field in which it shall suit their convenience'. At first the houses had earthen floors and were roofed with heather, though by the end of the century slate roofs were being used. The houses and attached crofts were held rent free with liberty to sell or bequeath as the miners wished though a small rent was charged if cows were kept. The women eked out their men's wages by embroidering muslin for Glasgow and Ayrshire manufactures.[9]

Growing economic activity under the aegis of a landowner often brought about the development of a town. A good example is that of the family of Erskine of Mar and the town of Alloa. Between 1689 and 1715 the town was transformed from a mean collier village: houses were demolished and rebuilt, roads were straightened and widened, and a broad, paved avenue lined with limes led from the town, past the castle gates and down to the harbour. Industry was introduced in the shape of saw mills, rope works, sail-cloth factory, woollen mill, breweries, distilleries, glass-works, brick and tile works and cabinetmaking works, all with access to the growing port. By 1825 Alloa was a respectable small town with a good mixed economy. Throughout, Alloa was a single-landlord town whose prosperity largely depended on the interests and personality of the owner of the time, and remained thus longer than most in an increasingly complex urban society.[10] Several other towns developed along similar lines as a result of mining activity and harbour building that acted as foci for further urban development: Port Seton was built by the Earl of Winton, Methil by the Earl of Wemyss, Bo'ness by the Duke of Hamilton, and Saltcoats was developed by Sir Robert Cunningham of Auchenharvie as the major coal port for the Irish trade.[11]

Not all towns developed in the seventeenth century were the result of economic stimulus. Because of the unsettled state of the

Highlands, Parliament ordained in 1597 'that there be erected and builded three burghs and burgh towns in the most convenient and commodious parts meet for the same, to wit: one in Kintyre, another in Lochaber, and the third in Lewis'. It was intended that these three, Campbeltown, Fort William and Stornoway, should become royal burghs, though in fact only Campbeltown did (Fig. 3.5). The Duke of Argyll obtained a feu charter in 1607 to the Crown lands of Kintyre on condition that he should 'plant a burgh to be inhabited by lowland men and trafficking burgesses'. The Duke shortly sub-feued and the name of Campbeltown was given to the new burgh, but, apart from the castle in the centre of the present-day burgh and a hamlet beneath its walls, very little building was undertaken before 1617. There was apparently no general eviction of old tenants, fewer than half the thirty names included in a rental of 1636 were those of incomers. The 'lowland men and trafficking burgesses' came first from Bute and Cumbrae, later from Ayrshire and Renfrewshire, and a charter of 1618 was signed by four men, 'all in Lochkilkerran and burgesses of Rothesay'.[12]

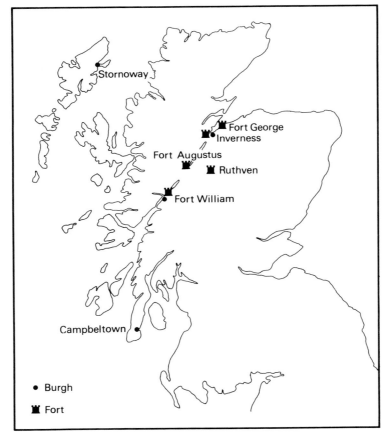

Fig. 3.5 Strategic forts and burghs used as bases in the pacification of the Highlands

The Convention of Royal Burghs opposed the granting in 1607 to the Duke of Seaforth of a charter of erection for Stornoway, fearing it would impair the position and ruin the prospects of the royal burghs, particularly Inverness, because 'the inhabitants of Stornoway would monopolise the fishing and so destroy all trade and the Haille shipping of the kingdom'. The Convention also feared, with justification, that with the encouragement of the earl 'straingeris' from Holland would monopolize trade. Stornoway's erection was cancelled in 1630, but a few months later the Convention recommended that the English be allowed to found a town in Lewis 'providing they fisch not in the reserved watters and haif no magasins nor plantations in any other of the West or North Illes'.[13]

Fort William, at the head of Loch Linnhe below Ben Nevis, was originally a temporary fortress built by General Monk in 1655, but rebuilt in 1690 in response to unrest in the area. The town was first called Gordonsburgh, being built on the Duke of Gordon's property, then Maryburgh, after William of Orange's consort, and finally took its present name from the fort itself.[14] Another Cromwellian fort was built at Inverness, using the stone from old ecclesiastical buildings at Chanonry Point, but it was demolished by order of the Scottish Parliament in 1662 and became a quarry for the town's buildings.[15]

During the seventeenth century there had indeed been a movement towards urbanization, and some industrial and trading settlements had been built, but these were only tiny pockets of burgh activity within a vast rural setting which had changed remarkably little. There had, however, been population growth and by the end of the century some of the straths and lowland areas showed signs of rural congestion. Inevitably change was in the air.

A journey through the Scottish countryside about the year 1755 would have revealed to the traveller a landscape completely different from that of fifty years later. In 1755, when the Rev. Alexander Webster made his census, nearly 90 per cent of Scots lived in small nucleated hamlets (fermtouns) and subsisted on the resources of the immediate neighbourhood. There were exceptions, for some landlords had already succumbed to the 'spirit of improvement' and were enclosing their estates and setting up their tenants in substantial farms. A trend towards commercial farming had been developing for some time, with emphasis on cattle in the Highlands, sheep in the Borders and grain on the lowland seaboard. Yet in general the Scottish countryside was a poor place.

The fermtoun was a cluster of farm houses, outbuildings and cot-houses, usually grouped without formal plan. Four to eight joint-tenants farmed together in runrig. The tenants had little or no security and paid their rent either in kind, services or money, or a combination of these. This antiquated system had a profound impact on the evolution of settlement. The proprietor could call on his tenants for labour, and there was thus no need for a free labour force housed in a village. Similarly, tenants were tied to the proprietor's mill and smithy so that there was little possibility of the rise of free villages such as had developed in England by this time. Only the magnate himself could take the initiative by obtaining a charter of burgh erection.

The fermtoun had an air of temporariness, reflecting the limited resources available. The house and byre in the south, and the black house in the north, were easily built. The low walls consisted of a drystone course filled with rubble. Timber was used only in the support for the roof, which was thatched with turf, heather or straw. There was no chimney, so the roof became impregnated with soot. The floor was of beaten earth and dung from the animals which shared the house. After five to seven years the roof timbers were retrieved, the house burned to the ground and the ashes, rich in nutrients, added to the dunghill. Twenty or thirty neighbours would then gather and erect a replacement in a day, followed by a feast called the daubing.[16]

The social structure of Scotland's rural population had all the components for a successful transition from a traditional economy to a growth-orientated society.[17] A few great aristocratic families owned vast areas and ruled their tenants absolutely. For example, the Countess of Sutherland owned over 400,000 hectares, albeit largely bare moorland; the Atholl estates consisted of 50,000 hectares of both hill and fertile lowland; and George, sixth Marquis of Annandale, owned 25,00 fertile hectares, mainly in the south-west. Many a parish had only one or two substantial proprietors. The smallest landowners (feuars or portioners) were found mainly near lowland villages or burghs of barony, but there were too few of them to be compared as a class to the English small farmer or yeoman. The tenantry, the next strata in society, held joint-farms of 2 to 5 hectares on lease and were the aristocrats of the rural proletariat. Below them came the mass of the rural population, amounting to around two-thirds of the total. This was made up of the male and female servants, crofters, cottagers, cotters and finally, the lowest of all, those dependent on parish welfare, mostly widows. The crofter occupied an intermediate position, possessing a half-hectare and having the privilege of keeping a cow and six sheep. The largest farms were worked by male and female servants (unmarried farm labourers). More often, however, farm labour was obtained from cottagers or cotters, who had the right to erect a cot-house at the end of the holding, with pasturage to keep a cow and a quarter-acre (0.1 hectares) to grow potatoes, giving in return such services as harvesting and rick building. The cotters also found temporary employment repairing roads, building dykes, working in the woods or fishing for herring. Cottagers are defined, somewhat artificially, as tradesmen — weaver, ditcher, thatcher, shoemaker, tailor — whilst cotters were merely labourers. Typical of the proportions of each category was the parish of Fortingall in Perthshire: 'The number of tenants is 354; of crofters 105; of cottagers, 250; of men servants, 152; of maid servants, 289.'[18] All but the tenants formed the pool of free labour that was to flow from the countryside to the towns in the coming industrial change.

Within this social structure the innovators began to implement agricultural change on a substantial scale from the mid-1750s. Innovation at first was undertaken by landowners, for they travelled abroad, read, exchanged ideas, had the advantages of wealth and, most important, regarded the proprietorship of their lands as a long-term responsibility. Once they were converted to improvement, very large areas were rapidly changed. Next, the tenant farmers, who had been privileged in the old regime, saw the opportunity for further improvement and copied the ideas. Where planned villages were built, cottagers could become feuars and gain a modicum of security. Thereafter the cotters gave the greatest boost to agricultural efficiency by leaving the countryside (Fig. 3.6).

The practice of inclosing, together with the increase of rents has occasioned the demission of herds and cottagers; and, of consequence, has materially affected the population of the district. Many persons of that description lived in the parish; and their services were particularly necessary while the ground was open . . . About twenty years ago there was hardly a tenant who had not one or more of these cottagers on his farm, whereas now there are very few of them in the whole parish. The cottages were the nurseries of servants, but their inhabitants have now been removed to towns, and having bred up their children to other employments, farm servants have become exceedingly scarce throughout the whole country.[19]

The result was a landscape devoid of cottages with the farm labourer leading a celibate existence in a bothy in the corner of the farm offices.

Towards the end of the eighteenth century there arose a movement for creating new villages which broke away from vernacular tradition and introduced the new concepts of the Age of Improvement.[20] Traditional burgh foundation was rejected in several ways: a chartered origin was no longer required, industry rather than trade was to be the main function, the aesthetics of planning were of great importance and, above all, the new villages were conceived as urban settlements within the reorganized landed estates. In Scotland, from the appointment of the Forfeited Estates Commissioners in 1755, through the 1760s until the collapse of the Ayr Bank in 1772, agricultural improvement raged like a fever. The

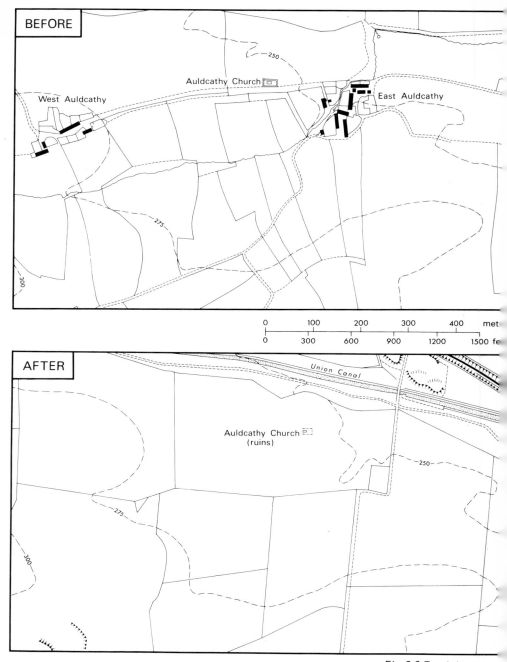

BEFORE

West Auldcathy

Auldcathy Church

East Auldcathy

— 250

275

300

| 0 | 100 | 200 | 300 | 400 | met |
| 0 | 300 | 600 | 900 | 1200 | 1500 fe |

AFTER

Union Canal

Auldcathy Church
(ruins)

— 250 —

275

300

Fig. 3.6 Rural de-
population in lowland
Scotland, Auldcathy,
West Lothian (based
on Hopetoun House
plans)

owner of a large estate wanted a new house, perhaps designed by Robert Adam, elegant policies in the manner of Capability Brown, and farms laid out in the regular and scientific manner recommended by the Society of Improvers; once these ambitions were realized he added a new village to show his complete mastery of the fashions of the age (Fig. 3.7).

The new village bore witness to comprehensive planning, with a spacious main street often opening out into a square in the centre of the village. When expansion took place a grid pattern was adopted, and the geometry was reinforced by the regular layout of house plots, gardens and lanes. Houses were built directly on the street, partly to discourage the habit of keeping a dunghill at the door; also the absence of front gardens gave the village a stronger 'urban' appearance than its size and function merited. Though much emphasis was placed on the aesthetic design of a planned village, behind it lay a strong economic *raison d'etre*. If the countryside was to be an efficient producer of surplus corn, it had to be balanced by food-demanding towns which at the same time could supply goods and services for the countrymen. Further advantages were envisaged by the landlord: rents would be enhanced by the relatively high density of buildings in the village, and he could raise the rent of surrounding farms which would have easy access to a new market. Linen manufacture was encouraged to give the village a firm economic base. The whole process is best illustrated by this account of the founding in 1763 of Cuminestown in Buchan:

> Joseph Cumine of Auchry . . . observing his tenants were frequently at a loss for a market, he determined to establish a permanent one on his own estate. For this purpose, he planned a regular village . . . upon the moorish part of a farm which in whole yielded only £11 a year. For a while, he felt in silence the sneers of his neighbours, who reprobated his scheme as wild and impracticable, but these temporary sneers soon gave way to lasting esteem. He prevailed on a few to take feus; he assisted the industrious with money; obtaining premiums for the manufacturer . . . Settlers annually flocked to Cuminestown (the name assigned to the chief of the clan) and the village, built of freestone, soon assumed a flourishing appearance. In connection with some neighbouring gentlemen, he established in his village a linen manufacturer.[21]

Sneers turned to envy and then emulation as landowners throughout Buchan built villages on their estates (Fig. 3.8).

The planned village movement had started in the North-East in 1720 when Alexander Garden of Troup founded the fishing village of Gardenstown. For a time progress was slow, but in the 1730s Earl Fife founded Macduff, Cockburn of Ormiston the

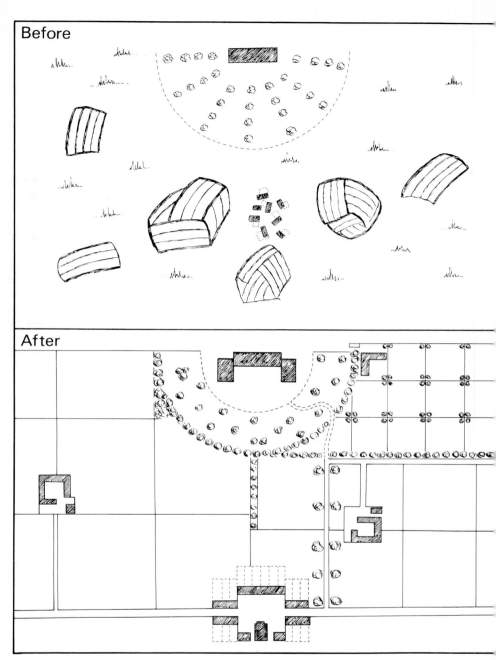

Before

After

Fig. 3.7 Schematic diagram of landscape change showing the revolutionary improvements brought in during the second half of the eighteenth century

62

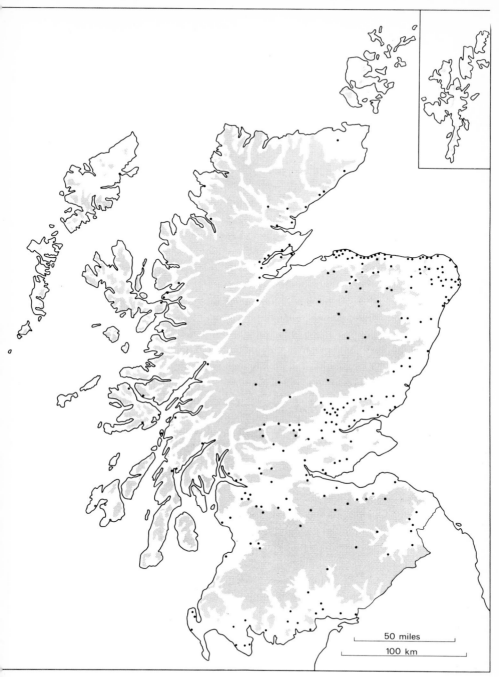

50 miles

100 km

Fig. 3.8 The locations
of planned villages of
Scotland 1720-1840

village of Ormiston and the Duke of Perth, Crieff and Callander. However, village foundation was a casualty of the economic and political disturbances in the 1740s (Fig. 3.9).

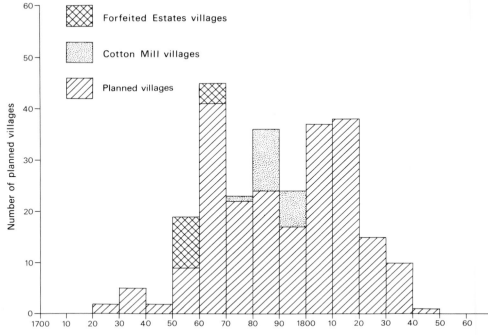

Fig. 3.9 The rate of village foundation in Scotland 1720-1840

Revival depended upon the re-establishment of confidence and this in turn depended upon the Government. The Hanoverian state set out to bring civilization to the Highlanders by 'promoting amongst them the Protestant religion, good government, industry and manufactures, and the principles of duty and loyalty to his Majesty, his heirs and successors'.[22] Government organization of the forfeited lands after the '15 Rebellion had brought little tangible improvement. Now the Government was determined to take positive action by appointing the Forfeited Estates Commissioners to administer the annexed estates under the leadership of some of the foremost agricultural reformers of the day. Thirteen estates were involved, ranging from the Duke of Perth's rich pastures along the River Earn to the bleak hillsides of Lovat.

The village was regarded as the ideal settlement to further the Government's aims, 'the perfect mean between the indolence of the deep rural peasantry and the profligacy of unregulated life in the big towns'.[23] The Commissioners set out to consolidate runrig and introduce individual farms and villages. Factors were asked by the Commissioners in the summer of 1755, 'What appears to you the most proper situations for villages upon the estate and your reasons for preferring these situations?',[24] and their replies, with the first reports by land surveyors, gave the Board a list of potential sites. William Monteath, factor on the Arnprior estate in west Perthshire, reported that 'the most proper place for a village is the ferme of Immararioch being the centre of the barony and in the king's high road',[25] this site became the village of Strathyre. Progress overall was very slow, mainly for political reasons, but the end of the Seven Years War in 1763 brought another wave of village foundation. The Government took the opportunity to settle discharged soldiers and sailors on the annexed estates, hoping to provide a core of loyal subjects in formerly rebellious areas, but this whole experiment collapsed very rapidly, for it was reported in 1769:

> The houses built for the soldiers at Callander will fall to the ground very soon unless the same are repaired by order of the Board as these soldiers neither can nor will keep up their houses, nor are they disposed to improve their grounds ... if these soldiers were treated with and either removed altogether or feus given to some of the best of them, the remaining houses might be sold to new feuars and carried down to the line of the village.[26]

The soldiers were not entirely at fault, for they were unwelcome visitors: 'The inhabitants are a sett of litigious, troublesome people, eternally at law with one another, and would rather hurt themselves than allow a stranger to settle peaceably among them.'[27]

Not all was failure: Crieff and Callander, originally built as planned villages in the 1730s and fallen into decay, were successfully rehabilitated by the Commissioners (Fig. 3.10).

New Keith was one of the key foundations in this second and more important phase of village foundation. Feu charters used in its foundation were followed as models by the Forfeited Estates Commissioners as well as by the Duke of Gordon. Land surveyors such as Peter May and his apprentices provided the professional corps who moved from proprietor to proprietor carrying with them a uniform set of ideas. Before the planned village movement exhausted itself, no less than 255 settlements were laid out on new sites or on old sites modified to such an extent that they could be called new (Fig. 3.11). Land surveyors were always on the lookout for possible village sites. On a survey in Badenoch for the Duke of Gordon in 1771, George Brown noted that if a 'village or new town' were to be erected in the area 'the haugh of Kingussie would be the most proper place and the most centricle in the country. It is well watered for the accommodation of bleachfields and manufactures of any kind.'[28] The suggestion was not taken up until 1799 when the duke advertised a new village.[29] Hopes that the spinning of yarn and manufacture of woollen cloths would encourage settlers were not

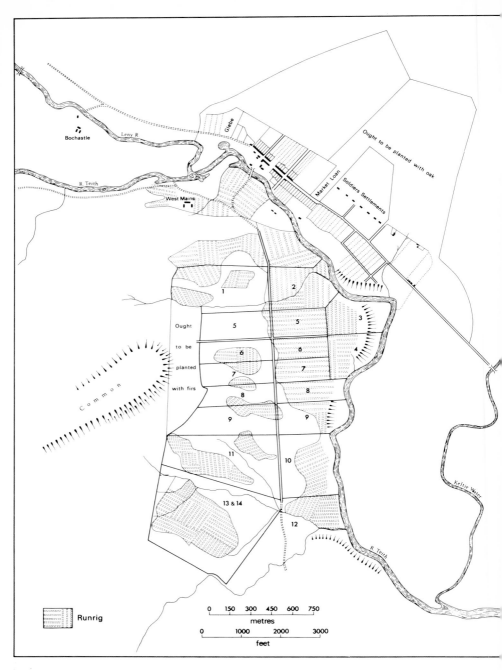

Bochastle

Leny R

R Teith

Glebe

Ought to be planted with oak

Market Loan

Soldiers Settlements

West Mains

Ought

to be

planted

with firs

Common

1

2

3

5

5

6

6

7

7

8

8

9

9

10

11

12

13 & 14

Keltie Water

R Teith

Runrig

| 0 | 150 | 300 | 450 | 600 | 750 |
metres

| 0 | 1000 | 2000 | 3000 |
feet

Fig. 3.10 Plan of the
fourteen lots of
Callander showing the
Duke of Perth's
planned village, the
soldiers' settlement and
the newly enclosed
farms

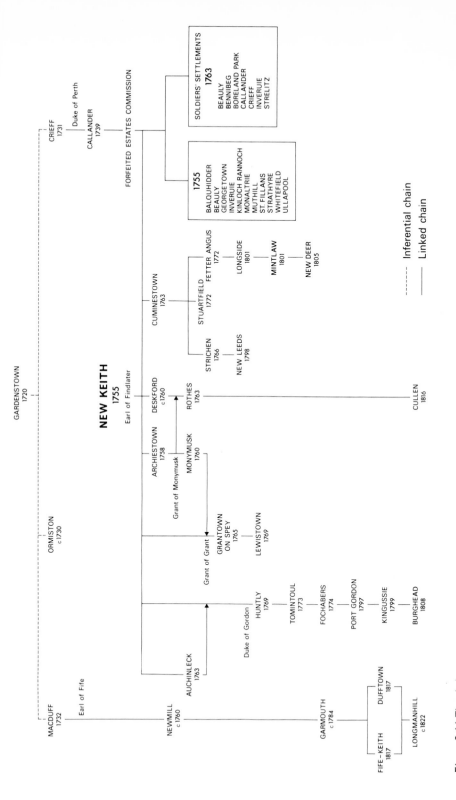

Figure 3.11 The chain of influence in the creation of planned villages

realized and the village eventually became a service centre for Badenoch.

Some towns were completely rebuilt in a new location to give the aristocrat privacy. Fochabers and Cullen are two cases which are worth examining in detail. The close proximity of the old Fochabers to Gordon Castle in 1774 annoyed the Duchess of Gordon, 'The Duchess has directed me to present her Compliments & to beg the Favour of you to come over here as soon as you can conveniently in order to take a precognition concerning three or four S[trumpets]s in Fochabers — who are notorious Thieves & are become so impudent as to steal several things from the washing house & to skulk frequently about the Castle.'[30] The Duke, already in the process of building large extensions to the castle, instructed the architect, John Baxter of Edinburgh, who 'made out a Sketch of a new Town agreeable to your Graces Idea of having it Square & compact'. As the time grew near for the removal to the new site they found that 'many of the present possessors are unwilling to part with their old Habitations, but as the Duke is determined and intent upon it, every method must be taken to force their removal — and among others a Process of Improbation and Reduction of their Rights, I imagine might help to forward His Grace's plan'. The old town was torn down and the new town started in December 1776 (Fig. 3.12).

Similar considerations prompted the Earl of Seafield to re-site the town of Cullen. In 1816 George Brown, a land surveyor with extensive experience in laying out planned villages, was ordered by the Earl of Seafield to 'set about the removal of the present town of Cullen and to have a new one gradually erected in order to save the heavy annual expence it costs to keep the swarm of worthless old houses from tumbling about the tenants' heads'.[31] Work started on the regularly planned town in 1822. All that remained of the old town of Cullen was the church and the fisherfolk settlement called Fishertown or Seatown (Fig 3.13).

The planned village movement was not restricted to the north of Scotland, for the identical process can be seen in the foundation of Ednam in Roxburghshire. When James Dickson MP became proprietor of Ednam estate, 'he inclosed all his lands, planned and built a neat village, the houses being all of brick, covered with pantile or slates — brought manufacturers from England and established woollen manufactures for cloth, particularly for English blankets. He also erected a waulk mill.'[32] A similar development took place in the same county in 1793:

As there is not a village in the parish, labourers and mechanics have long been very inconveniently situated for houses. For their accommodation, and no doubt to encourage manufactures, the Duke of Buccleuch has for some time past intended to build

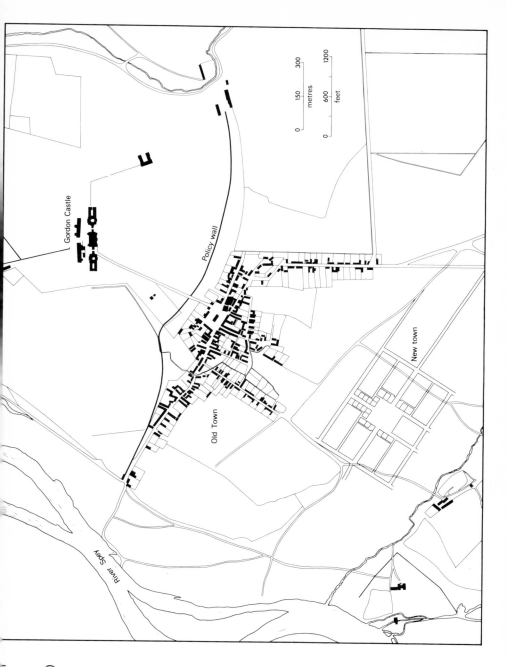

Fig. 3.12 The lost town of Fochabers and its planned successor (based on plans in the Scottish Record Office)

Gordon Castle

Policy wall

Old Town

New town

River Spey

metres
0   150   300

feet
0   600   1200

69

Seatown

Cullen

VICTORIA STREET

SEAFIELD STREET

NORTH CASTLE STREET

GRANT STREET

The Square

SEAFIELD STREET

SEAFIELD PLACE

CASTLE STREET

CASTLE TERRACE

Castle

Dovecot

Gallow Hill

Old Cullen

Church

Cullen House

0	60	120	180	210

metres

0	200	400	600	800

feet

a new town. At length a place was fixed on, and a plan made out. It is set down on the farm of Park, on the banks of the Liddel, in a field of upwards of 100 acres of fine land, and is named Castletown.[33]

With enclosure the whole pattern of rural society changed and many of the tasks and pleasures of life in the old fermtoun emerged in a commercial form in the village. The minister of Kirkcolm in the Rhinns, Wigtownshire, indignantly reported in 1792:

> Till within these three years, there was not the least vestige of a village in the parish, but, since that time, about thirty houses, contiguous to each other, have been built. They are, in general, inhabited by tradesmen, but some of them by common day-labourers. Unfortunately, however, more than one third of these houses may be called gin, or rather whisky shops, as they all sell that pernicious liquor.[34]

'A village cannot be expected to prosper unless it is advantageously situated and erected according to a judicious plan', wrote Sir John Sinclair in 1825. But these criteria were only a partial formula for success, for the increasing pace of industrialization was beginning to make its impact on the urban scene. The success of the planned villages was but fleeting, for their economic base was undermined by economic and technical developments elsewhere. The coming of the cotton factory produced a new type of planned settlement, the industrial village, whose main function was to house the factory workers, and the prime locational factor would now be adequate water power. The future development of towns lay in the complex and ever-changing interplay between sources of raw materials, markets, labour supply and transport: the industrial town was about to come into being.

Notes

1. *Extracts From the Records of the Burgh of Peebles 1652-1714* (Scottish Burgh Records Society, Edinburgh, 1910), p. 35.

2. F. J. Fisher, 'The Development of the London Food Market 1540-1640', *Economic History Review*, vol. 5 (1935), pp. 46-64.

3. I. D. Whyte, 'Agrarian Change in Lowland Scotland in the Seventeenth Century', unpublished Ph D thesis, University of Edinburgh, 1974.

4. T. C. Smout, *Scottish Trade on the Eve of the Union* (Oliver and Boyd, Edinburgh, 1963), p. 195.

5. Sir Robert Sibbald, 'Discourse Anent the Improvements May be Made in Scotland for Advancing the Wealth of the Kingdom 1698', MS (N.L.S. Ms. 33.5.16. cl.c2).

6. *Acts of the Parliament of Scotland*, VII, 492 (1663).

7. I. H. Adams, 'The Salt Industry of the Forth Basin', *Scottish Geographical Magazine*, vol. 81, no. 3 (December 1965), pp. 153-62.

8. Sir W. Brereton, *Notes of a Journey . . ., 1634-5*, ed. E. Hawkins (Newcastle, 1844).

9. T. C. Smout, 'Lead Mining in Scotland 1650-1850', in P. L. Payne, *Studies in Scottish Business History* (Cass, London, 1967), pp. 103-35.

10. T. C. Smout, 'The Erskines of Mar and the Development of Alloa, 1689-1825', *Scottish Studies*, vol. 7, pt 1 (1963), pp. 57-74.

11. T. C. Smout, 'Scottish Landowners and Economic Growth 1650-1850', *Scottish Journal of Political Economy*, vol. 11 (1964), pp. 218-34.

12. A. McKerral, *Kintyre in the Seventeenth Century* (Oliver and Boyd, Edinburgh, 1948), pp. 23-37.

13. Anon., *Stornoway and Its Charter: an Old Story Revived* (Inverness, 1899).

14. E. Macgregor, *The Story of the Fort of Fort William* (Inverness, 1954).

15. J. Fraser, 'Cromwell's Fort and Inverness Harbour', *Inverness Scientific Society and Field Club,* vol. 5 (1899-1906), pp. 93-102.

16. *OSA,* Kiltearn parish, Ross and Cromarty, 1, p. 289 and Dornock parish, Dumfriesshire, 2, pp. 22-3.

17. W. W. Rostow, *Stages of Economic Growth* (Cambridge University Press, 1960). The Rostovian model identifies societies in their economic dimensions as lying within one of five categories: the traditional society, the pre-conditions for take-off, the take-off, the drive to maturity, and the age of high mass-consumption.

18. *OSA,* Fortingall parish, Perthshire, 2, p. 453.

19. *OSA,* Colmonell parish, Ayrshire, 2, p. 65.

20. J. M. Houston, 'Village Planning in Scotland, 1745-1845', *Advancement of Science,* vol. 5 (1948), pp. 129-33.

21. *OSA,* Monquhitter parish, Aberdeenshire, 6, pp. 129-31.

22. Forfeited Estates Act, 25 Geo. II, c.41.

23. T. C. Smout, 'The Landowner and the Planned Village', in N. T. Phillipson and Rosalind Mitchison, *Scotland in the Age of Improvement* (Edinburgh, 1970), p. 78.

24. I. H. Adams, *Descriptive List of Plans in the Scottish Record Office*, 3 (HMSO, Edinburgh, 1974), introduction.

25. V. Wills (ed.), *Reports on the Annexed Estates* 1755-1769 (HMSO, Edinburgh, 1973).

26. Forfeited Estates records (SRO E721/24 p. 73).

27. *Ibid.* (SRO E721/9 p. 92).

28. Crown Estates records (SRO CR8/195 p. 29); see also Adams, *Descriptive List of Plans in the Scottish Record Office, 2,* p. xi.

29. *Scottish Notes and Queries,* 1, 3rd series, p. 22.

30. Gordon Castle papers (SRO GD44/52/39 and 40).

31. Seafield muniments (SRO GD248/1555 pp. 95-6).

32. *OSA,* Ednam parish, Roxburghshire, 11, pp. 305-6.

33. *OSA,* Castleton parish, Roxburghshire, 16, pp. 74-5.

34. *OSA,* Kirkcolm parish, Wigtownshire, 2, p. 49.

In the lull after the '45 Rebellion a handful of men planned the remaking of Scottish society and landscape. In the countryside the full fever of improvement was wiping out the past, but the towns were still straining their medieval bounds. The main force of the intellectual revival was centred on Edinburgh; every subject was explored, including contemporary problems of urban living.

The social geography of the town was the first feature to be remade. Social stratification of the medieval burgh was vertical, with merchants living on the ground floor, the well-to-do on the first floor and descending upwards to the poorest in the attic. Now the more prosperous wished to add physical distance to social distance, and their first move was to the one-class dormitory suburb of George Square, Edinburgh, built in 1766. 'Every person, whose recollection extends but a few years past', wrote William Creech the eminent publisher in 1792, 'must be sensible of a very striking difference in the external appearance of Edinburgh, and also in the mode of living, trade and manners of the people'.[1] The same correspondent from his vantage point in the Luckenbooths remarked of the Old Town in 1763 that

> ... people of quality and fashion lived in houses, which, in 1783, were inhabited by tradesmen, or by people in humble and ordinary life. The Lord Justice Clerk Tinwald's house was possessed by a French Teacher, Lord President Craigie's houses by a Rouping-wife or Sales-woman of old furniture, the house of the late President Dundas is now possessed by an iron-monger.

Large-scale social change could not take place, however, until the city was freed from the limitations of its crag-and-tail site and could expand into the fields to north and south. By 1830 these same fields bore a harvest of public buildings, miles of streets, squares, crescents, terraces and formal gardens on a scale that dwarfed the aspirations of later generations. Order was the essence of this urban revolution: streets were designed as a whole, the individual houses being subordinate to the general scheme. This regularity was in tune with the intellectual basis of the age. The conceptual leap forward is difficult to evaluate by today's standards. The goals of regularity and symmetry forced the planners to overcome physical barriers: Georgian townscapes swept over the topography, ignoring valleys, old loch beds and river channels. The North Bridge over to the New Town in Edinburgh was built for a society with only a few miles of proper roads and very few substantial bridges; outline plans were made for dozens of streets containing hundreds of houses in a country which had few stonemasons and no organized building industry. After nearly fifty years of painfully slow growth since the Union with England, capital projects were embarked upon without any clear indication that the economy would improve. The small circle of men who were to launch this cramped, inconvenient and evil smelling city into global pre-eminence in the world of letters had faith in an urban future, though the planning of the New Town of Edinburgh, which has been chronicled with such great devotion by A. J. Youngson in *The Making of Classical Edinburgh,* was brought about through the energy of one man, a local politician, Provost George Drummond.

A pamphlet entitled 'Proposals for Carrying on Certain Public Works in the City of Edinburgh', published in Edinburgh in 1752, led to the transformation of the city. The immediate cause for the proposals was the 'melancholy accident' of the collapse of a six-storeyed tenement in the High Street. After a survey, nearby buildings had to be pulled down so that 'several of the principal parts of the town were laid in ruins'. The anonymous author gained his inspiration from London:

> We cannot fail to remark its healthful, unconfined situation . . . no less obvious are the neatness and accommodation of its private houses; the beauty and conveniency of its numerous streets and open squares, of its buildings and bridges, its large parks and extensive walks . . . . When we survey this mighty concourse of people, whom business, ambition, curiosity, or the love of pleasure, has assembled within so narrow a compass, we need no longer be astonished at the spirit of industry and improvement, which, taking its rise in the city of LONDON, has at length spread over the greatest part of SOUTH BRITAIN, animating every art and profession, and inspiring the whole people with the greatest ardour and inspiration.[2]

Provost Drummond determined that the new Edinburgh should be modelled upon the metropolis and play a similar role in North Britain.

Results were quickly forthcoming. The Exchange, now Edinburgh District Council chambers, was started in 1753, the draining of the Nor' Loch began in 1759 and in 1763 George Drummond laid the foundation stone of the North Bridge. The way was now open for building the New Town. In April 1766 architects and others were invited 'to give in plans of a New Town marking out streets of a proper breadth, and by-lanes, and the best situation for a reservoir, and any other public buildings, which may be thought necessary'. James Craig's winning entry, according to Youngson, was 'entirely sensible, and almost painfully orthodox' (Fig 4.1). Youngson has

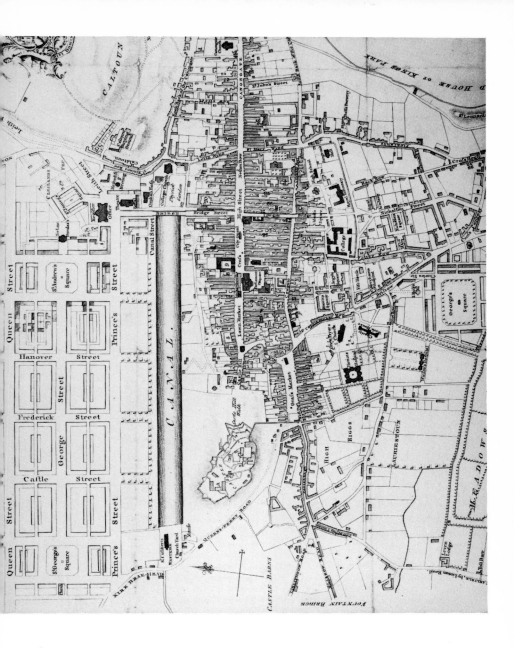

Fig. 4.1 Plan of the New Town of Edinburgh *c.* 1776 showing the progress in developing Craig's plan

suggested that Craig gained his inspiration from new town developments in Nancy. 'Nancy's ville de Stanislas is The Ideal City of France,' wrote E. A. Gutkind in his monumental history of city development, 'the consummation of the long line of trials and errors that had gone before and the last link in the unbroken chain of genuinely great artistic achievements.'[3] The ville de Stanislas was the creation of that great contradictory society, a closed decadent aristocracy in partnership with the men of the Age of Reason. Both seemed to understand the extravagance of excellence. Building at Nancy was accomplished in the years between 1751 and 1755, the very period when Edinburgh was contemplating her future. Craig's plan for Edinburgh succeeded because it was ideally suited to the site. The principal street, George Street, crowned the ridge, and dignity was added by a noble square at each end. Queen Street was adorned with pleasure gardens, though Princes Street had to make do with plain and rather modest buildings overlooking the huddle of the Old Town.

The Council kept control of the appearance of the New Town by a series of building regulations which progressively fettered the inclinations of the various architects, clients and builders. As the New Town progressed westwards the council insisted on the adoption of uniform elevations. Robert Adam was employed to carry on Craig's work, and his 'palace blocks' in Charlotte Square are masterpieces of urban design. Although their erection virtually completed the plans drawn up by Craig, the tradition of Georgian planning remained strong in Edinburgh for many years.

Georgian planners had not imagined that their exquisite residential suburbs would fall prey to commercial activities. The wealthy New Town residents demanded retail and other services which could be found by returning to the old town or by attracting these services to their own doorstep. Both prospects appalled them. In the end the rapid deterioration of the old town into slums encouraged small tradesmen, such as writers, stationers, milliners, haberdashers and chairmen to move to the basements and back lanes of the New Town to be near their clientèle. This infiltration was not without conflict, as Lord Cockburn observed. 'The growth of shops of all kinds in the New Town is remarkable. I believe there were half-a-dozen of them in the whole New Town in 1810. The dislike of them was so great, that any proprietor who allowed one was abused as an unneighbourly fellow.'[4]

Well into the second half of the nineteenth century Edinburgh retained a unique combination of medieval and Georgian compactness. The dignified townscape barely extended beyond the Dean Bridge (designed by Telford in 1831) before it petered out in the fields past Buckingham Terrace. The Victorian terraces of Coates and Atholl Crescents, Chester Street, Eglinton Crescent, Glencairn Crescent and Rothesay Place overlooked the steep slopes above the Water of Leith. Among these town houses rose, with ostentatious piety, a number of middle-class churches dominated by St Mary's Episcopal cathedral. Although this Victorian New Town lacked much of the elegance that had been captured in the earlier version, it retained all the geometrical symmetry, with curve replacing straight line, that had marked the eighteenth-century town.

About the same time another large development, mainly for lower middle-class occupants, was started in the lands of Bruntsfield House. The builders, John Watherston and Sons, joiners and cabinet-makers, did their own architectural work in order to save fees. This development became the Warrender Park district, of high-quality tenements in Scottish baronial style (the turrets and bay windows gave cheap extra space); very wide streets were laid out and the occasional shop included. Newington had long been the only garden suburb in Edinburgh but now new tastes encouraged the creation of villa suburbs. The policies of Grange House blossomed with villas and the process continued westwards for 3 km as far as Morningside and Merchiston. Comparing maps of the city in 1851 and 1871 one can see that most of the expansion took place in these southern districts.[5] This can be explained in part by the intrusion of the railways at the West End, Haymarket, Scotland Street and Leith Walk, bringing with them distilleries, maltings and other rather noxious enterprises, and the building of working-class housing. In a few peripheral areas such as India Street in Stockbridge, the middle class abandoned their spacious dwellings and subdivision soon reduced them to slums.

The era of Georgian town planning was opened in Glasgow by the tobacco barons who built their elegant residences around George Square between 1750 and 1775. Other streets followed, topically named Virginia, Havannah and Jamaica Streets (Fig 4.2). On the whole Glasgow had been contained within the historic outline of the old town until 1780. During the next half-century Glasgow's population leapt from 40,000 to 200,000 and the city expanded westwards. A new 'West End' was rapidly built on lands which had once belonged to Hutcheson's Hospital. Unlike Edinburgh's New Town the suburban developments in Glasgow were somewhat piece-meal and streets were often opened by the construction of a single house.[6] Soon the desire for suburban dwellings spread to the middle classes who lived above their counting houses, located mainly west of Glasgow Cross, then the city centre. Increasing industrial pollution, rising real incomes and changing fashions led to the wholesale movement of the middle class 1½ km west to a new suburb, Blyths-wood. Extensive land speculation began in 1802 and by 1830 a fine suburb of classical terraces had been laid out on a grid pattern. Even before Blythswood was fully built up, its earliest parts were being converted for business uses.

Expansion also took place south of the river. Until the 1790s

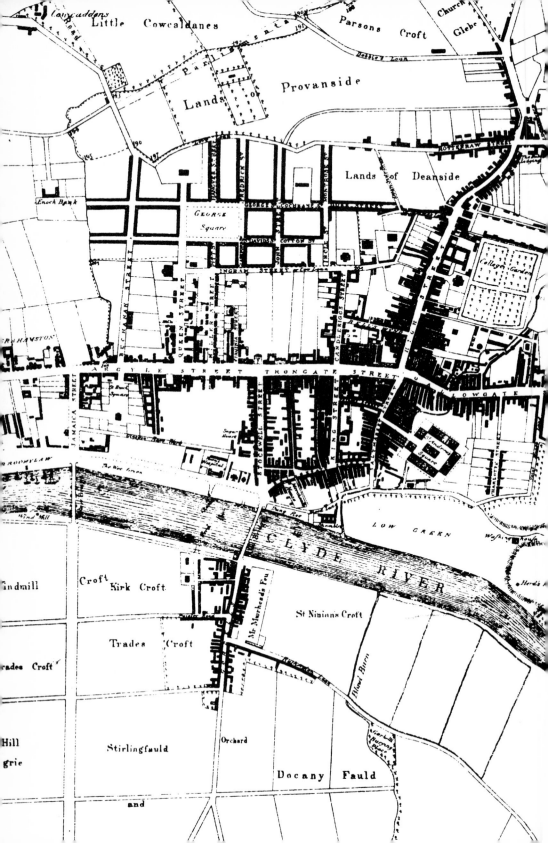

the old village of Gorbals (or Bridge-End) was still surrounded by fields. Speculative building produced a handsome Georgian suburb and there were ambitious plans for laying out a wide area as a high-quality estate. However, Laurieston fell victim to the rapid indus-trialization of the early nineteenth century; as in many other Victorian suburbs, houses became so mixed up with industry and railways that the middle class fled, leaving the poor with an elegant townscape decaying to slums. The hoped-for arrival of wealthy middle-class people never occurred and the spacious houses were soon 'made-down' or subdivided into warrens.[7]

During the second half of the nineteenth century the fashion-able residences in the West Central areas were abandoned to com-merce and business, and the middle classes left the regular geometry of St Vincent and George Streets to take up residence at Park Circus, Royal Crescent and Woodside or even further afield in Cathcart or the Lower Clyde resorts.

The medieval town of Aberdeen was clustered around the church, castle and market. Originally the burgh extended down the slope of the land, with the kirk at the north and the royal palace at the south end. Early in the thirteenth century a castle was built on Castle-hill and gradually the centre of the burgh moved from the Green to the Castlegate where the market was situated and a new tol-booth was built, though Robert III (1340-1406) insisted that it should be built at the side rather than the centre of the market place.[8] The town was never walled, although the main entries were guarded by half-a-dozen ports, which were demolished in the 1760s because they impeded traffic.[9] Development within the burgh took place in the principal streets — Shiprow, Broad Street and Gallowgate to Mounthooly, and by the Upperkirkgate to Schoolhill and Woolmanhill. This was virtually the entire burgh till the late eighteenth century, though unfortunately, as a result of later developments, little of the layout remains (Fig. 4.3).

Comprehensive development was started in 1799 with a proposal for a new town similar to that of Edinburgh and, as in the capital, physical obstacles had to be overcome to achieve regularity. The approach from Inverurie in the north-west was brought into the centre by the new straight thoroughfare of George Street, which was driven over the old bed of the Loch. The building of King Street entailed the removal of most of St Catherine's Hill and the construction of a high bridge across the Den Burn (Fig. 4.4). After the formation of these new streets expansion could proceed north-westwards; spacious streets and squares were laid out and many neo-classical buildings erected. A contemporary account reported that the buildings on the

. . . principal modern streets are so clean, so massive, so uniformly surfaced, and reflect the light so clearly from the glittering mica

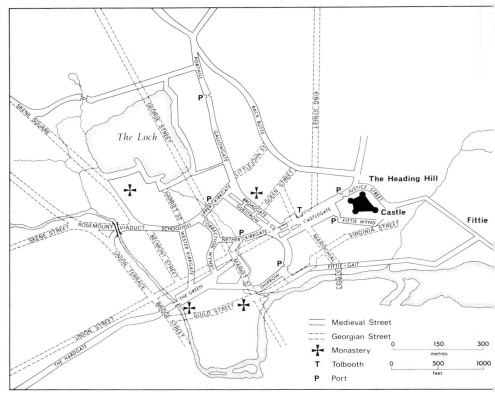

Fig. 4.3 Aberdeen: Medieval and Georgian street patterns (*after F. Wyness 1963*)

of the granite, as to look, on a sunny day, as if they had just been hewn and polished from the rocks on which they stand. Gardens are attached to many of the houses even in the compacter parts of the city, and to almost all in the suburbs, so that, even in the absence of any such spacious gardens as intersect the New Town of Edinburgh, they produce an effect of airiness and well-being.[10]

The bold planning of the early years of the nineteenth century was costly, and brought the city to bankruptcy for a time after 1817.[11] The disgraced councillors stood in 1819 before a committee of the House of Commons and repented that their management of the burgh's affairs had been 'radically defective and improvident.'[12] With these developments the old, once-popular residential quarters of the city — Gallowgate, Guestrow and the Shiprow — inevitably fell from grace. By the middle of the century, the fashionable districts were Belmont Street, Union Street and Union Place, Golden Square and Bon-Accord Square, and the east end of Albyn Place where a few country families had built town houses. By that time

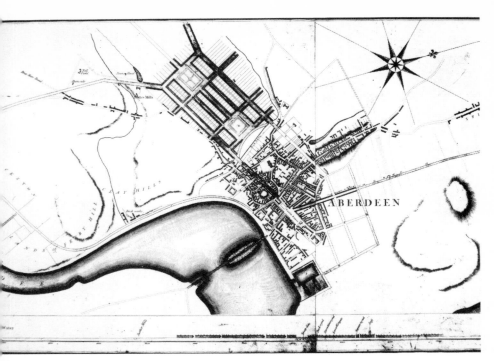

ﬕ. 4.4 The New Town
Aberdeen as
ﬕposed around 1800

the 'Granite City' tradition was firmly established, for much of the stone came from local quarries at Dancing Cairns, Sclattie, Kemnay and Rubislaw, which was eventually worked to a depth of 150 m (Fig. 4.5). The city had been soundly designed by two exceptional architects, John Smith (1781-1852) and Archibald Simpson (1790-1847), who appreciated the intractable material with which they created the new Aberdeen. Public buildings erected during this period included St Andrew's and St Mary's Cathedrals, the Royal Infirmary in Woolmanhill and the Assembly Rooms.

Georgian developments in Aberdeen resulted in a mixture of land uses different from that in other Scottish cities. The new streets, private and public buildings and harbour works produced imposing grandeur, but were interspersed with narrow lanes, courts and closes packed with people. Though the middle class moved westwards, the social stratification that characterized Edinburgh and Glasgow was not so marked, nor did the problems of massive industrialization, paramount in Dundee, appear in Aberdeen.

Dundee, unlike the other three cities lacked a distinctive phase of Georgian development. Physical limitations had restricted medieval building to the area parallel with the shore and in 1689 Dundee was 'a very pretty town' with 'buildings such as speak of the sub-

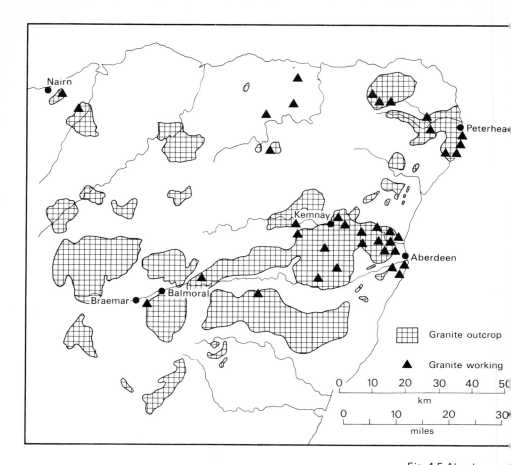

Granite outcrop

▲ Granite working

Fig. 4.5 Aberdeen and
the granite quarries of
the North-East. (After
Gaskin: North East
Scotland Survey.)

stance and riches of the place'. So it remained until 1760 when
change came rapidly under the stimulus of industrial growth[13] (Fig.
4.6). The townscape was dominated by large four-storeyed mills,
the design of which had been brought from Leeds in 1806. Otherwise there was little activity in reshaping Dundee to the norms of
the day: few public buildings were completed, the old street pattern remained largely intact and architects could hardly find work,
apart from designing factories.[14]

An attempt was made to reconstruct Dundee's medieval street
pattern, principally to improve access to the docks. The Edinburgh
architect William Burn was consulted and his advice lay behind the
Improvement Act of 1825. Reform Street was built in the 1830s
and with the Doric-styled High School gave Dundee 'uniformity
with elegance, rivalling, in the beauty of its buildings, some of the
admired parts of the Scottish metropolis'.[15] Development within
the burgh focused on the provision of working-class housing. Only
five Georgian terraces exist in Dundee, a sixth having been abandoned

Fig. 4.6 Dundee in
1777, by William
Crawford (*Scottish
Record Office*.)

after only two houses had been built.[16] Paucity of elegant townscape
was due to the absence of enlightened and strong-minded landowners like the Heriot Trust in Edinburgh or the Blythswood Camp-
bells in Glasgow.

Appalling water and sewage problems and the rate and scale
of industrialization led the small middle-class population to seek
new homes outside the city: the answer lay 6 km to the east in
the little fishing village of Broughty Ferry. Around 1801 Charles
Hunter of Barnside laid out a Georgian grid street plan on the slop-
ing links, and some terraces and semi-detached villas were built.
The opening of the railway in 1839 brought more incomers from
Dundee, though the real change in Broughty Ferry took place only
after 1860 when the jute magnates built their mansions.

The Georgian townscape was essentially a city phenomenon,
with the exception of Perth. From medieval times there were two
parallel main streets in Perth, and in the late eighteenth century
transverse streets were cut through the town to create a gridiron
pattern. Streets in Georgian style were completed some years later

as far as the Inches. The Palladian terraces of Atholl Crescent and Rose Terrace facing the North Inch, the view across the South Inch to the Greek revivial terraces flanking St Leonard's-in-the-Fields with its broach spire, and the tree-lined Tay Street with views to John Smeaton's 1771 bridge, create an atmosphere of grandeur which justifies the description of 'Fair City'.[17]

The appearance of Scottish towns reflects not only the climate but the prevalence of stone as the main building material. The granite buildings of Aberdeen sparkle in the sunshine, but the soft local sandstone in Edinburgh and the old red Dumfriesshire sandstone in Glasgow absorb soot, making these cities rather sombre. Recent cleaning of public buildings has given us an impression of the original appearance of these Georgian towns. The building of Georgian Edinburgh relied heavily at first on a few bands of sandstone to the west of the city (Fig. 4.7). As time went on, supplies were sought further afield, so that by 1886 a model tenement erected by Sir James Gowans had outside walls of dressed stone from Plean and Redhall, with stair steps and an eavescourse of old red sandstone from Angus.

Brick did not make a strong visual impression in the townscape,

Fig. 4.7 Quarries used in the building of Edinburgh's New Tow

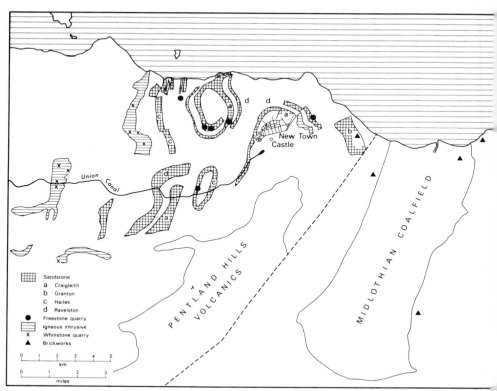

for it was used, as breeze block is today, mainly for internal partitions. However, many brickworks were established, especially in the coalfields, in the second half of the nineteenth century. Although Scottish brickmaking clays had the advantage of being virtually self-firing, the finished product with its pockmarks and uneven shape compared poorly with English brick. There was strong prejudice in the construction industry against its use, and even today bricklayers in Scotland handle this material less efficiently than their English counterparts.[18] The preference for stone cannot be explained in purely economic terms. Indeed, the startling difference between stone-built Langholm and the brick townscape of Carlisle, a mere 30 km away, can only be attributed to the Border and the resulting cultural differences.

The important contribution of Georgian town planners to urban Scotland was their ability to look at problems in spatial terms. Once burghs had broken out of their medieval bounds, large areas of single land use appeared. At first, upper-class residential suburbs were built, but these were often taken over by the central business district while the displaced residents had to renew their exclusive environment elsewhere. As transport systems improved, the whole process inevitably extended outwards, a process which accelerated with the rise of the industrial town.

Notes

1. A letter dated December 1792 to Sir John Sinclair, *OSA*, 6, pp. 581-620.
2. A.J. Youngson, *The Making of Classical Edinburgh* (Edinburgh, 1966), p. 4.
3. E.A. Gutkind, *Urban Development in Western Europe: France and Belgium, International History of City Development*, vol. 5 (The Free Press, New York, 1970), p. 140.
4. W. Forbes Gray (ed.), *Memorials of His Time by Lord Cockburn* (Robert Grant, Edinburgh, 1946), p. 252.
5. *Plans of Edinburgh and Leith with suburbs . . . for the Post Office Directory* by John Bartholomew provide an excellent series for comparative purposes. See W. Cowan, *Plans of Edinburgh* (Edinburgh Public Library, 1932).
6. W. Iain Stevenson, 'Some Aspects of the Geography of the Clyde Tobacco Trade in the Eighteenth Century', *Scottish Geographical Magazine,* vol. 89 (1973), pp. 27-9.
7. J. R. Kellett, 'Property Speculators of the Building of Glasgow', *Scottish Journal of Political Economy,* vol. 8 (1961), pp. 211-32; and *Glasgow: a Concise History* (Blond, London, 1967).
8. J.R. Coull, 'The Historical Geography of Aberdeen', *Scottish Geographical Magazine,* vol. 79 (1963), pp. 80-94.
9. F. Wyness, *City by the Grey North Sea: Aberdeen* (Impulse Books, Aberdeen, 1972), p. 67.
10. F.H. Groome, *Ordnance Gazetteer of Scotland* (London, 1903), p. 7.
11. *Municipal Corporations (Scotland). Local Reports of the Commissioners* (HMSO, London, 1835), pp. 27-8
12. *Report of the Committee of the House of Commons* (1819), p. 27.
13. W.H.K. Turner, 'The Growth of Dundee', *Scottish Geographical Magazine,* vol. 84 (1968), pp. 76-89.

14. D.M. Walker, *Architects and Architecture in Dundee 1770-1914* (Abertay Historical Society Publication No. 3, Dundee, 1955).

15. J.M. Wilson, *The Imperial Gazetteer of Scotland* (Fullarton, London, n.d.), p. 447.

16. D.M. Walker, 'The Architecture of Dundee', in S. Jones, *Dundee and District* (British Association Handbook, Dundee, 1968), p. 286.

17. D.C.D. Pocock, 'The "Fair City" of Perth', *Scottish Geographical Magazine,* vol. 85 (1969), pp. 3-8.

18. The *Scotsman*, 6 March 1968.

With the onset of the Industrial Revolution a new dimension was added to urban development. The craftman's skill gave way to the machine, and the scale of life was altered at every level: workshops were replaced by factories, villages became towns and everywhere men sought fuel to feed the new giants. During the last quarter of the eighteenth century the embryo industrial town emerged from the planned village movement. Settlements appeared whose sole function was to house industrial workers. Here cotters learned to become town labourers: the rewards were mechanical routines, rigid time-discipline and total dependence on wages.

The spinning inventions of the 1760s laid the foundations of the factory system. Full advantage was taken of the division of labour which could give countrymen urban skills with the minimum of training. The speed with which the new inventions were applied was remarkable. Richard Arkwright, the inventor of the water-frame, during a visit to Scotland in 1783-4 recommended the foundation of factories and villages at New Lanark, Stanley in Perthshire and Persley on the River Don. Enthusiasm at the sight of the Clyde Falls led Arkwright to predict that 'Lanark would in time become the Manchester of Scotland'. The constricted site, however, killed any hope of New Lanark rivalling that great cotton city, the symbol of the first industrial age.[1]

New Lanark was important in the story of Scotland's urbanization, for it provided a laboratory for social experiment. The first proprietor, David Dale, built a village to house one thousand people and which included a barracks capable of housing five hundred orphan children. Dale was regarded as a model employer even though children worked a thirteen-hour day in his factories. By 1799 New Lanark was the largest cotton mill in Scotland. Robert Owen, Dale's son-in-law, carried on in the same fashion and proved that a benevolent employer could make profits large enough to merit the title, 'Prince of Cotton Spinners'.[2] During the first thirty years of the nineteenth century, Owen, as partner-manager of the New Lanark Mills, pioneered reforms in the education of factory children, reduced the hours of labour, and hoped to bring about an industrial/urban harmony which he felt had been lost when people moved from rural communities. Owen was a man ahead of his time. Through his activities there developed a partial understanding of the social problems of the industrial town; but solving them was another matter. The value of his belief in the possibility of a harmonious organic community in contrast to unrestrained capitalism was not acknowledged until the twentieth century and his visions have yet to be realized.

Other settlements based on a single cotton spinning factory emerged. At Stanley on the River Tay several Perth merchants feued ground from the Duke of Atholl to set up a cotton mill in 1784 and soon built a village for the mill workers. Of the 100 families living there a decade later, about 350 people were employed at the mill, 300 of them being women or children under sixteen.[3]

It is clear that in these early years of the Industrial Revolution the key factor in location of factory and town was the necessity to harness water power: 'The First mills were built chiefly by Glasgow men but set up at a distance from Glasgow, a convenient supply of water power to drive the machinery being what mainly guided the choice of site for the works.'[4] Often the mill owner had to provide a large number of homes near the mill and occasionally this could lead to fruitful co-operation between industrialist and landowner. In 1782 George Houston of Johnstone feued land beside the Bridge of Johnstone to Corse, Burns and Company for a water-powered cotton mill five storeys high. At the same time Houston founded the village of Johnstone. By 1792 there were five cotton mills employing 1,020 people out of a population of 1,434.[5] The cotton industry prospered in Renfrewshire and a series of planned industrial towns was built to serve its needs (Fig. 5.1). Though some places, like New Lanark, remained no more than company villages others mushroomed into towns. In 1780 a co-partnership of Glasgow and Lancashire merchants built a cotton mill on the River Levern in Neilston parish, and at the same time 2 km to the south, Gavin Rawlston feued off the new town of Newton Rawlston which became one of the nuclei of Barrhead. The scale of change strained the credulity of contemporaries:

Barrhead, you must understand, has undergone a considerable metamorphosis with these thirty years back, when it may be said it was in its infancy; then it consisted of thirty families, now there is a street half a mile in length, built on each side .. there was perhaps but one small cotton factory on the Levern, and now there are six large ones within 2½ miles [4 km] of each other, besides three or four printfields, two weaving factories, and bleachfields numerous and extensive. Thirty years ago there was only one public house in this village and now there are certainly thirty. Thirty years ago there was but one school in it, and now there are in the village and neighbourhood six or seven.[6]

With a few exceptions, such as David Dale at New Lanark, cotton manufacturers had no real enthusiasm for urban experiments because of the capital costs involved. As James Watt saw in 1784, 'rotative engines, which we have now rendered very complete, are

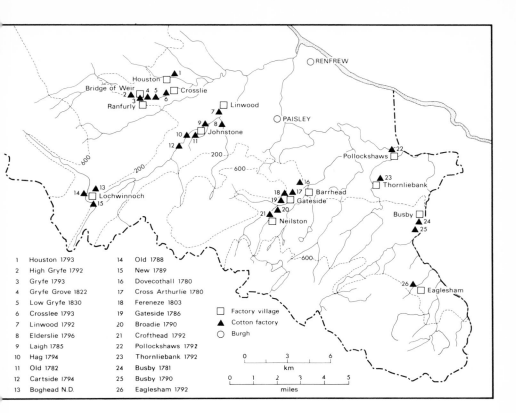

□ Factory village
▲ Cotton factory
○ Burgh

Fig. 5.1 Cotton mills and early industrial towns of Renfrewshire

certainly very applicable to the driving of cotton mills in every case where the conveniency of planning the mill in a town or ready-built manufactory will compensate for the expense of coals and of our premium'.[7] Watt's vision was ultimately realized although, throughout the initial period of cotton mill building in the 1780s and early 1890s, water power was favoured and Boulton and Watt did not sell a single textile mill engine in Scotland. In 1798 they sold one 16 horse-power engine, in 1799 three and in 1800 five, the total generating a mere 144 horse-power.[8] The early years of the nineteenth century saw a rapid growth in the application of steam power to cotton spinning, and in the 1820s there was a rush of mill building in Glasgow, Johnstone and Paisley, where available water power had long been used to capacity.

The rise of industrial Glasgow began in 1792 with the installation at Springfield on the south bank of the Clyde of its first steam engine used for spinning cotton. Two power looms were introduced a year later in an Argyle Street works and were powered by a large Newfoundland dog. Progress was still slow for only 40 looms were installed in 1794 and 200 more in 1801. Steam power then began to be applied and 'the extension of power loom factories, and of the cotton trade generally, became so rapid as almost to exceed belief.' By 1861 about one-eighth of the population of Glasgow between the ages of 10 and 40 was employed in textile factories. In addition several thousand more were still hand-loom weaving, between 3,000 to 4,000 were employed in printworks, as well as numerous others in bleaching, dyeing and wholesaling. 'The factories are a prominent architectural feature of the city, — or at least of its suburbs and out-skirts; and, not only by their number, but by their great size and their prevailing symmetry and neatness, they often strike strangers from agricultural districts with amazement.'[9]

The shift of textile manufacture from cottage to factory led to regional specialization, with cotton dominating in Renfrewshire and Lanarkshire, woollens in the Borders and linen in Fife, Perth-shire and Angus. In some cases old established towns were revital-ized, but in others completely new settlements arose. Urban expan-sion can be seen clearly in the Borders, an area which had from monastic times been a major producer of wool and woollen cloth. By the sixteenth century most Border towns and villages had their fulling mills, but little growth was experienced until the last quarter of the eighteenth century. Between 1774 and 1825 wool consump-tion at Galashiels rose from 7,718 kg to over 227,000 kg, and in response to the vast increase in the output of power-spun wool, the number of handloom weavers in the town increased from about 30 in the 1770s to 175 in 1828 (Fig. 5.2).[10] The market town of Hawick in 1800 had barely outgrown its boundaries mentioned in its charter of confirmation in 1537.[11] Four spinning mills were then built on flat land in the suburb of Wilton on the other side of the River Teviot and another five by 1859. The population of Hawick increased fourfold during that period, from 2,789 in 1801 to 8,191 in 1861, a reflection of the impetus gained from the burgh's functional change (Fig. 5.3). Alex Brodie, a local blacksmith who had made his fortune in the Shropshire iron trade, stimulated the growth of Innerleithen by building a five-storey woollen mill there in the 1780s. Water-powered woollen mills also led to the creation of new villages at Walkerburn and Earlston, and during the late 1790s a woollen manufactory was established in Peebles. Between 1790 and 1830 the Border towns, particularly Galashiels, led Britain in the range of processes which had been successfully mechanized. This ability to adopt new inventions was the foundation of the success of the Border towns, and the introduction of tweed in the 1830s assured their future.

In many ways linen formed a link between rural and urban industry in the eighteenth century. The industry grew under the tutelage of the Board of Trustees for Manufactures which had been founded in 1727 by pressure from the Convention of Royal Burghs. The Board's influence led to the building of lint mills, the laying out

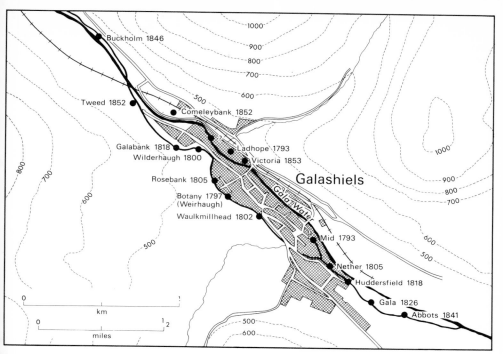

Fig. 5.2 The growth of
the woollen spinning
industry in Galashiels

Fig. 5.3 The growth of
Hawick and the
woollen industry 1771-
1861

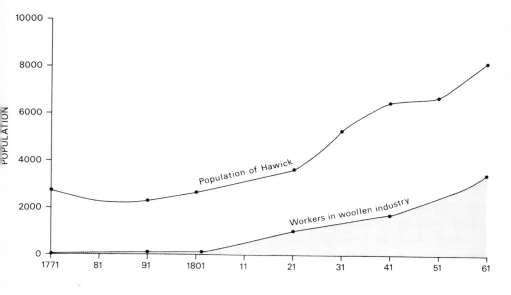

of bleachfields and numerous other innovations. Ultimately Dundee became the centre of the industry, whose influence spread through the valleys of Angus, Fife and Perthshire. Water-powered linen spinning was achieved and patented by John Kendrew and Thomas Porthouse of Darlington in 1787, and in the same year Scotland's first flax spinning mill was opened near Inverbervie, Kincardineshire.[12] Progress was fitful, for the flax fibres were brittle and snapped easily, but in the 1820s James Kay's process of wet spinning overcame the difficulty and made possible the efficient mill-spinning of flax. The abundant supply of water power at Blairgowrie led to the establishment of eleven mills employing 463 people (Fig. 5.4).

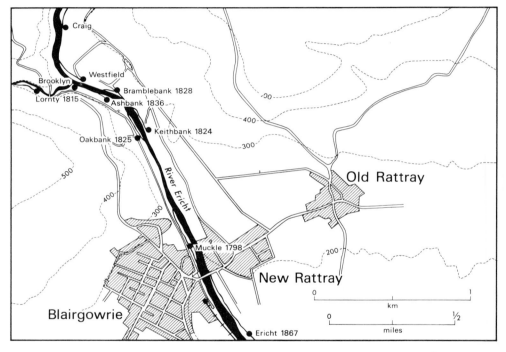

Fig. 5.4 Blairgowrie and the growth of linen spinning

Some employees lived beside the mills in tied houses but more lived in the town itself.

A little after the beginning of the present century, Blairgowrie was an insignificant village of mean thatched houses; but now it has a decided town appearance, with good streets, many good houses, and a considerable stir of business.... A good deal of business is done in the town, and much employment given to the inhabitants in connection with the spinning-mills.[13]

While Blairgowrie continued to prosper throughout the nineteenth century, most other rural mills closed after the introduction of steam power about 1820. There emerged a strong urban concentration — Dundee specialized in heavy flax and tow fabrics, Arbroath was the seat of the canvas trade, Forfar and Brechin produced heavy linens such as osnaburgs and northern Fife specialized in finer linens and bleached goods.[14]

Jute had been gradually introduced into Dundee's textile industry in the 1840s but the loss of Baltic flax during the Crimean War led to the complete changeover to this tropical fibre. Factory after factory was opened and labour for the great jute firms was drawn into Dundee from the Angus countryside, the Highlands and Ireland so that between 1854 and 1914 Dundee's housing stock never met the needs of the jute workers.[15]

Whilst textiles provided the economic base to the first industrial towns, iron and steel gave rise to fewer but more substantial towns thirled to local mineral resources. As long as iron smelting was a peripatetic industry dependent on charcoal no settlement of any note emerged. The little hamlet of Bonawe near Oban, now a national monument, illustrates the small size of even the largest of these industries at that time. The lighting of the first coal burning furnace at Carron in 1760 heralded a revolution in iron-making, both in techniques and size.[16] Carron was soon the largest foundry in Europe. A new settlement sprang up at Stenhousemuir, and Larbert changed from a small agricultural hamlet to an industrial town; the two towns housed 1,200 men working at Carron. Thereafter the location of ironworks was severely limited by the inadequacies of the transport system and new settlements were developed on out-of-the-way sites close to pockets of iron ore and coal. Settlements such as Shotts, Wilsontown, Muirkirk and Glenbuck had much in common with early cotton towns and mining villages: largely unplanned, with poor houses and minimum services, they were dominated by a single industry and often by one proprietor. By the 1820s the Scottish iron industry was in poor shape, relying on poor quality clay-band ores and coking coals. Dramatic change came in 1828 with James Beaumont Neilson's patent hot blast process which allowed the use of the more abundant blackband ores.[17] Pig iron output rose from 38,300 tonnes in 1820 to 274,254 tonnes in 1842 (Fig. 5.5). By 1835, 65 of the 88 Scottish blast furnaces were situated in or about the Monklands (Fig. 5.6). The speed and size of these developments left little scope for good town planning. One result was Coatbridge, a town straggling between foundries, railways and canal.

Coatbridge did not retain its monopoly, for Motherwell grew to considerable importance:

Founded in the early years of the nineteenth century, having previously had no existence even as a village, it consists largely of

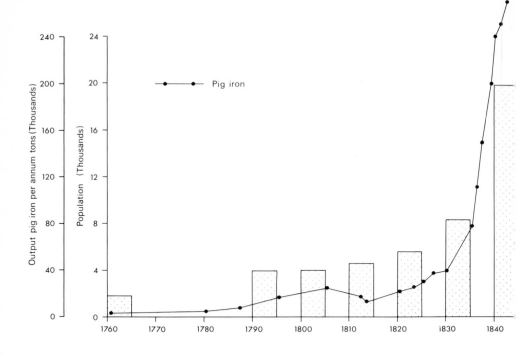

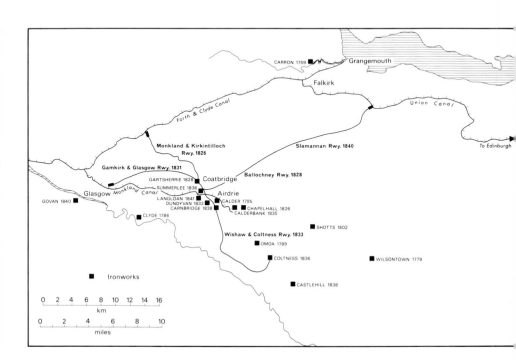

ig. 5.5 Pig iron output
d the growth of
oatbridge

the dwellings of miners and operatives employed in the neighbouring collieries and ironworks, and serves, in connection with
the railway junctions, as a great and bustling centre of traffic...
No Scottish town has grown so rapidly as Motherwell, such
growth being due to the vast extension of its mineral industries.
Besides the works of the Glasgow Malleable Iron and Steel
Company — the largest in Scotland — there are several other
extensive iron and steel works. In and about the town are also
boiler works, bolt and rivet works, brick, tile and fire-clay works,
quarries, steam crane works, and spade and shovel works.[18]

After 1871 the ironmasters invested heavily in open-hearth steelworks, especially for ship plate, and by the late 1880s Scotland was
the leading open-hearth steel district in Britain. Up to World War I,
when shipbuilding was the chief growth point of the Scottish
economy, the sheer volume of work kept these steel towns growing
(Fig. 5.7). Thereafter this supremacy was challenged and lost,
through failure to integrate the various steel-making processes.
Motherwell's continuation has been maintained only by huge government grants between 1958 and 1963. Ultimately the British Steel
Corporation will have to build on a green-field site on the Clyde
estuary. This will mean a considerable upheaval of population but
on the other hand will provide an opportunity to plan anew.

g. 5.6 The growth of
e iron industry and
e Monkland Railways
59-1842

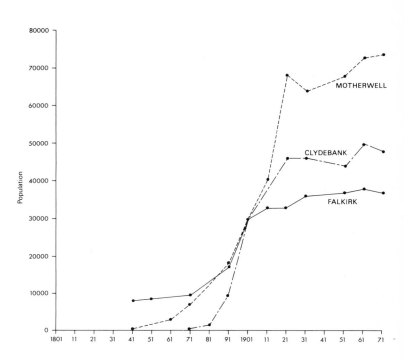

g. 5.7 Population
owth in iron and
eel towns. Note
e rapid rise between
390 and 1914

95

Rapid growth also occurred in Falkirk where the population rose from 9,547 in 1871 to 17,282 in 1891. Nineteen foundries had been established in or near the burgh, and three more were under construction. The period was one of immense boom but wages never rose high enough to enable the working man to pay an adequate rent. No workers' houses had been erected in the burgh for many years, so that overcrowding was excessive. In 1898, when the town council made a desperate plea to the Secretary of State to be allowed to build forty *one-roomed* houses, even this modest programme was refused (Fig. 5.8).[19]

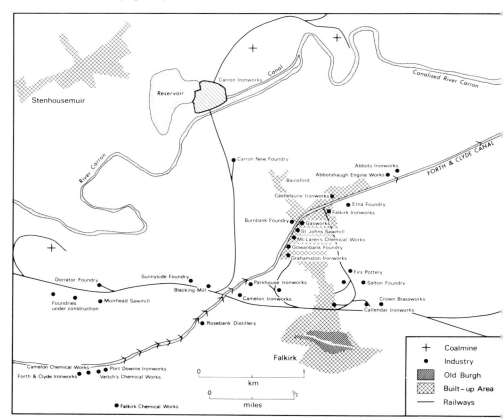

Fig. 5.8 Burgeoning industry around Falkirk 1898. Workers from Carron Ironworks lived in Stenhousemuir (Source: SRO British Rail records MPS(S)2/35.)

Shipbuilding entered the industrial scene late, making its first major contribution to the growth of the Scottish economy after 1870 with its consolidation on the Clyde.[20] To expand, the industry had to break out of the confines of the city. In 1872 J. and G. Thomson's yard moved to a new site on the north bank some 11 km downriver, which possessed neither housing nor transport for the labour force. The Glasgow, Yoker and Clydebank Railway Company built a line to serve the new shipyard and a sewing machine factory, and began a spectacular commuter operation without parallel in the country. Between six and seven o'clock of a morning fourteen trains converged on Clydebank from as far east as Airdrie and as far west as Balloch. Clydebank, a small village of 816 people in 1871, became a police burgh in 1886 and a town of 30,000 people by 1901. In the rush to house so many people, standards were minimal, for in 1911 four-fifths of the houses had two rooms or less.[21] Clydebank's rapid growth was uncoordinated, unplanned, and almost entirely dependent on two major industries so that in the inter-war slump the town had one of the highest unemployment rates in Britain. War dealt a savage blow when 35 per cent of the housing stock was damaged or destroyed.[22] The post-war years have not been easy, for Clydebank's blighted inheritance has been added to by the failure of the shipbuilding industry.

The tidemarks of industrial activity can be seen in the industrial dereliction of several towns in Central Scotland — Fauldhouse, Forth, Harthill, Newmains, Shotts and Whitburn — but the purely mining settlements were vulnerable and suffered most. Parallel to the rise of the industrial towns, a large number of unplanned village-like settlements grew up around pit-heads. Nineteenth-century coal-mining was transitory, and the inevitable exhaustion of seams and closure of pits led people to regard the mining village as temporary. Physical isolation reinforced social isolation, a relic of serfdom. Although housing standards were worse than in the towns, conditions were ameliorated by a rural location and a deep sense of community. Numerous such villages sprang up in southern Ayrshire, central Fife and the uplands of the central coalfield. The Royal Commission on Housing in Scotland in 1917 found conditions in other coalfields no better than at the Rosehall rows in Whifflet, Lanarkshire:

> Four long parallel rows of single-storey hovels; most of them have no rhones to carry the rain from the roofs. Rainwater simply runs down the roof and then runs down the walls. . . There are no coal-cellars; coals are kept below the beds. There are no wash-houses. Water is supplied from stands in the alleys. The closet accommodation is hideous. A number of these hovels are built back-to-back.[23]

At the turn of the twentieth century about 13,000 men were employed in mining in Ayrshire. The total mining community was 40,000, of which 75 per cent lived in mining rows or villages belonging to the mining companies. Most of the dwellings were single storeyed with just a room and kitchen. Conditions were appalling, with overcrowding the rule rather than the exception. Dampness was widespread and in Burnbrae, Tarbolton, the space under beds was not floored. Sewage disposal was rudimentary — waste water emptied into open channels and thence into cesspools near the houses, and the privies were emptied on to large privy middens which were cleaned out monthly.[24]

James Young's discovery and patenting of the low temperature distillation of coal in 1850 brought a new era of geological exploitation in Scotland with the extraction of rich oil shale at Torbanehill, near Bathgate. The expiry of Young's patent in 1864 led to a remarkable proliferation of oil-works and by 1866 there were 120 in operation (Fig. 5.9). The shale oil boom was accompanied by extensive building of employees' houses. Broxburn became a large linear settlement flanking the old turnpike road to Glasgow, and the population doubled each decade from 660 (1861), to 1,457 (1871), to 3,066 (1881) and to 5,898 (1891). Winchburgh changed from a farming to a mining village. Prosperity was shortlived, for American crude petroleum first arrived in Britain in 1861, though it was relatively unimportant until after the American Civil War. Thereafter the number of works declined to a mere seven in 1910 but the industry struggled on, only finally ceasing in 1961.

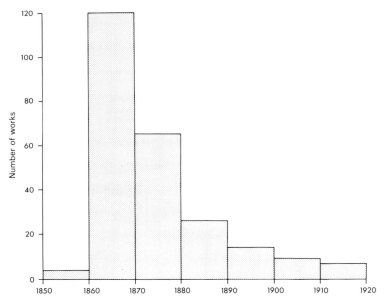

Fig. 5.9 Maximum number of shale works in operation in each decade 1850-1920

Agriculture also benefited from the rise of the industrial town. Adam Smith forecast this inter-relationship, for industrial towns, 'by affording a great and ready market for the rude produce of the county . . . gave encouragement to its cultivation and further improvement'.[25] The increasing numbers of mouths to be fed led to completely new methods of marketing, with emphasis on large, steady flows of staple foods. Throughout the nineteenth century perishability and current means of transport determined the level of specialization at which farmers could serve the urban market. The production of milk remained in or near towns, mainly in urban dairies with their town milk being retailed through the streets in pails. Cattle were purchased in calf and stall fed by cowkeepers often in extremely congested conditions. In 1865 and 1866 there were epidemics of cattle plague and town herds began to disappear. Government regulation in 1865 curtailed the operation of town diaries and thenceforth railways played an increasingly important role by transporting railway milk from specialized dairy districts. The pastures of Ayrshire began to produce milk for Glasgow, and when this market was saturated, especially during the summer, the surplus was converted to less perishable products. The first factory for the manufacture of dairy foods was established in Derby in 1870, but the most important technical development was the introduction of the centrifugal separator in 1877. At Lockerbie, creameries and cheese factories were set up close to the railway by the Annandale Dairy Company in 1899 and the Edinburgh and Dumfries Dairy Company in 1919. Other factories were built at Kirkcudbright, Dumfries, Sanquhar and Stranraer.

Horticulture had similar problems regarding perishability. These were overcome by surrounding the city with a tight belt of market gardens and nurseries which met the demands on the soil by heavy inputs of urban manure. The volume of sewage increased as water supplies improved, and was put to good use by the market gardeners of Edinburgh. The common sewers of the city emerged to the east of Holyrood Palace as the Foul Burn, which carried its rich load to the sea at Craigentinny. The irrigated meadows beside the stream were some of the most valuable farmlands in Scotland.[26] Even when the sewage systems were improved the large horse population of the towns provided valuable manure. Street sweepings were taken to manure sidings, such as at Meadowbank and Dary in Edinburgh, and thence to dung depots in the countryside. Areas in the vicinity of these depots used so much cheap manure that the structure of the soil has been permanently altered. At times the scale of these operations was quite awesome; for example, Glasgow Corporation reclaimed 40 hectares of Fulwood Moss, Renfrewshire, for a potato farm with 12,192 tonnes of street sweepings, the product of three hundred men's labour for one year.

Town markets came under severe pressure with the growth of population, resulting in a concentration on the wholesale trade. Change also came geographically for there was no room for growth on the constricted sites at the edge of the medieval towns, so markets were moved in a series of steps outwards, each time being established at the edge of the built-up area, only to be engulfed again by suburban expansion (Fig. 5.10). Glasgow's markets were one undertaking until 1845 and formed part of the common good of the city. In that year the Glasgow Market and Slaughter-houses Act transferred the cattle market, slaughter houses and horse market from the common good to the corporation as trustees, at the same

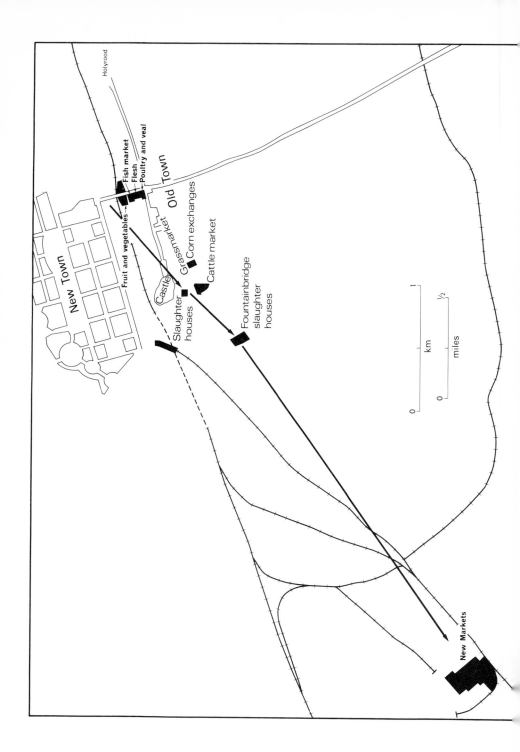

New Town

Old Town

Holyrood

Fish market
Flesh
Poultry and veal

Fruit and vegetables

Castle

Grassmarket

Corn exchanges

Cattle market

Slaughter houses

Fountainbridge slaughter houses

New Markets

km

miles

½

0

0

of Edinburgh's markets

Fig. 5.11 The migration
of Glasgow's markets

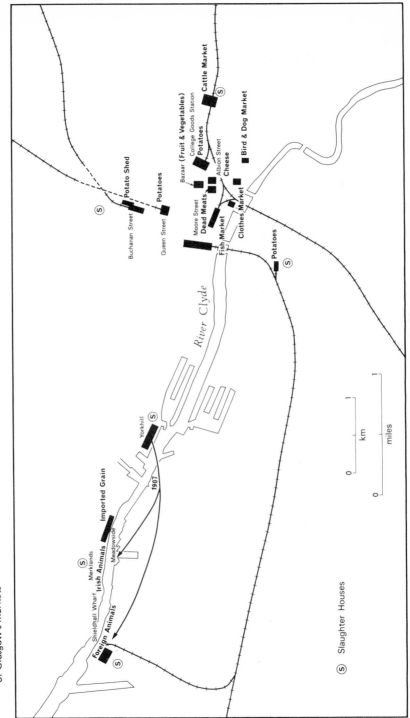

Potato Shed

Buchanan Street

Potatoes

Queen Street

Bazaar (Fruit & Vegetables)

College Goods Station

Potatoes

Albion Street

Cheese

Bird & Dog Market

Cattle Market

Moore Street

Dead Meats

Fish Market

Clothes Market

Potatoes

River Clyde

Imported Grain

Yorkhill

1907

Irish Animals

Merklands

Sheldhall Wharf

Meadowside

Foreign Animals

Slaughter Houses

km

miles

0   1

0   1

time abolishing private slaughter houses; a new Act in 1865 brought in the fish market. In 1905 the Markets Act transferred the fruit and vegetable bazaar, cheese market, bird and dog market and old clothes market to the corporation. The import of livestock was at first concentrated at Yorkhill but fluctuations of trade, outbreaks of foot-and-mouth disease and the need for a harbour extension at Yorkhill wharf led to a move downstream, to Merklands for the Irish and to Shieldhall for the North American trade (Fig. 5.11). A similar concentration of marketing and storage occurred in the grain trade when the repeal of the Corn Laws in 1846 brought into economic range wheat from the Black Sea region and the farmlands of the American Great Lakes. Massive grain elevators rose above the quaysides at Meadowside in Glasgow and Leith Docks in Edinburgh, to become symbols of the world of industry and trade which was reached by the end of the nineteenth century. At the same time production of food ceased to be a national concern, but relied heavily upon an imperial system to provide cheap food for the urban masses.

Acceptance of the foundation and growth of industrial towns and a faith in social progress became more general during the latter half of the nineteenth century as the towns became more prosperous and socially stable. Economic individualism was seen by many people as the ethic of urban society, with improvements being made through municipal regulation, philanthropic effort and, above all, self-help.[27] At the same time, local government stumbled from palliative to panacea, each piece of legislation taking it a step further along the path of urban reform.

Notes

1. See Asa Briggs, *Victorian Cities* (Penguin, Harmondsworth, 1968), ch. 3. pp. 88-138 for a vivid account of Manchester's influence on attitudes towards the growing industrial town.

2. J. Butt, (ed.), *Robert Owen, Prince of Cotton Spinners : A Symposium* (David and Charles, Newton Abbot, 1971).

3. *OSA,* Aughtergaven parish, Perthshire, 17, p. 556.

4. Autobiography of Peter Carmichael, in Enid Gauldie, *The Dundee Textile Industry 1790-1885* (Scottish History Society, Edinburgh, 1969), p. 5.

5. *OSA*, Abbey Parish of Paisley, 7, p. 88.

6. *Glasgow Free Press,* 8 September 1827, quoted in C. Taylor, *The Levern Delineated* (Glasgow, 1831), p. 72.

7. SRO (GD1/612/1).

8. R.L. Hills, *Power in the Industrial Revolution* (Manchester, 1970), p. 159.

9. J.M. Wilson, (ed.), *The Imperial Gazeteer of Scotland* (London, n.d.), p. 755.

10. C. Gulvin, *The Tweedmakers* (David and Charles, Newton Abbot, 1973), p. 40.

11. R. Murray, *History of Hawick from the Earliest Time to 1832.*

12. J. Butt, *Industrial Archaeology of Scotland* (David and Charles, Newton Abbot, 1967), p. 61.

13. J.M. Wilson (ed.), *The Imperial Gazetteer of Scotland* (Fullarton, London, n.d.).

14. W.H.K. Turner, *The Textile Industry of Arbroath since the Early Eighteenth Century* (Abertay Historical Society Publication No. 2, Dundee, 1954).

15. B. Lenman, C. Lythe and E. Gauldie, *Dundee and its Textile Industry 1850-1914* (Abertay Historical Society Publication No. 14, Dundee, 1969), p. 78.

16. R.H. Campbell, *Carron Company* (Oliver and Boyd, Edinburgh, 1961).

17. K. Warren, 'Locational Problems of the Scottish Iron and Steel Industry since 1760', *Scottish Geographical Magazine,* vol. 81 (1965), pt 1, pp. 18-37, pt 2, pp. 87-103.

18. F.H. Groome, *Ordnance Gazetteer of Scotland* (London, 1903), p. 1203.

19. 'Housing of the Working Classes. Proposed One-Roomed Houses in Falkirk 1898' (SRO DD6/254).

20. R.H. Campbell, 'Scottish Shipbuilding: Its Rise and Progress', *Scottish Geographical Magazine,* vol. 80 (1964), pp. 107-13.

21. Return showing the housing conditions of the population of Scotland 1908 (SRO DD6/265).

22. Home and Health Department records. Air raids on Clydeside (SRO HH50/91-103).

23. *Report of the Royal Commission on the Housing of the Industrial Population of Scotland Rural and Urban* (HMSO, Edinburgh, 1917), para. 948. See also paras 917, 918, 921, 938, 941, 951 and 953. For papers of Royal Commission (SRO DD6/172-199, 1171).

24. 'Housing conditions in mining districts in Scotland 1898-1914' (SRO DD6/1170).

25. Adam Smith, *The Wealth of Nations,* ed. E. Cannan, 5th ed. (Methuen, London, 1930), p. 382.

26. The offensive odours rendered the Palace of Holyrood uninhabitable and gave rise to litigation to control these practices (SRO, Court of Session process, The Lord Advocate, *v.* Fletcher & ors, 1845 CS232 A/22/3); see also P.J. Smith, 'The Foul Burns of Edinburgh: Public Health Attitudes and Environmental Change', *Scottish Geographical Magazine,* vol. 91 (1975), pp. 25-37.

27. B.I. Coleman, *The Idea of the City in Nineteenth-Century Britain* (Routledge and Kegan Paul, London, 1973).

6

Transport systems have always exerted an influence upon the success or failure of towns. In each age the dominant form of transport has reflected the limits of technology at the time. Until the end of the eighteenth century, the sea satisfied most of the country's transport requirements and most burghs were situated on or near the coast, each with easy access to a natural harbour. However, changes began when more specialized harbours were required especially for the coal trade. Bo'ness, Alloa and Saltcoats Harbours were founded in the seventeenth century, St David's and Charlestown in Fife in the eighteenth century and Methil a century later. The urban implications of these foundations are best documented in the case of Methil which was an insignificant burgh of barony of little over 700 people until Methil Number One Dock was opened to traffic in 1887. Four years later the population had more than doubled. A second dock was opened in 1899 and a third in 1913 when coal exports exceeded 3 million tonnes (Fig. 6.1). The town expanded to over 17,000 people in the interwar period when Methil remained Scotland's leading coal export port. The collapse of the coal export trade since the Second World War has left the town with an obsolete harbour and chronic unemployment. All those ports founded earlier collapsed as their mining hinterland either found new markets or became exhausted.

The old natural harbours began to decline in the eighteenth century when large capital outlay was expended on more modern docks. The first dry dock at Leith, for instance, was built in 1720 and the second in the 1760s (Fig. 6.2). David Loch observed in 1778 that these dry docks were 'well-employed ... and of great benefit to all the shipping on the east of Scotland'.[1] The town's proximity to Edinburgh was the spur to growth which was reflected in its expanding population: 5,500 in 1706, 9,405 in 1755 and rising to 13,841 in 1791. Thereafter the real impetus to growth came from the series of wet docks — East and West, Victoria, Albert, Edinburgh and Imperial — built between 1799 and 1911 to serve the markets of the Empire.

Different patterns could be observed on the west coast, for Glasgow was divorced from the sea by an unnavigable channel in the River Clyde. The city's need for a harbour prompted the town council in 1668 to purchase land at Newark on the south bank of the Clyde, where quays and docks were built. The new town, Port Glasgow, remained the chief port of the Clyde until the late eighteenth century.[2] Shaw of Greenock erected a burgh of barony in 1635 on an ideal site to serve shipping in the Clyde estuary, but

Fig. 6.1 Methil Docks, Fife. In the background the burghs of Buckhaven and Methil and Leven. (Photo: John Dewar.)

Greenock's harbour was not built until 1710 when basins occupying an area of 3 hectares were completed.[3] Although extensions were completed in 1734 and 1751, Greenock never attracted as much traffic as Port Glasgow, the royal burgh's outport.

The Union of the Parliaments in 1707 opened up the tobacco trade of Virginia, Maryland and North Carolina to Scottish merchants. The Clyde ports were handling 10 per cent of the British tobacco trade in 1741, had doubled this by 1744 and had captured 52 per cent by 1769.[4] This massive increase in trade necessitated large extensions to harbour facilities, such as graving docks at Port Glasgow in 1763 and Greenock in 1783. Yet the facilities remained inadequate and most vessels were forced to anchor in the roads and tranship their cargoes into lighters. Clearly Glasgow itself would have to be opened to ocean navigation.

Glasgow magistrates appointed a committee in 1737 to study 'the ways and means for deepening the river and foords' but little was done. A report prepared by John Smeaton in 1755 initiated a

Fig. 6.2 The prosperous port of Leith. The dry docks can be seen north of The Shore. (Scottish Record Office.)

107

scheme to 'cleanse, amend and improve' the river, but again the city fathers took no action. The turning point came in 1768 when John Golbourne of Chester recommended that the existing channel be narrowed by the construction of a series of jetties which would stimulate tidal scour and thus deepen the river. The scheme was a success and by 1781 ocean-going vessels of 200-300 tonnes were berthing at the Broomielaw (Fig. 6.3). The tobacco trade had already been lost in the American War of Independence, but its place was taken by a new cargo, cotton, which was to change the whole basis of urban life in Scotland.

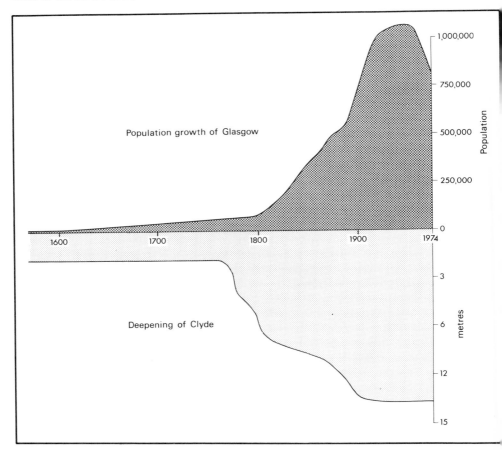

Fig. 6.3 The deepening of the River Clyde and the growth of Glasgow

The Glasgow tobacco merchants also played an important role in the Canal Age in Scotland. They were the principal shareholders in the Forth and Clyde Canal which was begun in July 1769 on mud-flats at the mouth of the Grange Burn on the Forth. The canal reached the northern outskirts of Glasgow in 1777 but the collapse of the tobacco trade stopped work until a grant from the Commissioners of the Forfeited Estates allowed completion in 1790. Port

Dundas, on the northern outskirts of Glasgow, developed into a bustling inland port, though the canal's western terminus at Bowling remained a small cluster of employees' houses. Sir Lawrence Dundas of Kerse saw an ideal opportunity to augment his rents by laying out a town at the eastern terminus. The site chosen was a narrow neck of land between the Sea-Lock (the town was known by this name until 1784) and the new cut of the River Carron (Fig. 6.4). With the customs house, transferred from Bo'ness in 1810, the canal to Glasgow and low shore dues, Grangemouth prospered at the expense of its neighbour, Bo'ness. New docks and timber basins built in the nineteenth century gave continuous prosperity and with the early adoption of containerization and the continuing expansion of the oil refining industry Grangemouth has become Scotland's premier east coast port. Urban expansion was also stimulated at Falkirk and Kirkintilloch, but it is clear that the Forth and Clyde Canal and its branch, the Monkland Canal, were not so important in this sphere as was the canal system in England.[5] Their most valuable contribution was to Glasgow, for without the benefit of cheap, bulk transport the fuel situation in Glasgow would have become critical in the years before railways. The canal and its cheap coals allowed the continued building of steam-powered factories within the city limits.

Probably the most ambitious canal town was the Earl of Eglinton's Ardrossan, with a harbour designed to be the terminus of the Glasgow, Paisley and Ardrossan Canal (Fig. 6.5). The harbour was begun in 1806 but its extravagant design brought work to a standstill by 1815 and at the same time it was clear that financial difficulties would force a premature termination of the canal at Johnstone. The town of Ardrossan was laid out in a spacious grid pattern with a good many elegant villas. Few burghs could benefit from canals so men turned to roads which were more suited to Scotland's topography.

In medieval times movement by road was very restricted and effectively limited any burgh's chance of establishing a strong regional market. Roads were bad because there was no real authority to provide a proper system. The first important legislation designed to improve them is found in the two Acts of 1617 and 1661, under which Justices of the Peace were directed to mend roads leading to market towns, seaports and parish churches. These Acts, however, proved ineffective, and in 1669 a further and more comprehensive Act was passed, appointing the Sheriff and one of his deputes — 'being always ane heritor' — and Justices of the Peace as the local road authority, and requiring them to meet yearly to prepare a list of highways, bridges and ferries to be repaired. They were given power to appoint overseers, who in turn were authorized to call on the service of tenants, cottars and servants with horse and cart for up to six days service each year. Naturally this compulsory service,

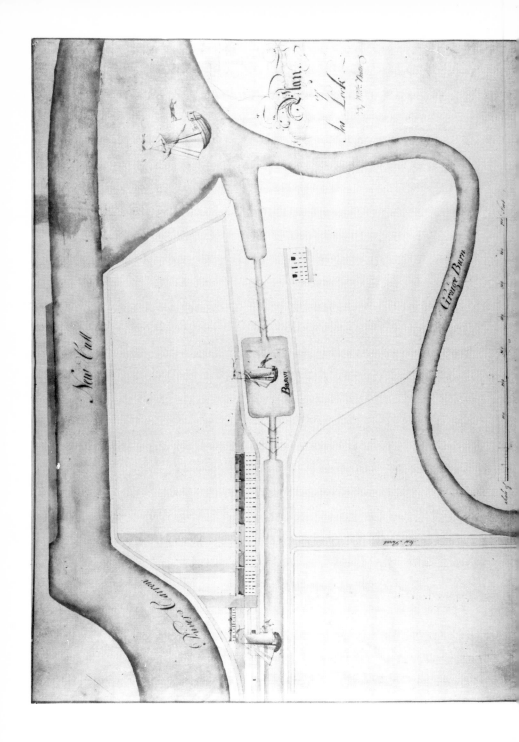

110

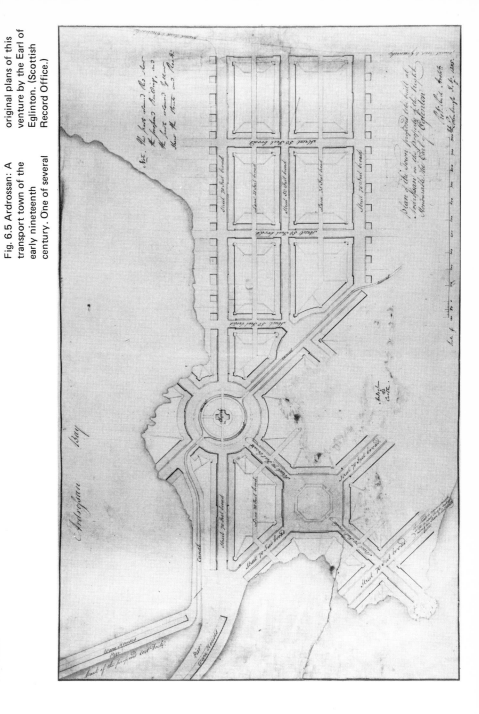

Fig. 6.5 Ardrossan: A transport town of the early nineteenth century. One of several original plans of this venture by the Earl of Eglinton. (Scottish Record Office.)

map of Grangemouth (c. 1772).

usually known as statute labour, was grudgingly given, for it often meant that men had to leave urgent work at home.

Examples of inefficient road transport abound. At the end of the eighteenth century it still required two days' work with a cart and two horses to carry four or five bolls (250 to 300 kg) of grain from the west end of the county to the markets of Berwick or Eyemouth, a distance of 30-50 km.[6] It was considered a good winter day's work for a horse to carry 100 kg of coal 6½ km from the coal mines to Haddington.[7]

After 1750 the era of the turnpike trusts opened up inland country towns. The initiative was generally taken by local proprietors and business people, who made preliminary surveys and estimates and raised a subscription to defray the expenses of obtaining a private Act of Parliament. Typical of a turnpike trust was one for Ayrshire formed in 1767 which improved the links between towns, either by repairing and widening existing roads or by constructing new roads between such places as Kilmarnock and Irvine, Ayr and Irvine, Irvine and Saltcoats, and Ayr and Sanquhar.

City expansion too was facilitated by the improvement of roads. Villa suburbs sprang up with their prominent stables intimating the possession of a carriage. Turnpikes like those of Minto Street in Edinburgh and the Great Western Road in Glasgow gave easy access to town. Speculation was rife, for the landowners had a vested interest in these roads. The success of Glasgow's West End, made up of exclusive upper middle-class houses and covering an area of 5 by 1½ km, was one such case. To attract prospective house buyers the landowners laid on a subsidized horse bus service.[8] The horse-drawn omnibus remained a privileged form of transport for its fares were out of reach of most of the population; it was the railways which brought transport to the masses.

As the eighteenth century neared its close the steam engine was already firmly established at the pit-head and soon led to profound changes in urban Scotland. The rudimentary links provided by the turnpikes and canals did not merit the designation 'network', although both helped to alleviate transport problems, the most pressing of which was the cost of coal. This was notoriously high in Edinburgh for carters and coal merchants added 150 per cent to the price of coal on a 10 km journey from the Lothian collieries.[9] Wagonways had been used for taking coal from pit to private harbour, and it was only a matter of time before they were pointed towards the city. In 1826 the Garnkirk and Glasgow Railway Company obtained an Act to build a direct line from the Monklands coalfield to Glasgow in competition with the canal. With its opening in 1831 speedy, efficient and convenient transport was introduced, and it captured much of the increasing traffic.

It was the influence of the railways, more than any other single

112

agency, which gave the Victorian city its compact shape, which influenced the topography and character of its central inner districts, the disposition of its dilapidated and waste areas, and of its suburbs, the direction and character of its growth . . .[10]

H. J. Dyos went further, maintaining that 'the changes they brought were not, however, confined to the physical layout of the urban landscape. Railways also influenced the daily lives of the townspeople themselves'.[11]

As railways penetrated cities their demand for land had a profound influence on urban land use, though Scottish cities did not suffer to the same extent from the demolition of houses as did London and the English provincial cities. The glacial geomorphology of Edinburgh gave the railways considerable advantages and central locations were found close to the heart of the city. The Edinburgh and Glasgow Railway terminated at Haymarket and the Caledonian Railway built a modest station in open fields at the west end of Princes Street; only under the North Bridge did the railways compete with existing uses (Fig. 6.6). Similarly in Dundee, the first railways in the 1830s terminated at the end of the medieval burgh and even when connected across the town, reclamation beside the Tay provided ample land for railway yards. In Aberdeen, Guild Street station was built on land being reclaimed from the River Dee; when a northwards extension was required, the Den Valley provided an uncluttered routeway. Glasgow was the exception, for the railway companies situated just outside the central area embarked on large-scale penetration of the centre with the building of Central and St Enoch's Stations and the College goods yard complex.

After the main phase of railway construction the public no longer accepted the railway companies' activities with uncritical admiration. Henceforth the companies were on the defensive and city schemes were publicized with care. In Edinburgh, the Caledonian Railway, anxious to gain access to the east coast, planned an extension to their line from Princes Street station under George Street to a new station in St James Square and then on eastwards. Initial publicity stressed that the scheme would be accomplished 'without injury to the amenity of the city'.[12] This and similar projects failed but the railways enjoyed an orgy of conspicuous rebuilding. Several city main line stations were reconstructed and above each rose a splendid hotel whose gross solidity reflected the railways' corporate image at the turn of the century. The future still seemed assured.

Railways also gave rise to specialized settlements. In Scotland the railway town as a nineteenth-century phenomenon rarely reached the dimensions of Crewe, Doncaster or Swindon, though possibly Perth, with its plethora of railway companies and its station, could be classed as a railway town (Fig. 6.7).

Fig. 6.6 The Calton Hill, Calton Jail and The North British Railway station, Edinburgh.

The major railway workshops were established at the edge of cities, at Cowlairs in Glasgow by the Edinburgh and Glasgow Railway, and at St Margaret's Works in Edinburgh by the North British Railway. These were the cores of communities devoted solely to railway life. The ancient burgh of Inverurie was greatly changed with the establishment between 1898 and 1905 of the Great North of Scotland Railway's locomotive and carriage works which covered 10 hectares. The population increased by 1,200 and a new suburb was built at the north end of the old town.

Remote termini and junctions generated sufficient employment for new settlements to be created. Before the coming of the North British Railway, Riccarton in Roxburghshire was a bare hillside some 3 km from the nearest public road. After the station was built a railway community developed to service trains of the Waverley route on their passage over the Border Hills.[13] Carstairs Junction village was laid out by Joseph Locke in 1848 at the time of the opening of the Caledonian Railway, with a school and schoolmaster provided by the company. Mallaig was an isolated township at the tip of the North Morar peninsula which came to life as the terminus of the extension of the West Highland line. The construction of a pier, both for the ferry to Skye and as a landing point for the west coast

114

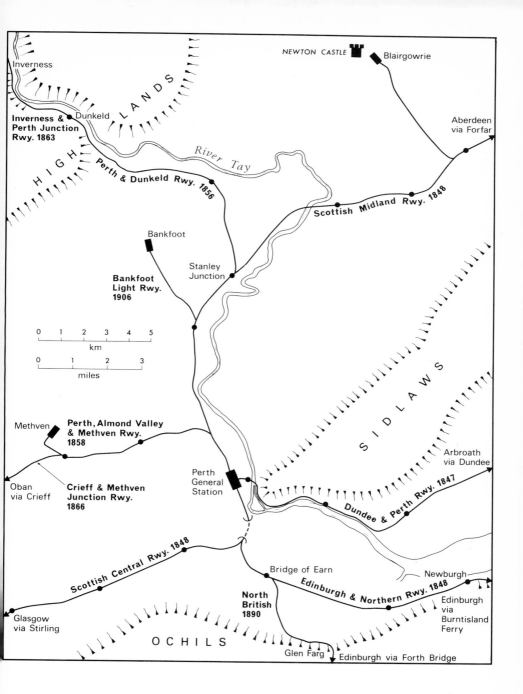

Fig. 6.7 Perth as a
railway centre

115

herring fleet, enabled a village to prosper on this rocky coast. Similarly, Kyle of Lochalsh grew up around a steamboat landing stage at the Highland Railway's terminus for Skye. The hamlet of Crianlarich nestles beneath the junction of the lines to Oban and Fort William.

Although Scotland benefited greatly from the initial phases of railway construction, many towns — Alyth, Crieff, Callander, Jedburgh, Peebles, St Andrews — were still without rail connections after the collapse of the 'railway mania' in 1847. In many smaller burghs civic improvement and rising self-esteem were apparent in the development of new streets and public buildings, and in the desire for a rail connection. But there was little chance of their hopes being realized for Scotland's railway companies were not in the position to commit themselves to new projects. Thus if any lines were to be built they had to be cheap and sponsored by local proprietors. Major H. L. Playfair, provost of St Andrews, encouraged his constituents to build their own line in 1852; this put new life into the town which had been declining as a result of its isolation at the tip of Fife, its lack of an agricultural market and the silting up of its harbour. The new railway enabled the residents to use their potential facilities for the fashionable recreations of golf and sea-bathing and the town became a favourite refuge for exiles returning from the Empire. The success of the project was due to the efforts of a young engineer, Thomas Bouch, whose 'cheap railway' philosophy was followed elsewhere (Fig. 6.8).[14]

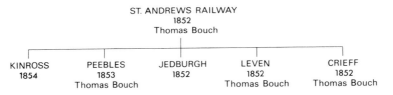

Fig. 6.8 Towns where railways were built on the St Andrews model

From the opening of the first railways, people used them to escape from the economic bondage of towns to more congenial surroundings. This was, however, regarded by the railway companies themselves as a privilege of the first-class rather than as a right for the third-class traveller:

> The working classes are not likely to be the first to enjoy the double benefit of city employment and wages and country residence to boot. There are thousands of persons of means superior to theirs who need country air as much as they. The working classes will be well off if the migration from the city of a large number of the wealthier classes gives to them a better choice of dwellings in the city.[15]

The process of the well-to-do moving out from the centre was not new, but the distance that could be travelled by train was revolutionary. An example of the transformation is the suburb of Trinity some 5 km north of Edinburgh. Before 1846 Trinity consisted of extensive flat lands formed by raised beaches and occupied by a few mansion houses whose owners had leased some of their land to brewers for growing barley or to market gardeners serving the city. With the opening of the Edinburgh, Leith and Newhaven Railway in 1846 the district became a fashionable quarter for 'the wealthy and more affluent class, many of them retired merchants and writers to the signet from the city, with a goodly sprinkling of rich and genteel families from many other places and countries'.[16] Further afield, North Berwick was promoted as a high-class residential outer suburb of Edinburgh by means of 'line of residence tickets'. These were issued to new residents who worked in Edinburgh but occupied a house within 1½ km of a North British station. Only first-class traffic was promoted, but results were so discouraging that the line reverted to horse-drawn rail vehicles.

The Blane Valley and Kelvin Valley Railways failed to induce the Glasgow merchant community to build their large houses in the countryside north of the city. But Glasgow did succeed in developing commuter traffic from residential villages around the shores of the Clyde, the Holy Loch and Loch Long. Few industrial cities as large as Glasgow have on their doorstep areas of such surpassing beauty as the Firth of Clyde.[17] Quiet burghs like Rothesay and Dunoon grew to prosperous towns where the well-to-do could escape the congestion and pollution of Victorian Glasgow. Ground was feued and magnificent villas built in these estuarine suburbs (Fig. 6.9). The only way to the Clyde coast was by steamer until 1841, when the railway reached Greenock. Railway and steamer services were not at first co-ordinated, but once this had been overcome the long-term development of the Clyde resorts was possible. The companies extended their joint operations to Wemyss Bay in 1865, Prince's Pier, Greenock in 1869, Fairlie in 1882 and Gourock in 1889; so that by the end of the 1880s the Clyde steamer fleet was unsurpassed in British coastal waters for size and quality of service.[18] A combination of Clyde steamer and rail, with very low fares, gave the businessman a leisurely existence. At Rothesay he caught the steamer at 7.20 am and arrived in Glasgow at 9.00 am; the day's work done, he joined the train at 4.13 pm and landed at Rothesay pier at 5.48 pm. On the other hand working-class commuter travel was very different. The transfer of Thomson's (later John Brown's) shipyard 11 km down river to a green-field site brought workers from as far afield as Airdrie and the Glasgow, Yoker and Clydebank Railway was opened in 1882 to meet this demand. Between six and seven o'clock in the morning fourteen trains converged upon Clydebank with workers crammed into unlit compartments.

Whilst railway management easily identified these two extremes of passenger traffic, they found it difficult to create an intermediate

type of customer who would reside sufficiently far out to need the railways and in sufficient numbers to make the service pay. There was a rash of suburban railway schemes in the 1880s: the Dundee Suburban Railway and the Edinburgh, Stockbridge and Leith Railway, for example, adorned the face of a map but progressed no further.[19] Stations were planted in open country but all too often custom did not appear. The Edinburgh and Glasgow Railway tried to attract commuters with the introduction of 'villa tickets', free season tickets granted to people who agreed to build houses at any undeveloped location on the railway. Following this inducement, Lenzie, 2 km south of Kirkintilloch, grew up as a community of substantial villas beside a junction on an empty moor. Similarly, the less well-to-do began to move into neighbouring towns. Numerous stone-built villas appeared after 1880 in Bearsden, Bishopbriggs, Helensburgh, Kirkintilloch, Milngavie and Uddingston, although railways had served these towns long before then, and by the time of the Glasgow Boundary Commission Inquiry in 1888, middle-class residence in these places had become normal.

Living conditions for the middle classes in Edinburgh were so much more pleasing than in Glasgow that there was little inducement to escape from the city. However, the railway companies took part in joint speculation to open up new areas for commuter dwellings. One such example was the co-operation of the Caledonian Railway and Sir James Maitland of Barnton. A line had been laid to Granton in 1861, and a small community had developed near the intermediate station of Craigleith. The company decided to build a branch westwards into a countryside of magnificent policies and prosperous farms, with the final 2 km and two stations within the walls of Barnton Park. The Edinburgh Burgess Golfing Society's course lay immediately beside the Cramond Brig terminus and a hotel was built conveniently next to the station. A magnificent feuing plan was drawn up in anticipation of the more prosperous members of Edinburgh society taking up residence near their favourite golf course.[20] The branch opened on 1 March 1894 but only a few houses were built along Barnton Gardens. The railway company learned that people did not desert the city without good cause. Indeed if new and pleasant surroundings were sought, 8 sq. km of high-quality housing was already available on the south side of the city, alongside the Edinburgh, Suburban and Southside Junction Railway. This line, authorized in 1880, exemplifies the difficulties faced by railways serving a compact city. Parts of its circuitous route swung far out into non-revenue producing country and some stations, such as Newington and Blackford Hill, were too near town to make the roundabout journey worthwhile.

The underground railway made a considerable contribution to urban transport problems in late Victorian times and Glasgow was one of the first places in the world to experiment with the subway. A private Act was granted in 1890 to the Glasgow District Subway Company to construct a circular route of two endless tunnels. The Act specified that 'any method other than steam was to be used for traction power' and cable haulage was adopted.[21] The subway opened in January 1897 in competition with the trams, but it did not live up to expectations for the electrification of the tramway system began within a year. Appearances did not help as the stations were dingy and difficult to find. After a short closure in 1922 the enterprise was taken over by the corporation and although the subway was electrified in 1938 the public still was not enthusiastic about it (Fig. 6.10). World War II brought a short-lived rise in the number of passengers, which fell again in the late 'fifties as the population moved out beyond the reach of the subway (Fig 6.11).[22]

During the inter-war period municipal tramway systems provided the pinnacle of cheap urban transport. Yet like the suburban train and omnibus, the trams had an early high-cost phase which restricted their use to the well-to-do. Most early tramways were privately constructed, but the seeds of municipal control were contained in the compulsory purchase powers of the Tramways Act 1870.

The period 1870-1914 was the great age of tramway building. Scottish cities developed systems of considerable individuality, and Glasgow was one of the first to invest in this new form of urban

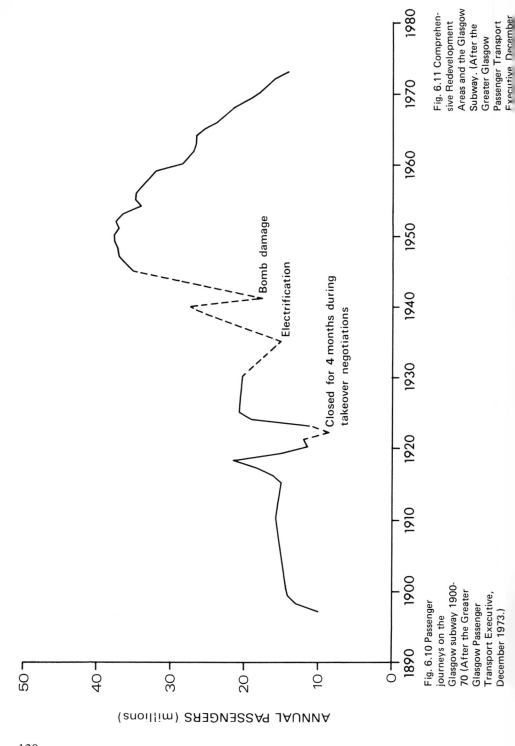

Fig. 6.10 Passenger journeys on the Glasgow subway 1900-70 (After the Greater Glasgow Passenger Transport Executive, December 1973.)

Fig. 6.11 Comprehensive Redevelopment Areas and the Glasgow Subway. (After the Greater Glasgow Passenger Transport Executive, December

ANNUAL PASSENGERS (millions)

Bomb damage

Electrification

Closed for 4 months during takeover negotiations

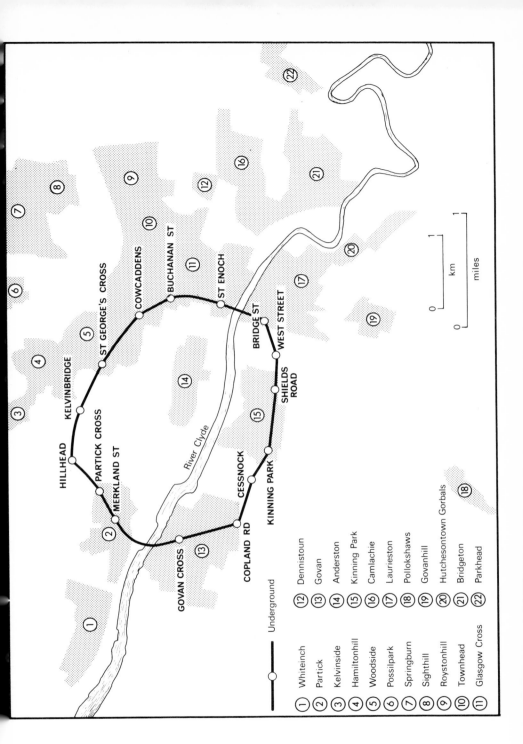

Underground

① Whiteinch
② Partick
③ Kelvinside
④ Hamiltonhill
⑤ Woodside
⑥ Possilpark
⑦ Springburn
⑧ Sighthill
⑨ Roystonhill
⑩ Townhead
⑪ Glasgow Cross
⑫ Dennistoun
⑬ Govan
⑭ Anderston
⑮ Kinning Park
⑯ Camlachie
⑰ Laurieston
⑱ Pollokshaws
⑲ Govanhill
⑳ Hutchesontown Gorbals
㉑ Bridgeton
㉒ Parkhead

HILLHEAD
KELVINBRIDGE
PARTICK CROSS
ST GEORGE'S CROSS
COWCADDENS
BUCHANAN ST
ST ENOCH
BRIDGE ST
WEST STREET
SHIELDS ROAD
MERKLAND ST
KINNING PARK
CESSNOCK
COPLAND RD
GOVAN CROSS
River Clyde

km
miles

transport. The corporation promoted an Act in 1870 which allowed it to construct and lease lines to a private company to run horse-drawn trams. The routes kept to the principal roads and never ventured beyond the built-up area although they did extend over the city boundary (Fig. 6.12). Municipal operation started in 1894 and the new management embarked upon a programme of modernization and extension. Cheap popular fares were made possible around the turn of the century following widespread municipalization and electrification, for the latter alone gave something like a 40 per cent reduction in operating costs over horse traction. Economy of scale clearly played its part, for the larger the city and more extensive the system, the lower the fares per mile.[23] The idea that the tram was a means of cheap transport for the working class is clearly belied by the fact that although the 1870 Act provided for at least two cars on each route before 6 am and after 5 pm on each working day at fares of a halfpenny a mile (with a penny minimum) for the benefit of 'artisans, mechanics and daily labourers', all too often this provision was ignored by the tramway companies. Municipal control changed this and by 1902 the fares in Glasgow were so low that statutory workmen's fares were not needed. The tramway system with its city centre orientation benefited shop and office workers rather than industrial workers whose places of employment were not so centrally located. The tramway did bring in an era of cheap passenger transport, but the best bargains were available to the more affluent members of the community living in the outer suburbs.

Edinburgh's search for an efficient mode of public transport had to meet its citizens' aesthetic standards. The corporation had built tramways but had leased them to private companies to run horse-trams. When the time came in 1888 for a decision about future modes of power, the already proven electric traction was rejected because the overhead wires would be an eyesore.[24] So Edinburgh adopted cable haulage which had recently been developed in San Francisco.

Network	Date	Engineer and assistant
San Francisco	1873	A. S. Hallidie and
		E. S. Eppelsheimer
Highgate Hill, London	1884	E. S. Eppelsheimer and
		W. Newby Colam
Edinburgh Northern Tramways	1888	W. Newby Colam

For complexity and mechanical ingenuity, the Edinburgh system had no British rival; but cable breakages and other mishaps earned the cars an unenviable reputation, so that when the companies' leases ran out in 1919 the corporation took over and electrified the lines.

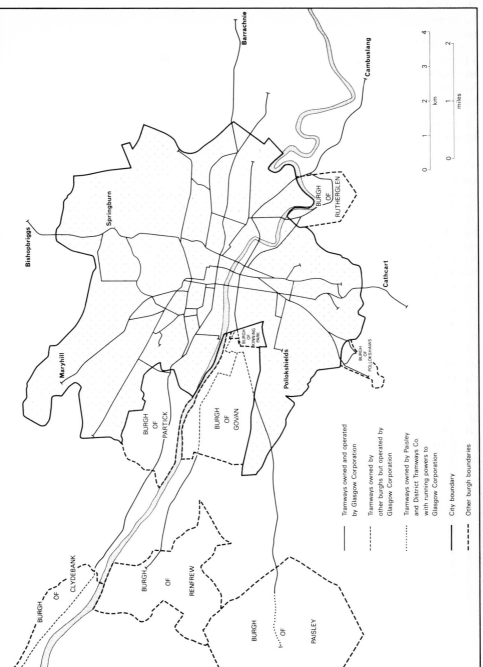

Fig. 6.12 Map of
Glasgow tramways
1910

Tramways owned and operated
by Glasgow Corporation

Tramways owned by
other burghs but operated by
Glasgow Corporation

Tramways owned by Paisley
and District Tramways Co.
with running powers to
Glasgow Corporation

City boundary

Other burgh boundaries

123

By the beginning of the twentieth century, cheap fares and more efficient urban transport caused a marked outward movement of population which diminished the pressure for housing in the central districts and led to the rapid growth of suburbs. This is illustrated by the drop in population of 45,000 in the central area of Glasgow between 1901 and 1911. At the same time the population in the outer suburbs included in the municipal boundaries increased by 7,481. These trends seem to reflect the experience of the London County Council in attracting the working classes to suburban travel in search of lower rents, but a detailed analysis shows the reverse to be true. Despite high site values in the central parts of the cities, many older houses were let at comparatively low rents, while the rise in the standard of accommodation and the cost of building had raised the rents of newer properties in the suburbs to a generally higher level.

Competition between tramway and train, though often unequal, was so fierce that only one system could survive and railway management grudgingly welcomed the shifting of responsibility. Trains catered for the morning and evening rush hours with very little traffic between, while passengers filled the trams throughout the day, making it easier to finance the peak travel periods. The Granton branch of the London and North Eastern Railway with its two stations at Trinity and Granton was a typical urban line running parallel to electric trams when the railway company determined to close the line to passenger traffic in October 1925. The only justifiable objections came from the fishwives of Fisherrow who found the trams less convenient for their early morning journey to the fish market.[25] Occasionally the railways tried to fight back. On Clydeside the London, Midland and Scottish Railway proposed electrification of the Cathcart Inner and Outer Circles as early as 1929. Many homes had been built adjoining the lines and it was estimated that they served a quarter of a million people. However, the railway was already under severe competition from trams and buses and the scheme was not approved. The Greenock, Gourock and Wemyss Bay line had been similarly hit by competition from the buses. The drop in rail traffic from Glasgow Central to Paisley was particularly big after the introduction of a cheap 2d fare by Glasgow Corporation on their Glasgow and Paisley Tramways. Again electrification was rejected for financial reasons. Ironically both these schemes were revived, as we shall see later, and the lines now prosper in spite of the trams' ephemeral victory in the 1920s.

The tramcar vanished with the large-scale transfer of inner zone dwellers to peripheral council estates in the late 1950s. The authorities had to decide whether to scrap their almost obsolete systems whose various peripheral termini were unrelated to the new urban limits, or invest considerable capital to bring the system up to date. To the admirers of the efficient tramcar systems of Basel, Zurich,

Cologne and elsewhere the summary rejection may seem to have been shortsighted, but there were few objections when the last trams ran in Edinburgh and Dundee in 1956, Aberdeen in 1958 and Glasgow in 1962.

While most people relied on public transport, urban development was limited by the fixed routes provided by the various transport systems, but with the move towards universal ownership of the car options changed so that man could develop the regional city.

Notes

1. D. Loch, *Essays on the Trade, Commerce, Manufactures and Fisheries of Scotland* (Edinburgh, 1778).

2. W. F. Macarthur, *History of Port Glasgow* (Glasgow 1932).

3. I. A. G. Kinniburgh, 'Greenock: Growth and Change in the Harbours of the Town', *Scottish Geographical Magazine*, vol. 76 (1960), pp. 89-98.

4. W. Iain Stevenson, 'Some Aspects of the Geography of the Clyde Tobacco Trade in the Eighteenth Century', *Scottish Geographical Magazine*, vol. 89 (1973), pp. 19-35.

5. Jean Lindsay, *The Canals of Scotland* (David and Charles, Newton Abbot, 1968).

6. A. Lowe, *General View . . . of the County of Berwick* (Edinburgh, 1794), p. 25.

7. G. Buchan Hepburn, *General View . . . of East Lothian* (Edinburgh, 1794), p. 152.

8. M. Simpson, 'Urban Transport and the Development of Glasgow's West End, 1830-1914', *The Journal of Transport History,* new series, vol. 1, no.3 (February 1973), pp. 146-60.

9. B. T. Duckham, *A History of the Scottish Coal Industry* (David and Charles, Newton Abbot, 1970), I, p. 204; see also John A. Hassan, 'The Supply of Coal to Edinburgh 1790-1850', *Transport History*, vol. 5 no. 2, (July 1972), pp. 125-51.

10. J. R. Kellett, *The Impact of Railways on Victorian Cities* (Routledge and Kegan Paul, London, 1969), p. xv.

11. H. J. Dyos, 'Railways and Housing in Victorian London', *Journal of Transport History,* vol. 2, no. 1 (May 1955), pp. 11-21; vol. 2, no. 2, November 1955, pp. 90-100.

12. British Rail records (SRO RHP 25352).

13. John Thomas, *The North British Railway* (David and Charles, Newton Abbot, 1969), I, pp. 104-5.

14. C. J. A. Robertson, 'The Cheap Railway Movement in Scotland: The St Andrews Railway Company', *Transport History,* vol. 7 (March 1974), pp. 1-40.

15. *The North British Railway and Shipping Journal* (1848), quoted by John Thomas, *A Regional History of Railways of Great Britain,* vol. 6, Scotland: Lowlands and the Borders (David and Charles, Newton Abbot, 1971), p. 191.

16. W. Ballingall, *Edinburgh Past and Present* (Edinburgh, 1877), p. 94.

17. A. J. S. Paterson, *The Victorian Summer of the Clyde Steamers (1864-1888)* (David and Charles, Newton Abbot, 1972); and idem, *The Golden Years of the Clyde Steamers (1889-1914)* (David and Charles, Newton Abbot, 1969).

18. T. R. Gourvish, 'The Railways and Steamboat Competition in Early Victorian Britain', *Transport History,* vol. 4, no. 1 (March 1971), pp. 1-22.

19. British Rail records (SRO RHP 25445 and 25450 respectively).

20. British Rail records (SRO RHP 10331).

21. 'Glasgow District Subway 1889-1915' (SRO DD5/70); D. L. Thomson, and D. E. Sinclair, *The Glasgow Subway* (Scottish Tramway Museum Society, Glasgow, 1964).

22. Greater Glasgow Passenger Transport Executive, *Modernisation of Glasgow Underground: Application to Secretary of State for Scotland for Infrastructure Grant* (December 1973).

23. G. C. Dickinson, and C. J. Longley, 'The Coming of Cheap Transport — a Study of Tramway Fares on Municipal Systems in British Provincial Towns 1900-14', *Transport History,* vol. 6, no. 2 (July 1973), pp. 107-27.

24. D. L. G. Hunter, 'The Edinburgh Cable Tramways', *The Journal of Transport History,* vol. 1, no. 3, May 1954, pp. 170-84.

25. British Rail records (SRO BR/LNE/8/712).

At the beginning of the nineteenth century the archaic nature of local government and the explosion of population focused attention on man's inadequacies in coming to terms with the new scale of urban life. The self-perpetuating oligarchy in charge of burgh affairs acted in time-honoured ways which did little damage in small independent communities; but with growth, this somewhat casual approach collapsed in the face of empirical problems that arose out of the remorseless pressure of population on urban fabric and services. The transition from oligarchic incompetence to bureaucratic omnipotence was only achieved after numerous commissions and inquiries into every aspect of urban life.

To find the origins of the incompetence one must go back to 1469 when a statute, which has been described as 'the most damning Act of the Scottish Parliament', was enacted to make the council a self-perpetuating oligarchy.[1] The old method of election of the burgh councils at the annual meeting of the head court of the guildry was then set aside and it was ordained that each council should elect its own successor, thus giving the council absolute control. By the early nineteenth century corruption and inefficiency had led to burghal bankruptcy, and a Royal Commission appointed to inquire into the state of municipal corporations in Scotland reported in 1835. Their general conclusion was devastating:

> In regard to the actual state of the real property conferred on or entrusted to the royal burghs of Scotland . . . with comparatively few exceptions its administration has been most unfortunate and even ruinous; and what was originally bestowed by the Crown, for public purposes, and inalienably devoted to the support of municipal establishments, has, in the greater number of cases, been lost by management the most reckless and shortsighted. Prior to the beginning of the sixteenth century, there is no trace of any dilapidation of the property of the burghs. If waste of any kind existed, it must have been confined to the annual produce of the common property; and the property itself would appear to have been sufficiently protected by the inalienable quality of the original gift.[2]

The Commissioners regarded the introduction of feu-ferme tenure in the burghs as a fundamental cause of corruption. In earlier times leases were frequently granted for only one year, rarely as long as five years. During the sixteenth century a number of burghs alienated their common property in feu-ferme in order, originally, to augment the revenue from such property. As early as 1535 Parliament was aware of the existence of abuse and one of the immediate causes of its increase, the fact that provosts, bailies and magistrates within the burghs were using the common good for their own purposes. The Report exposed numerous subterfuges by which the individual could profit from office. Indeed there was hardly a burgh that did not contribute an example of corruption. In Midlothian numerous superiorities were quietly sold by the town council of Edinburgh to members and their friends; the provost of Renfrew instigated a number of sales to himself; and houses were granted privately to council members for inadequate rents. Burgh property was greatly over-valued and public buildings such as churches and courtrooms were wrongly included in valuations. Sometimes mere revenues, such as petty customs, market and fair dues and street manure, were valued as property. In many burghs expenditure exceeded the proper resources; public officers were overpaid and undue profits were allowed to tradesmen or public works contractors who were often council members. Aberdeen town council borrowed funds on the security of heritable property belonging to charities, of which they were the sole trustees, and then sold part of the property to pay the debts of the city. Again, the accounts of many treasurers were irregular in the extreme: the Dumbarton treasurer received from members of the council cash advances which he spent, and was then authorized by the council to grant bills for the total amount. In some smaller burghs, although the revenue was very small, the treasurer had no clear idea of his duties. In larger burghs the printed abstracts of accounts tended to be both inaccurate and deficient. Sometimes money was kept in the treasurer's private bank account, while the account book was regarded as a private record and not passed on to his successor. Some account books had been lost, indeed there had not been one kept in Kelso for forty years, and no satisfactory reason was found for the burning of the Dunbar book nearly thirty years previously. The other chief area of corruption was in the matter of patronage or the right of bestowing offices, privileges or church benefices. A boy of twelve years of age was appointed town clerk of Forfar in 1803; when it was realized in 1822 that he was an imbecile he could not be removed from office because he had been appointed for life. In other cases offices were sold, for example in 1833 the town clerk of Leith paid £1,200 to the magistrates and council of Edinburgh .for his appointment.

Exclusive privileges were the perquisite of merchant freemen and guild brethren. They had trading privileges within the burgh and its liberty and, in order to keep foreigners out of the burgh, the fee for entry into burgess-ship was raised dramatically in many cases and the corporations were quite capricious in the granting or refusing of licences. The corporations and the community also suffered from the multiplicity of unnecessary lawsuits that had siphoned funds away from their proper charitable purposes. A number of burghs were overburdened by magistrates and councillors, the number having been fixed at an earlier date without any principle. Dornoch, for instance, with a population of 504 and a revenue in 1822-3 of £1 15s had 26 councillors; New Galloway with a population of 500 and a revenue of £3 8s 2d had 18 councillors but only 14 qualified electors; at the other extreme Aberdeen had a population of 58,000, a revenue of £11,000 but only 11 councillors. The published evidence destroyed the credibility of the existing system of local government. The question, however, had become academic for the whole archaic system had been swept away by the three Reform Acts of 1833.

The old oligarchies had not been beyond instigating reform when pressed through untoward circumstance. Fire was a periodic visitor to most medieval towns with their wood and thatch buildings, but it was in the high 'lands' of Edinburgh that it was most feared. The congestion within the city walls led to fearful conflagrations in 1700 and 1824. After the fire of 1700 new regulations led to the appointment of twelve burgesses to act as firemasters. During the century fire insurance was developed and, to protect their interests, the various insurance companies set up their own fire brigades. A metal plaque bearing the insurance company's mark was fixed to a client's building so that the company's brigade did not waste its efforts on competitors' or uninsured buildings (Fig. 7.1). A series of fires in 1824 led the Commissioners of Police to establish a municipal fire brigade. It was none too soon, for that November Edinburgh's worst ever fire raged for three days (Fig. 7.2). Edinburgh's lead was copied throughout the United Kingdom.

The policing of towns was another subject difficult to ignore. Attention was increasingly focused on the lack of a formal system of policing the growing towns. Fears for a breakdown in law and order overcame age-old prejudices about interference with personal liberty. The medieval concept of watch and ward affirmed the principle of local responsibility for policing a district, by which each burgess was expected to take his turn of duty or send a substitute, and could be fined for failure. Officially this system continued until the nineteenth century but it had inevitably broken down long before then. The first efforts to regulate the office of constable were made by statute in 1617; in royal burghs, constables were to be appointed for six months and were to keep the king's peace. This Act was largely a failure because of the vast number of private jurisdictions in Scotland in which the landlord had the hereditary right of administering justice; these were not abolished until 1747.

A small professional police force was established in Glasgow in 1778 to supplement the traditional city guard, but was soon dis-

Fig. 7.1 A fire insurance company's plaque. (Photo: C.A. Somerville.)

banded because the citizens were unwilling to bear the cost. From this time the situations in Scotland and England were similar but the main debate on the responsibility of the state in relation to the rights of the individual took place in London. During the second half of the eighteenth and early part of the nineteenth centuries there was a steady deterioration in the watching services and a fear of mob rule, but public opinion was with Fox who 'would much rather be governed by a mob than a standing army' or by armed policemen as in France. After a number of bills to inaugurate a police force had been thrown out of Parliament the Metropolitan Police Acts were passed in 1829; these marked the beginning of the modern police force.

The Burgh Reform Acts of 1833 and 1834 introduced new principles and established effective authority in the growing towns. The existence of nearly standard burgh constitutions made the reformers' task very much easier in Scotland than in England where there was a great variety of customs and tenures. This difference explains the delay of borough reform in England until 1835. The first two Acts conferred on householders who paid a rateable value of £10 the right to elect town councils in 66 royal burghs and 13 parliamentary burghs. One-third of the councillors were to retire each year and the number of councillors was stipulated for each parliamentary burgh, but no change was made in the powers of either the royal or parliamentary burghs. The third statute, and in many ways the most important, authorized the £10 householders in a royal burgh or burgh of barony to adopt a 'police system' and to choose 'commissioners of police'. The commissioners were to levy rates for the purposes of watching, lighting, paving and cleansing the streets, the improvement of water and gas supplies and the prevention of infectious diseases. Furthermore they were to regulate slaughterhouses, apprehend vagrants and name and number streets and houses. The existing burgh did not become a police burgh, rather the residents initiated a new local authority (with much wider powers than the old), so that the burgh was subject to a system of dual administration. Legislation extended these powers to all parliamentary burghs in 1847, to places with populations over 1,200 in 1850 and over 700 in 1862. Many industrial towns first achieved independence in this way and became known as police burghs.

Fig. 7.2 Ruins in Parliament Square, Edinburgh, after the Great Fire in November 1824 (from a contemporary print).

To what extent was local government reform translated into tangible improvement? Throughout the *New Statistical Account,* published in 1838, there is a feeling of improvement and advancement since the time of Sir John Sinclair's *Statistical Account,* published in the 1790s. This optimism was due partly to agricultural improvements and growing industrialization, but also to the improvements which were originated either under a local police act or the burgh reform acts. In Moffat 'the police were lately very inadequate, but has been improved'. In Inverness, a new efficient system of police, due attention to cleanliness and a great improvement in the paving of the streets had been noticed, and common sewers had been constructed under the streets. In Bathgate much had been done in the previous four years to improve the pavements and causeways, while Haddington 'has been greatly improved of late by side pavements in the streets and gas lights'.

Sanitary reform became possible when the political reforms provided a suitable structure for local government to extend its sphere of responsibility. For centuries the removal of filth from the streets was a subject of only occasional interest. In 1505 Edinburgh Town Council provided a horse and cart to cleanse the streets 'when need is'; the streets were to be cleared every eight days and the fulzie (manure) sold for the common good. Individuals were to cleanse the causeway to 'myd channel fornent their dwelling place or booth' in time of plague and the refuse was to be removed by the tacksman. By 1619 the citizens brought all refuse from their houses twice a week to the head of the close or street and the council paid to have it removed. After the outbreak of plague in 1645 the high constables were fined if their bounds were not cleansed. Though a cleansing committee was set up in 1678, it was a failure. In spite of repeated efforts by magistrates, ranging from fines and imprisonment to banishment, the old habit of 'gardyloo' continued in both Edinburgh and Glasgow.[3]

Slaughterhouses and fish markets were a particular nuisance in towns, for butchers sometimes slaughtered in booths attached to their dwelling houses. In 1621 slaughterhouses were erected at the Nor' Loch, but the first public slaughterhouse was not built in Edinburgh until 1850. The keeping of stall-fed cattle was a nuisance which diminished after stringent inspection regulations were enacted in 1865, by which time a plentiful supply of milk could be brought into towns by rail. The shambles marked the limit of the medieval burgh, but as the city grew they became trapped. So the blood, bone and soap boiler, the tallow and fat melter, the knacker, tanner, glue and size manufacturer, gut or tripe cleaner, skinner or hide factor and manufacturer of manure continued his trade to the increasing discomfort of the townsfolk. By the end of the nineteenth century a series of by-laws squeezed these noxious activities out of their traditional sites.[4] There is no better description of a shambles than that of Glasgow Green at the end of the eighteenth century:

The Laigh Green lay so low, and was so irregular in its surface, that a slight swell on the river or a smart shower laid it under water, which had to be carried off to the Camlachie Burn by an open drain. The entries to the Laigh Green by the Saltmarket Street, Cow Lane, and the Old Bridge were so narrow, irregular, and dirty, from their vicinity to the Slaughter-House, that, with the exception of the first, they were chiefly used by cattle and fleshers' dogs . . . the bottom of the Laigh Green was surrounded by offensive pits, used by skinners and tanners. The Slaughter-House spread over a large and irregular surface on the bank of the river, and was bounded by crooked lanes on the north and north-east ports, than which there was no other entry to the Green from the west.

The dung of the Slaughter-House and the intestines of slaughtered animals were collected in heaps, and allowed to remain for months together, till putrefaction took place, to the great annoyance of the neighbourhood. A gluework, and a work in which tharm was manufactured from the intestines of animals in a recent state, was erected at the bottom of the Laigh Green; and to complete the nuisance, the adjoining houses were occupied for cleaning tripe; and rees were fitted up for the retail of coal and coal-culm. The space on the bank of the river at the cattle market, came now to be used by the police as a receptacle for filth from the streets.[5]

Although efforts were made to keep the towns clean, little could be achieved until sewage and drainage systems were improved. The Cowgate in Edinburgh had only surface drains till the 1840s when a committee of private gentlemen built an underground sewer 758m long to the Foul Burn. Lord Cockburn complained that the Cowgate had lost half its character — such was public opinion. In the Old Town three sewers discharged into the Foul Burn through Craigentinny meadows where pits were dug for the collection of sludge for manure; the meadows were irrigated by the foul water as it flowed slowly enough to be absorbed by the soil over a wide area. The drains in the closes were still very poor in the 1860s because the tenements were so subdivided and in such poor condition that it was difficult to join them up to the common sewer. The volume of sewage reduced rivers like the Water of Leith to fetid channels. The Royal Commission on the Sewage of Towns heard in evidence that this small stream received the sewage of 100,000 people, 'the bed of the Water of Leith is rocky and uneven, and in the pools thus formed much of the solid matter conveyed by the sewage stagnates, and, passing into a state of putrescence, evolves abundantly offensive gases'. These 'hot-beds of decomposing filth' gave rise to the disturbing situation in that houses bordering the stream had a child mortality rate of 160, taking as a base of 100 those streets a little away from it.[6] Other towns were little different. Glasgow's first sewer was built in 1790. In Inverness the few common sewers and drains in the poorer parts of the city were often obstructed in order to increase the production of fulzie for the potato patches. The nineteenth-century streets in Aberdeen had large common sewers though there were still many cesspools. By Police Act, the 'whole manure', except that of stables and a few streets in the suburbs, was the property of the police. It was collected every morning at their expense from the doors at the heads of closes and any profit went to police funds.

Sanitation and sewage systems remained almost non-existent until there was a sufficient and pure water supply. People were beginning to realize that there might be some connection between disease and bad housing, but it was not yet understood that foul water led to infectious diseases and general debility. In early days water was collected from a well or standpipe in the street, the supply being restricted to a few hours two or three times a week, or it was just another commodity bought from hawkers in the street. Such wells or pumps frequently ran dry and were as frequently contaminated by sewage. Throughout the nineteenth century the situation worsened as the rapid growth of towns outstripped the capacity to organize an adequate water supply. Giving evidence in January 1847, James Simpson, an advocate turned lecturer on sanitary matters, had this to say:

> I have visited over 40 cities in Great Britain and, with perhaps two or three exceptions, the supply was so exceedingly stinted, as to form the principal barrier to the improvement of the conditions of the working classes. I made it my business in coming to any particular town to inquire into two matters — water and sewerage. I considered water to be rather a misfortune in a house without sewerage; but with sewerage, and with free supply, the chief obstacles to the improvement of the working classes, and the health of towns, would be removed.[7]

When asked specifically about how the poorer classes in Edinburgh fared, he replied:

> Wretchedly. Living, many of them, in floors of very high altitudes, they labour, particularly when sickness is in their families, under privation so great that they content themselves with a driblet of water that would surprise you — probably their little tea-kettle full. Anything like personal cleanliness in such a condition is rare, while domestic cleanliness is quite out of the question. Their recourse to public wells is not only a very great hardship on themselves, but is a source of public nuisance, moral as well as physical. I should be sorry to see any attempt to increase the number of these wells; and I hope to live to see the time when they will be a matter of history alone.

The 'moral hardship' encountered at the public wells appears to have been based on Victorian paternalism: 'Families complain of sending their servants or children to the wells as one of the greatest of evils. These make the wells excuses for every absence and every delinquency. The excuse is "waiting their turn". It is a very bad school for them.'

Edinburgh relied on a meagre supply of water from Comiston which was distributed through two town cisterns and numerous public wells until the Edinburgh Water Company obtained its first Act in 1819. The Company introduced water for a population of 112,000, but by 1842 the population had risen to 166,000 without any expansion of facilities so that even under the most favourable circumstances the domestic supplies could not exceeed 45 litres per head daily. No provision had been made for manufacturing processes, the fire service or watering the streets, nor for future sources of demand such as the introduction of water closets in the houses of the poorer classes. In the summer of 1842 the supply failed for several weeks and this forced the Water Company to seek new supplies from the Pentland Hills. In 1843 daily consumption in Edinburgh was 100 litres per head, but after the General Police Act of 1862, which compelled proprietors to introduce water into houses, the demand jumped to 141 litres (in 1971 Edinburgh used 195 litres per head per day for domestic purposes, and a further 123 litres by industry).

Glasgow showed a similar trend. Before 1806 there were 29 public and a few private wells to provide water for its citizens. In that year the Glasgow Water Works Company was formed to supply the city and its suburbs from the River Clyde. In 1808 this company was joined 'in a spirit of competition' by the Cranstonhill Water Works Company which also drew its supply from the Clyde below Glasgow. Far more serious was the manoeuvring of the Glasgow Water Works Company for a monopolistic supply of this vital commodity. The company obtained an amendment of the 1833 Burgh Reform Act which excluded Glasgow from the clauses allowing the 'inhabitants of a town to supply themselves with water at prime cost, to escape being taxed for a profit to joint stock speculators'.[8] Taxed they were, for the two companies amalgamated to form the Glasgow and Dalmarnock Water Works, and with full monopolistic control doubled the water rate. The howl of anguish forced the authorities to commission Thomas Grainger and John Millar, civil engineers in Edinburgh, to seek out possible alternative supplies along the Earn Water, as a source of a gravitational supply on the model of that adopted 'at Edinburgh, Greenock, Manchester, Portsmouth and many other places' and which had been recently recommended by Thomas Telford for the London water supply. Nothing came of it, but large-scale building operations on the south bank of the Clyde led to the first tentative introduction of a modern water supply. The Gorbals Direct Water Supply Company ensured that water would be constantly available, relying on a head of water from reservoirs on tributaries of the Avon Water rather than town cisterns.[9] Furthermore, this service was provided for a much wider social spectrum than previously. 'There are a great many buildings going up for the working classes, mechanics and cotton mill people and such like, where the introduction of water-closets is universal.' The first scheme, in 1845, to bring water from Loch Katrine was withdrawn when, in the following year, the Loch Lubnaig scheme was passed by Parliament. Technical reasons led to the failure of this scheme so the Loch Katrine project was revived. Opposition was very strong and the Corporation commissioned Robert Stephenson and I.K. Brunel to prepare a report in support of their case. An Act was eventually passed in 1855 and water reached the city in the extraordinarily short time of four years. Glasgow's provision of ample water for all its citizens now set a standard for British cities to follow.

In terms of sheer inefficiency in the provision of adequate water supply and sewage disposal, Dundee would be hard to beat. In 1861 the town, with a population of 91,664, had but five water closets, three of them in hotels. All the water either came from wells, of which the chief, the Lady well, was heavily polluted by the slaughterhouse, or came from barrels on carts, sold at $\frac{1}{2}d$ or $1d$ a bucket. In 1831 and 1835 plans for an adequate supply were put before Parliament by the town council, but they were frustrated by private companies and an oligarchy formed by the Guildry and the Nine Trades. An advocate for the water company, putting his case successfully to the House of Lords, said that his clients 'did not see the peculiar circumstances that should make men idiots enough to prefer paying by taxation what ought to be a vendible article in the market like any other commodity'. From want of good water and drainage, smallpox was endemic, cholera frequent, and typhus and typhoid annually brought many deaths to a population of whom two-thirds lived in tenement houses of one or two rooms, at a density of from 960 to 2,400 persons per hectare. The private company supplied Dundee from 1845 to 1869, when it was taken over by the municipality. The following year the supply was exhausted and it was not until 1875 that an adequate supply was achieved when the Lintrathen scheme brought water by aqueduct from the Sidlaw Hills.

From the fourteenth century Aberdeen's water was drawn from the Loch of Aberdeen in a stone-lined channel, and by 1840 only 6,000 of the population of 48,000 had piped water in their houses. River water was also pumped at the Bridge of Dee until 1862 when a new scheme, designed by James Simpson, civil engineer in London, tapped the river 37 km upstream at Cairnton. Both this case and those of the other cities illustrate the growing outward influence of the town on rural resources. The urban reservoir perched in surrounding hills enabled towns to be supplied by gravity with an adequate head of water.

Although the cities secured adequate water supplies by the 1870s, smaller burghs lagged far behind. In this they were aided by a labyrinth of inadequate and contradictory legislation. Virtually powerless, the Local Government Board had to consider legal proceedings in the Court of Session to press the burghs of Inverbervie, Kelso, Lochmaben, Pulteneytown (Wick) and Stromness to provide adequate water supplies. Kelso, for example, felt little need to undertake the expensive business of putting in a gravity supply when it had the Tweed to draw from. Even though the townsfolk knew the river was acting as a sewer for Galashiels, Peebles and Innerleithen, they showed their defiance by electing an anti-water-supply council. The whole matter stirred central government into action and a bill was produced to clarify the legislative muddle. Lord Balfour, however, raised a somewhat deeper question, 'Is it worthwhile considering whether in the proposed Bill we should not try for more power over Burghs?'[10] This bold suggestion was not pursued in the resulting Burgh Police and Public Health (Scotland) Act 1898.

Within the crowded and filthy streets of the average burgh there was little chance of escape from infection, but indeed every encouragement was found for disease-carrying organisms to spread through the overhanging timber-framed houses that crowded in on the narrow lanes. Despite the prohibiting town ordinances, household refuse flowed down the streets to be joined by offal and other waste. This garbage usually drained into a stream that was at the same time a source of drinking water, a place for domestic laundering and perhaps the unsavoury workplace of a fuller whose collecting pots by the wayside acted as a public urinal. Not surprisingly most towns had an excess of deaths over births in many years and were able to maintain or increase their population only by ever-increasing immigration.

Attempts had been made to control infectious diseases by forcible isolation and harsh repression. In the sixteenth century death was the penalty for the master of a house who did not report illness in his household. Leprosy, at its height during the eleventh to thirteenth centuries, led to the sufferers' expulsion from the community. Small settlements of lepers grew up, for instance the one at Liberton near Edinburgh. Lepers were forbidden to enter towns except occasionally to buy food; pork or salmon that was found unfit in the markets was sent to them. The inmates of the Greenside Hospital outside Edinburgh were encouraged to keep the rules by the sight of a gallows at the door. Although plague was first noticed in Glasgow in 1330, the first regulations did not appear till 1453 when a plague hospital was built on the island of Inchkeith in the Firth of Forth. There were several epidemics of plague through the centuries but the efforts made to restrict the disease were ineffective. During outbreaks, owners of dogs and swine were often forbidden to allow the animals to wander at will, meetings were forbidden, schools were closed and children under fifteen could be put in the stocks and scourged if they used their enforced leisure to play 'on the gaitt or in the streets or in the kirk'. In Edinburgh if any member of a family succumbed to the plague, the whole family was forced to live in temporary huts erected on the Burgh Muir.[11]

Certain diseases flourish in urban conditions and those which are waterborne, such as cholera and typhoid, increased with the rise of the industrial towns. Cholera, a disease which paid no regard to class, for urban filth was common to all men, first appeared in epidemic form in Scotland in 1831 and was especially bad in 1833 and 1848 (Fig. 7.3). Medieval methods were reintroduced to control the disease and beggars and tramps were prevented from entering towns. Only in 1849 was it proved that cholera was waterborne. In an effort to control the disease, boards of health were set up and some public money was spent in cleaning the worst parts of the towns. In Glasgow the closes, staircases and lanes were cleansed and fumigated, and water was supplied to remove the dunghills. Cleanliness, ventilation and a proper diet were recommended. However, the epidemics did not last long enough to create a consistent demand for new social policies, the boards of health were quickly disbanded and the filth accumulated again in the streets.[12]

The medical profession was aware of a correlation between dirt and disease and men such as Neil Arnott, James Kay, Southwood Smith and William Farr in England, and Dugald Stewart and William Alison in Scotland were trying to set medical problems in their wider social setting. They had gained their experience by visiting the slums during epidemics. Knowing that generalities would be ineffective in producing reforms, they carried out local surveys. These new statistical surveys were now possible in England as a result of the setting up of the Registrar-General's Office in 1837, and of the actuarial studies that were sponsored by friendly societies, life assurance societies and the National Debt Office. Also emerging was a band of professional administrators with access to facts, as a result of laws dealing with factories, prisons, emigrant shipping and the Poor Law. The working of the Poor Law and the excessive expenditure on poor relief led directly to the setting up of the commission to report on sanitary conditions, as Edwin Chadwick, one of the poor law commissioners in England, hoped that this would lead to the authorization of expenditure for the removal of 'nuisances', i.e. refuse and sewage, supplemented by a building act which would involve the substantial extension of powers of local and central government. The report took three years to compile, with the help of Poor Law medical officers, Assistant Commissioners of Poor Law, local relieving officers, Guardians, and clerks to the Boards of Guardians. Originally the Report was only to deal with conditions of towns in England and Wales. After a visit to Edinburgh

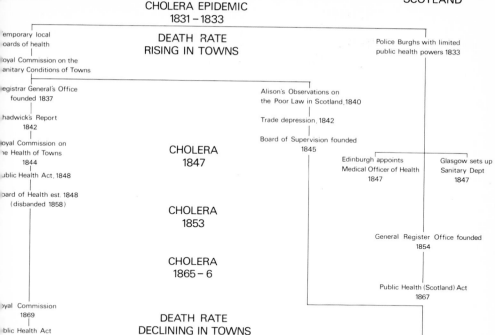

CHOLERA EPIDEMIC
1831 – 1833

DEATH RATE
RISING IN TOWNS

Temporary local boards of health

Royal Commission on the Sanitary Conditions of Towns

Police Burghs with limited public health powers 1833

Registrar General's Office founded 1837

Alison's Observations on the Poor Law in Scotland,1840

Chadwick's Report 1842

Trade depression, 1842

Royal Commission on the Health of Towns 1844

Board of Supervision founded 1845

CHOLERA 1847

Public Health Act, 1848

Edinburgh appoints Medical Officer of Health 1847

Glasgow sets up Sanitary Dept 1847

Board of Health est. 1848 (disbanded 1858)

CHOLERA 1853

General Register Office founded 1854

CHOLERA 1865 – 6

Public Health (Scotland) Act 1867

Royal Commission 1869

DEATH RATE DECLINING IN TOWNS

Public Health Act 1872

Public Health Act 1875

Public Health (Scotland) Act 1897

by Chadwick, Dr Alison asked that Scotland should be included in the survey, and in 1840 he issued his own 'Observations on the Poor Law in Scotland'. Scotland was included in the Report and merits a volume to herself in the Local Reports. Its statistical base, however, was less authoritative because there was no civil registration nor did the Poor Law administration extend north of the Border.

Edwin Chadwick's *Report on the Sanitary Condition of the Labouring Population of Great Britain* was published as a House of Lords paper in 1842. Chadwick enunciated four main principles in his Report: first, the correlation between insanitation, defective drainage, inadequate water supply and overcrowding, and disease, high mortality rates and low life expectancy rates. Secondly, the economic cost of ill-health as administered by the Poor Laws. Thirdly, the social cost of squalor and bad housing in morals and bad habits (this was a major breakthrough in the attitudes of the day which regarded the miseries of the poor as due to some defect of character). Fourthly, again dealing with the Poor Laws, the inefficiency of the existing legal and administrative machinery, which needed centralizing. Parliament was not convinced. A further Report was called for and the Health of Towns Association was set up to inform public opinion through propaganda. Although some local councils had already started reforms, it was only in 1848 that the Public Health Act was passed, under which a new Central Board of Health was set up. Scotland was not included in the Act because she was caught in the trap of having no civil registration of births and deaths and thus could not establish where the death rate exceeded the statutory figure of 23 per 1,000. When the Scottish Act was finally passed in 1867 the Board of Supervision, which had previously been responsible for the supervision of the relief of the poor, became the central authority in Scotland for public health matters. The 1867 Public Health Act had relatively little impact as town councils continued to enforce sanitary reforms either through the general Police Acts or private legislation. Indeed, considerable sections of the Act remained a dead letter. This is not surprising as 'there was a little awkwardness in the wording caused by the fact that the draughtsman seems to have taken the words of the English Public Health Act and applied them to Scotland, ignoring the fact that the word "house" has a different meaning in the two countries'.[13]

The medical profession in Edinburgh, which had done so much to pioneer the better education of physicians, was sceptical of the advantages that might accrue from the activities of non-medical bureaucratic bodies (though they had supplied information) and were reluctant to submit to supervision from London. The Royal College of Physicians in Edinburgh had recognized the need for the appointment of medical officers of health and in 1847 measures were proposed for the creating of a board of health. After the collapse of a house in the High Street, Edinburgh, involving the deaths of thirty-five people, a public meeting successfully urged the town council to appoint a medical officer of health, and in the same year a special sanitary department was set up in Glasgow.

It must have come as some relief to the city fathers when mortality rates began to decline in the 1870s. In Edinburgh the average death rate from 1865 to 1875 was 26.26 per 1,000, and from 1875 to 1885 was 19.94 per 1,000. This improvement was greater than in almost any city of the United Kingdom, but within the city, St Giles ward had rates double that of the residential New Town. Up to 1870 the average death rate in Glasgow was 30.5 per 1,000, thereafter it averaged 28.5 for a decade falling to 26.5 per 1,000 by 1885. Dundee's average death rate from 1864 to 1875 was 28.86 per 1,000. but after the beginning of the 'great demolition' in 1874 and the inauguration of its new water supply in 1876 the average rate fell to 21.09 from 1875 to 1884. The death rate in one of its central wards with as many as 1,800 persons to the hectare had reached the horrific level of 58.4 per 1,000 in 1870.

Edinburgh's pre-eminence in public health was reinforced when the world's first tuberculosis dispensary was set up at 13 Bank

Street by R. W. Philip in November 1887. The dispensary aimed at the detection and treatment of tuberculosis which raged through the congested tenements of the Old Town, and the prevention of infection in other members of the families of the affected persons. Philip suggested that the treatment of TB was a public health matter and advocated his 'co-ordinated Edinburgh system.'[14] In 1912 his concept of a uniform tuberculosis system was adopted by the Government. But for many years the ever-open tenement window remained a symbol of the sufferer's battle with the disease until mass radiography and the development of new drugs in the late 1940s made this a memory.

Disease was not the only urban evil that terrified the middle class. Chartist agitation between 1838 and 1848, anti-Poor Law unrest, especially in the industrial towns of north England between 1834 and 1845, and the Anti-Corn Law League which organized massive demonstrations between 1838 and 1846, revived memories of the excesses of the French Revolution. Furthermore a series of bad harvests before 1842 and a severe trade depression from 1839 to 1843 aggravated the discontent of the urban poor and the landowning class felt their political stewardship of the country at risk. 'If there is anything more to be dreaded in this country, than another, it is a class war', wrote Sir Charles Fergusson in 1843.[15] The fear of crime also contributed to suburban insecurity. The criminal class (an object well established in the Victorian mind) was substantially a phenomenon of cities, where there were districts of sufficient extent to be nurseries and hiding places of criminals. Poverty, too, led to crime as Robert Owen pointed out, 'If the poor cannot procure employment, and are not supported, they must commit crimes, or starve.'[16] The exodus of merchants and craftsmen to the suburbs was a further incitement to crime, as city shops and warehouses were unoccupied at night and weekends. Growing urbanization led to great changes in dealing with crime. Punishment was harsh up to the early nineteenth century, for over 200 offences carried the death penalty, and miscreants were executed for the theft of a few shillings. Every jail acted as a recruiting depot and the army gained a significant proportion of its recruits from the steps of the gallows, 'This day received a Letter from General Smith . . . desiring me to inform you of the Names of the Several Convicts who had received Sentence of Death but were pardoned on Condition of entering into the Service.'[17] Transportation to the colonies was another way of reducing the need for jail space. The reduction of capital offences to a short list by 1837, penal reforms of the 1840s stressing isolation of the individual cell, and the abolition of transportation in 1853, all meant a massive increase in prison population. The demand was met in the 1840s when Thomas Brown designed urban prisons (Fig. 7.4).[18]

Up to the nineteenth century the poor were relatively evenly

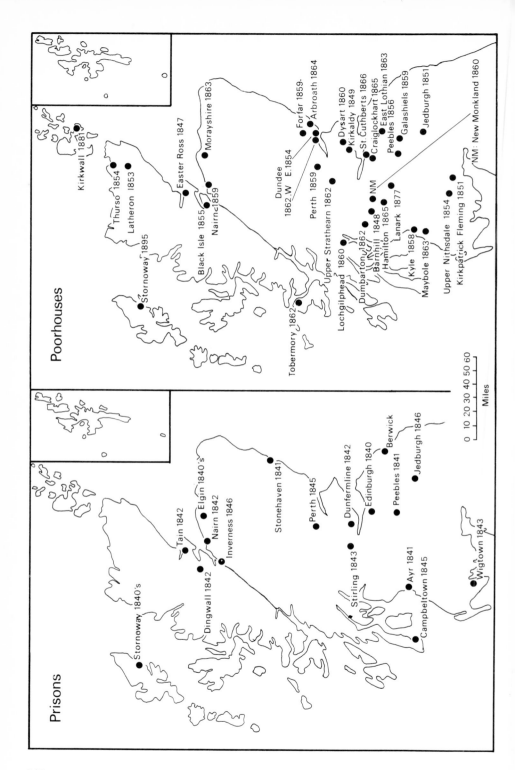

Poorhouses

Kirkwall 1881

Thurso 1854
Latheron 1853

Stornoway 1895

Easter Ross 1847

Morayshire 1863

Black Isle 1855
Nairn 1859

Tobermory 1862

Lochgilphead 1860

Upper Strathearn 1862

Dumbarton 1862

Barnhill 1848

Hamilton 1865

Kyle 1858

Maybole 1863

Forfar 1859
Arbroath 1864

Dundee
1862 W E.1854

Perth 1859

Dysart 1860
Kirkaldy 1849

St.Cuthberts 1866
Craiglockhart 1865

East Lothian 1863
Peebles 1856

Galashiels 1859

Jedburgh 1851

NM

Lanark 1877

Upper Nithsdale 1854

Kirkpatrick Fleming 1851

NM: New Monkland 1860

Prisons

Stornoway 1840's

Tain 1842
Dingwall 1842

Nairn 1842
Inverness 1846

Elgin 1840's

Stonehaven 1841

Perth 1845

Dunfermline 1842

Edinburgh 1840

Berwick

Peebles 1841

Jedburgh 1846

Stirling 1843

Ayr 1841

Campbeltown 1845

Wigtown 1843

0 10 20 30 40 50 60

Miles

142

spread throughout the country, and each parish looked after its own widows, orphans, sick and destitute. With the growth of towns, however, poverty took on a new form. Now it became more concentrated in areas which were suddenly hit by trade recession as, for example, in Paisley in 1842, when 25 per cent of the population depended for subsistence on relief funds. The problem was brought to the public's attention by Dr William Alison. In 1840 he wrote *Observations on the Management of the Poor in Scotland and its Effect on the Health of the Great Towns*, and concluded,

> Thus it appears, that in Edinburgh (and I believe the same holds of other large towns in Scotland), while there has been much disposition to relieve the SICK POOR, there has been a very general discouragement of institutions for the relief of MERE POVERTY — of the unemployed poor, the aged or permanently disabled poor, and the widows and orphans of the poor. The whole sum applied to these purposes is much smaller than in all the English towns. The kind of assistance to the poor, which all medical men know to be of the utmost importance for the PREVENTION of many of their most formidable diseases, has been as much as possible withheld.

As a result of the campaign in which Alison played such a prominent part, the Government set up a commission of inquiry into the working of the Poor Laws in Scotland. Government acted by passing the Poor Law Amendment Act for Scotland in 1845, but the provisions disappointed the reformers. A Central Board of Supervision was to be set up in Edinburgh for the general administration of the Poor Law in Scotland. However, the Act only *recommended* that poorhouses should be built in all big cities and that money for poor relief should be raised by assessment. Relief for the able-bodied was considered 'neither necessary nor expedient', and even the aged and infirm were subject to a test for entry. Discipline and restraint were designed to make life in the institution more irksome than poverty outside.

New poorhouses were to be of such a scale that men were forced to England to gain inspiration. Messrs Mackenzie and Matthews, architects in Aberdeen, visited several recently built workhouses in England (note the differing national terminology) and reported to the Board of Supervision. 'In urban parishes,' they suggested, 'the poorhouse should be so situated as to be perfectly convenient and easy of access for all parties being sufficiently removed from the crowded city, and yet in close proximity thereto . . . It is necessary for the health of the inmates, that it should not be surrounded by a dense population, nor in the immediate vicinity of any noxious trade, or other nuisance.'[19] On the whole recommendations like these were ignored by city fathers, for they desired the whole

g. 7.4 Housing the
iminal and poor in
ictorian Scotland. The
ites are based on the
ans in the Scottish
ecord Office for the
iilding or major
novations and ex-
nsions of these
timidating institu-
ons.

143

problem to be located at the furthest boundary of their administrative area.

Large sites were needed for the new poorhouses, and these were usually found in remote country spots, often some distance from the nearest railway station. These large penal-like institutions had a geography of their own, and their very isolation and cold grandeur must have brought terror to the heart of many a destitute person. The main exception was Glasgow, which housed its poor in the city between the clattering of trains at Buchanan Street station, the sooty clamour of an iron foundry and the toxic effluent of the largest chemical works in Europe. This admixture of land uses reflects the Victorian attitude towards misfortune.

By 1862 there was much uneasiness about poor relief. It was recognized that poorhouses had two aims: to enable local authorities to administer more effectively to the needs of the aged and infirm and to furnish a test of poverty. They were singularly successful in the second aim. Entry into the poorhouse was for many, both young and old, on a one-way ticket: 23 per cent of paupers in residence died and 9 out of 100 died within a year of entry. The diet was calculated merely to sustain life, if that.

The nineteenth-century city attracted footloose flotsam who, in earlier times, had plagued the countryside. The down-and-out, drunkard and single man looking for work irritated the orderly Victorian mind. The solution was to build barrack-like institutions, the lodging houses, which if they did not reform did at least discipline the inmates.

Glasgow went further than any other British city in the building of municipal lodging houses. The model lodging house was created to divert lodgers into more 'moral and sanitary' surroundings and away from the already overcrowded one- and two-apartment houses. Under the Improvement Act of 1866 the city built seven lodging houses and a family home. The family home was intended for widowers and widows with families but 'the association of the two sexes in the one building was found to be dangerous' and the home was restricted to widowers and their families. For both the family home and lodging houses, admittance was by test of respectability rather than need. But at that time the Corporation felt it was not their business to participate in these activities and built no more lodging houses, leaving to private enterprise the provision of this type of accommodation. 'House-farmers' provided furnished accommodation of a rudimentary kind in the poorer parts of Glasgow. A large house was subdivided into a number of rooms which were let on a nightly basis to an individual or a family. The places were taken by people who had been refused accommodation by private landlords, the corporation lodging houses or the family home: 'No provision has been made for this section of the population, and it is understood that the Corporation do not intend to make provision for them, and hold that it is not their duty to do so.' The extent of municipal policy and responsibility had yet to be defined, but it is clear that doubts were present in some minds as to the limits of acceptable involvement. A question raised at the inquiry into the 1902 Improvement Act, 'at what point is municipal enterprise to commence, and if commenced where is it to end?' still needs to be answered.

Whatever their political complexion local authorities have shown little diffidence in expanding their interests into public or private amenities. No better case can be provided than that of the provision of lighting in towns. Gas lighting was pioneered by William Murdoch, one of Boulton and Watt's leading mechanics. In 1806 this great firm began to market the new lighting in cotton mills but soon its use spread to street lighting. However, the unreformed burghs did not adopt gas lighting on any scale until the middle of the 1820s and only extensively after the Reform Acts (Fig. 7.5). Gas was regarded at first solely as a means of providing illumination. Permission to lay mains was obtained by private Acts of Parliament which in effect created local monopolies. The Edinburgh Gas Light Company was formed in 1812 and soon the shops in the Old Town were lit by this novelty. Oil street lamps were replaced by gas in 1820 and the system was gradually extended throughout the growing town. Gas lighting was introduced into Glasgow shops in 1818 by the Glasgow Gas Light Company, to Aberdeen in 1824 and soon spread through many burghs (Fig. 7.6). In Annan the provost was one of the principal instigators and his enthusiasm extended to offering to feu part of his back garden for the gasworks when all other proprietors had rejected approaches for a site. Twenty of the provost's neighbours, more sensitive to the potential pollution, petitioned against this site but they were brusquely over-ruled and in October 1838 the streets of Annan glowed from the light of forty lamps.[20] Early attempts to control the growing industry were ineffective to counter its monopolistic nature but in 1876 the Burghs Gas Supply (Scotland) Act authorized municipal control, and town councils began taking over the gasworks. Thereafter gas was increasingly used as a fuel, not only for domestic cooking and heating but also for industrial processes.[21]

The Victorian Age settled down to the hissing glow of the gas mantle until electricity challenged its ascendancy towards the end of the nineteenth century (Fig. 7.5). The switching on of four arc lamps in 1879 at the opening of St Enoch's railway station in Glasgow inaugurated the era of public electric lighting. But it was Joseph Swan's patented carbon-filamented electric lamp the following year that launched widespread electric lighting. Within three years the brilliance of the new light encouraged the crowned heads of Europe to illuminate their palaces, exhibitions and opera houses with it. Yet the burghs stayed their hands until the innovation had

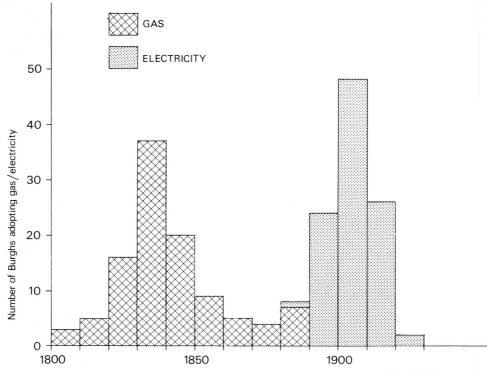

Fig. 7.5 The rate of adoption of gas and electric lighting by burghs

been thoroughly tested.

Government legislation (Electricity Supply Act 1882) recognized that town councils must be involved in regulating the new industry, and the Victorian town fathers did not need ideological reasons to protect it from the hazards of the market place. A further Scottish Act in 1890, empowering burghs to instal electricity plant, was adopted by Glasgow where street lighting appeared in 1893, and two years later Edinburgh's Princes Street glowed with the novel light. Transmission distances were at first short; the concentration of demand in the city centres and the need for coal to drive the steam generators effectively limited the earliest power stations to sites near the central railway termini. Edinburgh's burgh engineer designed a red sandstone generating station at Dewar Place:

> ... the foundation here is rock, and the station being on the railway, coal is brought direct into the boiler-house in the railway trucks at a minimum expense. The position of the site is such that, while being fairly central, it is in a neighbourhood where there is little chance of complaint as to nuisance, real or otherwise.[22]

Distribution, too, was based on socio-economic criteria: the New Town was laid with mains for house and shop lighting, while the

Fig. 7.6 Burgh gas-works in nineteenth-century Scotland. Provisional dates give the earliest known reference to a gaswor. (Based on Private Acts of Parliament, Gas Board records in the Scottish Record Office and various printed sources.)

146

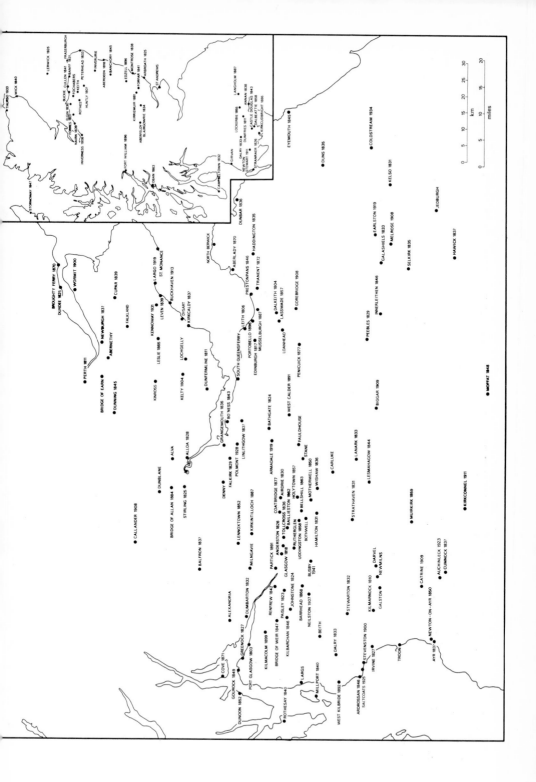

major thoroughfares in the Old Town were provided only with street lights (Fig. 7.7). As demand increased, larger generating sets brought problems of cooling, and the next series of power stations were built near ample cooling water such as the River Clyde and the Firth of Forth. Only with the development of a National Grid after World War II could the electricity industry break away from its urban origins (Fig. 7.8).

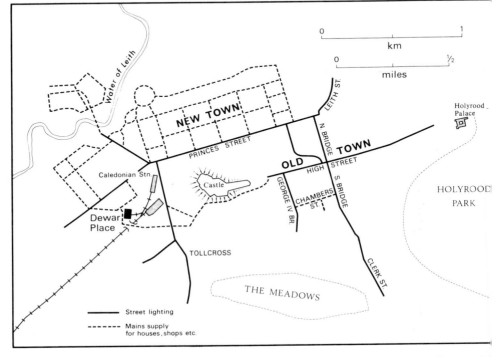

Fig. 7.7 Edinburgh Corporation's electr city supply system swtiched on 11 Apr 1895. (*Engineering* November 1895.)

Urban reform had its more pleasant aspects and the Victorian enthusiasm for parks created valuable assets in the expanding towns. The burgh common was often a piece of ground which had defied development through some physical defect. Ill-drained sites, often beds of old glacial lakes, bogs or riverside lands survived, as at the Inch in Perth, Glasgow Green, The Meadows and Princes Street Gardens in Edinburgh and Magdalen Green in Dundee. The technical problems of developing these central pieces of open land were overcome very late, by which time civic awareness was sufficient to prevent their disappearance. The same was generally true of rocky outcrops such as Dundee Law or Edinburgh's Bruntsfield Links. Quarrying tended to ruin these burgh commons for building purposes, and at the same time provided an economic argument against such building. These unattractive sites were gradually surrounded by development so that they were no longer continuations of the open countryside and, mainly during the Victorian era, they were turned

concentration of
Scotland's early
power stations

Arbroath 1899
Carnoustie 1902
Broughty Ferry 1900
Wormit 1900
St Andrews 1902
Dundee 1883
Leven 1911
Methil 1911
Buckhaven 1911
North Berwick
Dysart 1911
Kirkcaldy 1899
Musselburgh 1899
Inveresk 1906
Falkland 1911
Kinghorn 1911
Burntisland 1911
Leith 1897
Dalkeith 1901
Markinch 1911
Edinburgh 1891
Lochgelly 1910
Cowdenbeath 1910
Dunfermline 1906
Inverkeithing 1911
Perth 1898
Bo'ness 1903
Linlithgow 1912
Uphall 1905
Crieff 1901
Dollar 1901
Saline 1911
Carnock 1911
Torryburn 1911
Grangemouth 1905
Dunblane 1900
Stirling 1895
Alloa 1899
Falkirk 1901
Coatbridge 1905
Airdrie 1899
Bellshill 1906
Motherwell 1895
Wishaw 1904
Denny 1905
Kirkintilloch 1903
Uddingston 1906
Bothwell 1906
Kelvinside 1890
Partick 1893
Hamilton 1898
Kilpatrick 1906
Blantyre 1906
Fochabers 1906
Aberdeen 1890
Cults 1905
Ellon 1914
Montrose 1898
Lossiemouth 1913
Aboyne 1914
Ballater 1914
Brechin 1898
Nairn 1902
Inverness 1899
Galashiels 1901
Melrose 1901
Jedburgh 1901
Dunoon 1901
Rothesay 1898
Hawick 1899
Dumfries 1899
Maxwelltown 1913
Portpatrick 1904
Ayr 1914
Dumbarton 1902
Renfrew 1905
Govan 1892
Paisley 1891
Pollokshaws 1905
Barrhead 1908
Eastwood 1906
Gourock 1901
Greenock 1923
Port Glasgow 1913
Clydebank 1901
Kilmacolm 1900
Skelmorlie 1910
Ardrossan 1910
Saltcoats 1903
Irvine 1903
Kilmarnock 1899

1 Kinning Park 1902
2 Glasgow 1890
3 Rutherglen 1905
4 Cathcart 1906
5 Shettleston 1906
6 Cambuslang 1903

Km 0   10   20   30   40
Miles 0   6   12   18   24

149

to great advantage in the urban landscape.

In the second half of the nineteenth century a more positive approach developed regarding the provision of public parks. Glasgow began to purchase ground for parks on the edge of the built-up area. The first of these was Kelvingrove Park (34.5 hectares) purchased in 1852. Five years later Queen's Park (59 hectares) was purchased far to the south of the city. There was considerable opposition because of its remoteness but the scheme was part of a wider one to encourage residential building in the southern outskirts. The City Improvement Trustees purchased Alexandra Park (42 hectares) to serve the north-east of the city, although air pollution was so bad that only the hardiest species of trees and shrubs could survive. Maintenance of these parks was a growing problem and the Corporation obtained an Act in 1878 establishing the Parks Department on a formal basis. After this date the city added numerous open spaces to its inventory, the most important being the Botanic Gardens, acquired in 1891. On the whole the new parks of this period enhanced the middle-class villa suburbs springing up on the edge of the city, while for most, the cobbled street or Glasgow Green had to provide a substitute for the countryside.

As urban growth continued through the nineteenth century, municipal boundaries rarely synchronized with the spread of buildings and population. This was nowhere more apparent than in Glasgow. The boundaries of the burgh were extended in 1846 to coincide with the 1832 parliamentary boundaries. Under the General Police and Improvement (Scotland) Act of 1862, any area with a population of more than 700 could be formed into a police burgh, and nine of the wealthier suburbs took advantage of this to form independent police jurisdictions and become what were in effect 'villa burghs' (Fig. 7.9). Clearly the Act had not been framed with this in mind. Govan, comprising 452 hectares, was constituted a police burgh in 1864, followed in 1869 by the district of Hillhead, with an area of 52 hectares of residential property.[23] This fragmentation was contrary to current trends. The Corporation had initiated the Loch Katrine water supply in 1855 and a City Improvement Act in 1865, had municipalized the gas supply in 1869 and tramways in 1870 and 1875, and abolished tollgates within the boundaries. All these activities depended on a strong and dynamic city government. Glasgow's city fathers felt that the middle classes in their separate suburbs wanted only the advantages of the economic activity generated by the city but none of the responsibility. By the 1880s the boundary anomalies had become excessive and the Glasgow Boundaries Commission of 1888 found unanimously that the city's boundaries should be extended under one administration and this was enacted three years later.[24]

For the individual the city could throw up pleasures which fleetingly reduced the everyday squalor. Government made a contribu-

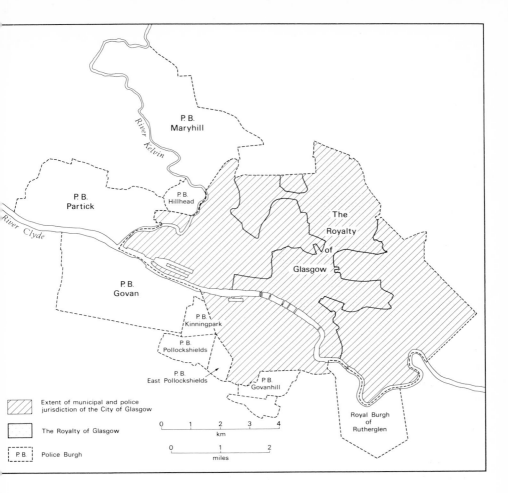

Fig. 7.9 Villa burghs in the vicinity of Glasgow in the 1880s.

tion by passing the Bank Holiday Act in 1871. But the urban contribution was the rise of mass entertainment which sprang from the working man's sporting interests. Association football emerged towards the end of the century as a great spectator sport. Queen's Park Football Club, founded by boys at a Glasgow YMCA in 1867, were the pioneers of Scottish football. Professionalism and the hardy Scottish footballer went on to convert this sport from an English public school pastime to the working man's religion. The football stadium was a city phenomenon for only there could tens of thousands be gathered together for a couple of hours Saturday by Saturday through the bleak winter months. Even in the warmth of the music hall, reality broke in when a great entertainer like Will Fyffe sang:

151

I belong to Glasgow, dear old Glasgow town!
But what's the matter wi' Glasgow?
For it's going round and round
I'm only a common working chap
As anyone here can see,
But when I get a couple of drinks on a Saturday
Glasgow belongs to me.

Buried deeper in the song is the pent-up rage and bitterness of urban deprivation which was often vented upon some broken woman.

There's nae harm in taking a drappie,
It ends all your trouble and strife;
It gives you the feeling, that when you get home
You don't care a hang for the wife.

It has been suggested that there were fundamental reasons why Victorian cities should develop differently in England and Scotland. First, much of the legislation passed by the British parliament at this time was unworkable in Scotland because of the different legal system. 'Only in the 1860s did the general government of Scotland attain, in respect of public health, the state which England had been in since 1848, and only in the 1890s did the Scottish laws of public health really catch up with the English.'[25] By 1897 the standard of public health was about the same in the four Scottish cities as in English cities, but lamentably behind in smaller urban areas and in country towns and villages, largely because these were the very local authorities who did not bother to pass by-laws or try to put the national legislation into effect. Secondly, Scottish municipal authorities probably had greater powers of interference in citizens' lives under their Police Acts, and this authoritarianism led to less voluntary or private effort in self-help. Dundee and Glasgow were the first authorities in Britain to introduce public lighting into private courts and common stairs. Glasgow was the first authority to build tramlines and then lease them to private companies. Glasgow, Edinburgh, and Dundee were well ahead of the other British cities in the clearing of slum dwellings. Thirdly, the appalling overcrowding was possibly the result of the indestructible stone from which the tenements were built. Because the structures were still sound there was little incentive to demolish them and instead they were 'made-down' by more and yet more subdivision. Fourthly, the Dean of Guild courts could legislate only on the exterior of houses. Thus the courts had no power over nuisances in the common stair or the subdivision of houses.

By the end of the nineteenth century reform had spread through most aspects of city life and administration. Only housing had been left outside this broad spectrum of reform, and in this sphere Scotland had an enormous backlog to catch up. Few would have guessed at the beginning of the twentieth century that within seventy years the state would be responsible for housing the majority of the population of Scotland. Scotland was on the verge of the Socialist century.

Notes

1. The Act was entitled, ' . . . as touching the election of Aldermen, bailies and others . . .', *Acts of Parliament of Scotland* 1469, II 95, c.5. The criticism was made in an address by the Lord Dean of Guild, G. L. Orchard, *Guildry and Local Government* (Edinburgh, January, 1962).

2. *General Report of the Commissioners Appointed to Inquire into the State of Municipal Corporations in Scotland* (London, 1835), p. 40.

3. T. Ferguson, *The Dawn of Scottish Social Welfare* (Nelson, Edinburgh, 1948); for a good description of this custom see H. G. Graham, *The Social Life of Scotland in the Eighteenth Century* (Black, London, 1928), p. 83.

4. The Scottish Record Office has a considerable number of records relating to by-laws (DD13/1356 etc.).

5. Senex, *Glasgow Past and Present* (Glasgow, 1884), III, pp. 58-9.

6. *Royal Commission on the Sewage of Towns* 1st Report 1857-8, 2nd Report 1861, 3rd Report 1865; *Edinburgh Water-works Bill. Minutes and Evidence Taken before the Surveying Officers* . . . (Edinburgh, 1847), p. 104 (SRO RHP 17124).

7. *Report for the Supply of Water to Glasgow from Water of Earn and Water of Cart* (1834) (SRO RHP 5394).

8. Gorbals Direct Water Supply Company's plans (SRO Sheriff Court plan).

9. Records relating to the Burgh Police and Health (Scotland) Bill (SRO DD13/1145).

10. W. Moir Bryce, *The Burgh Muir of Edinburgh* (The Book of the Old Edinburgh Club, Edinburgh, 1919), pp. 167, 184-9, 234.

11. E. Gauldie, *Cruel Habitations: A History of Working Class Housing 1780-1919* (Allen and Unwin, London, 1974), p. 109.

12. M. W. Flinn, (ed.), *Edwin Chadwick's Report on the Sanitary Conditions of the Labouring Population of Great Britain* (University Press, Edinburgh, 1965), pp. 21-31. For a detailed analysis of reactions to the cholera outbreak of 1832 see R. J. Morris, *Cholera 1832* (Croom Helm, London, 1976).

13. *Royal Commission on the Housing of the Working Classes*, 2nd Report, *Scotland*, 1885, Cmnd.4409, p. 102.

14. *British Medical Journal*, 1 December 1906.

15. Earl of Glasgow's papers (NRA (Scot) 94 box 6 bdl.7).

16. Select Committee on Police, Parliamentary Papers 1816, v., p. 234.

17. Edward E. Curtis, *The British Army in the American Revolution* (Yale University Press, 1926), p. 164.

18. The original plans are in the Scottish Record Office.

19. They were commissioned to build the Black Isle Poorhouse (SRO RHP 30852).

20. Minutes of the Annan Gas Light Company (SRO Gas Board records GB1/1/1).

21. Representations to the Gas Undertakings Bill, 1934 (SRO DD11/92).

22. *Engineering*, 8 November 1895.

23. Glasgow Corporation, *Statement by the Lord Provost, Magistrates and Town Council of the City and Royal Burgh of Glasgow of the Grounds on which They Urge the Appointment of a Royal Commission . . . to Consider the Whole Question of the Extension of Municipal Areas in Scotland*

(Glasgow, 1879) (SRO DD5/1).

24. Glasgow Boundaries Bill 1888-1891 (SRO DD5/2).

25. G. F. A. Best, 'Another Part of the Island', in H. J. Dyos, and M. Wolff, *The Victorian City: Images and Realities* (London, Routledge and Kegan Paul, 1973), pp. 389-411.

A Scotsman's home is not his castle but his council house. When J. B. Cullingworth remarked recently that 'Scotland has a lower proportion of owner occupation than any European country west of Russia' there were no ideological implications. Scots live in a land where the State houses the majority of the population and they think little of it; no less than 57.6 per cent of the population live in state housing compared to 29 per cent in England. The Scottish city became socialized not from any specific political ideology but through the need to rectify urban injustices created in the nineteenth century. Whilst Glaswegians provided ships and locomotives for the Empire and soldiers to police it, those who remained at home lived in conditions that made the Second City the Calcutta of Europe.

Of all the problems in towns, housing was by far the most pressing. Reports, committees and royal commissions brought their collective attention to the horrors suffered by the labouring class. The problem had many facets: the condition of buildings was often poor in the extreme; overcrowding was the rule rather than the exception; sanitation was non-existent. The stress did not end there, for the houses were often near evil-smelling, dirty and noisy industry. Conditions in the wynds of Glasgow in 1839 were described in the report of the Commission for Inquiring into the Conditions of the Hand-loom Weavers:

I allude to the dense and motley community who inhabit the low districts of Glasgow, consisting chiefly of the alleys leading out of the High Street, the lanes in the Calton, but particularly the closes and wynds which lie between the Trongate and the Bridgegate, the Salt-market and Maxwell-street. These districts contain a motley population, consisting in almost all the lower branches of occupation . . . . I have seen human degradation in some of its worst phases, both in England and abroad, but I can advisedly say, that I did not believe until I visited the wynds of Glasgow, that so large an amount of filth, crime, misery and disease existed on one spot in any civilised country. The wynds consist of long lanes, so narrow that a cart could with difficulty pass along them; out of these open the 'closes', which are courts about 15 or 20 feet [4.5 or 6 metres] square, round which the houses, mostly of three stories high, are built; the centre of the court is the dunghill, which is probably the most lucrative part of the estate to the laird in most instances and which it would consequently be esteemed an invasion of the rights of property to remove. The houses are for the most part let in flats, either to the lowest class of labourers or prostitutes, or to lodging-keepers. . . . In the more costly of these abodes, where separate beds are furnished at the price of 3d per night, the thieves and prostitutes chiefly congregate. . . .

In the lower lodging-houses ten, twelve, and sometimes twenty persons of both sexes and all ages sleep promiscuously on the floor in different degrees of nakedness. These places are, generally as regards dirt, damp, and decay, such as no person of common humanity to animals would stable his horse in.[1]

If conditions like these were exceptional then that report must be dismissed as mere sensationalism. Surely the reward for being one of the foremost industrial nations in the world, partner in the greatest empire the world has ever seen, would have yielded a decent home for the working man? It was not until the 1861 census that sufficient data were at hand to answer the question. According to the census, 34 per cent of families in Scotland lived in one room and 37 per cent in two rooms; 1 per cent of all families occupied single rooms without windows (Table 1). In parts of Edinburgh there were from 525 to 850 persons per hectare. Of the single-roomed houses in the city, 121 had no windows and 1,530 housed from 6 to 15 persons each. The average size of the rooms was 4.3 m by 3.5 m. All this did not go unnoticed by the city fathers. Indeed in Edinburgh, with the council chambers set in St Giles ward, one of the worst in the city, the problem was hard to avoid. When a police report submitted in 1889 showed one arrest for every six inhabitants of the ward and the presence of one drink shop for every 139 persons, the councillors felt that municipal licensing of drinking places would mitigate the problem. They were aware of the terrible conditions, for one of their number, Councillor Macpherson, reported on the 76 one-roomed houses in the ward (Fig. 8.1).[2] 'The single-room system appears to be an institution co-existent with urban life among the working classes in Scotland', was the despairing conclusion of the commissioners inquiring into the working classes in Scotland in 1885.

Housing became a prominent political problem in the last quarter of the nineteenth century. In part, however, it cannot be separated from the general economic climate of the period; depression started in 1877 and lasted in varying degrees for twenty years.[3] As usual it was the unskilled labourer earning less than £1 a week who suffered most: in economic terms it was not worth building a house for him. Although 1876 had been a boom year for Scottish house production when 28,531 houses were built, the annual production sank to between 5,000 and 10,000 (Fig. 8.2). The boom of the 1870s gave rise to a great deal of jerry-building. A jaundiced professional eye observed: 'The character of the carpentry or joiners work of these four

Table 1. Distribution of houses in Scotland by size 1861-1911 per cent of total houses

	Houses without windows	1 room	2 rooms	3 rooms	4 rooms	5 rooms and over
1861	1.2	34.0	37.0	11.4	5.5	10.9
1871	0.2	32.1	37.2	12.6	6.0	11.9
1881	0.1	26.0	38.9	14.7	6.8	13.5
1891	0.1	22.1	39.1	16.4	7.5	14.8
1901	—	17.6	39.9	18.5	8.5	15.5
1911	—	12.8	40.4	20.3	9.3	17.2

Source: Census (SRO DD6/265).

or five storey flats needs no description. It might have been executed by an amateur casual. The mason and the plasterer do the principal work, and when the sashes are hung, the doors hinged, the flats are ready for their victims.'[4] The types and quality of buildings provided cannot be separated from the financial system that backed them. Lenders of money to builders and small-time investors demanded structural strength but showed little concern for the internal layout of the houses. The more families a proprietor could squeeze in, the better was the chance that his bonds would be honoured. High land prices necessitated building to very high densities. The result was the tenement block of three or four storeys, built to a fairly standard design. The dwellings were approached by a narrow passageway or close leading from the street to a stone stair at the back of the building and this gave access to the upper floor flats. The houses were badly planned; rooms were often awkwardly shaped and windows so placed that artificial light was necessary. Common water closets, which were added later, were usually at either side of the stair and entered from the half-landing. In the older properties where the water closets were on the inside of the stair, the only ventilation came from a few holes bored in the doors.

During the nineteenth century the principle of state interference in housing, which usually left rights of property intact, was insinuated into the statute books. Several Acts of Parliament were passed giving local authorities the power to deal with the housing problem. The Dwelling Houses (Scotland) Act 1855 gave power for associations of persons acting in the public interest to acquire dilapidated property at a price fixed by the sheriff; this was the forerunner of compulsory purchase. The Nuisances Removal Act 1855 empowered and obliged local authorities to provide adequate privies, maintain

LIST OF ONE-ROOMED DWELLING HOUSES in St Giles' Ward, personally visited and measured by Councillor Macpherson, and submitted to Sub-Committee of the Lord Provost's Committee, 21st January 1889.

Name and No. of Street or Close.	Name of Proprietor.*	Cubic Capacity per Head.	Name of Tenant.	Size of House.	Rent per Week or Year.	No. of Persons in House.	No. of Apartments.	Remarks.
				FEET.				
Craig's Close		137·8	Ward	13½ × 10½ × 5-10	1s. 6d. per week	Six	One	No water, no W.C.
		378	Ferrier	14 × 12 × 9	2s. 6d. „	Four	One	
Covenant Close		198	Hady	11 × 8 × 9	1s. 4d. „	Four	One	Very dark.
		254·5	Anderson	{12 × 9 × 9 and / 15 × 6 × 9}	1s. 11d. „	Seven	Two	
		264	Gibson	11 × 8 × 9	1s. 8d. „	Three	One	
Stevenlaw's Close		270	Hamilton	15 × 10 × 9	2s. 6d. „	Five	One	
„		660	Smith	11 × 8 × 9	1s. „	Two	One	Dark, and three feet belo- [street
„		330	Thornton	11 × 9 × 10	1s. 3d. „	Three	One	
„		288	Renshaw	12 × 12 × 10	2s. „	Five	One	No W.C. or water in stair
„		405	Hunter	10 × 9 × 9	1s. 2d. „	Two	One	
„		237·6	M. Flannigan	12 × 11 × 9	2s. 2d. „	Five	One, and dark closet	
„		198	Kechan	12 × 11 × 9	2s. 3d. „	Six	One, and dark closet	
„		115·2	M'Raw	9 × 8 × 8	1s. 4d. „	Five	One	Miserable dens, garrets, n gas.
„		261·3	M'Ginty	14 × 7 × 8	1s. 4d. „	Three	One	
„		504	Henderson	12 × 12 × 7	1s. 7d. „	Two	One	
Robertson's Close		416	Burns	13 × 12 × 8	2s. 6d. „	Three	One	
„		476	M'Bride	17 × 7 × 8	2s. 6d. „	Two	One, and dark closet	Very dark.
„		770	M'Condy	11 × 10 × 7	1s. 6d. „	One	One	Damp.
„		176·8	M'Greenen	15 × 11 × 7½	2s. 3d. „	Seven	One	
Hall's Court		374	M'Bride	17 × 11 × 8	1s. 9d. „	Four	One	
„		280	Degnan	14 × 12 × 10	1s. 9d. „	Six	One	Very dark.
Baxter's Close		288	Gallagher	8 × 8 × 9	1s. „	Two	One	
„		189	Girty	9 × 7 × 9	1s. 6d. „	Three	One, and dark closet	
„		324	Brown	12 × 6 × 9	10d. „	Two	One	
„		216	M'Lauchlan	14 × 12 × 9	2s. „	Seven	One	
„		526·5	Napier	13 × 9 × 9	1s. 2d. „	Two	One	Attic.
„		283·5	Taylor	14 × 9 × 9	2s. „	Four	One, and dark closet	Miserable hovel, no plaste
„		320	M'Ewan	15 × 8 × 8	1s. „	Three	One	
„		228	H. Devine	19 × 9 × 8	2s. „	Six	One	
Anderson's Close		200·5	J. Stewart	{12 × 9 / 12 × 9} × 6-6	1s. 9d. „	Seven	Two Rooms	
Castle Wynd		360	Smith	15 × 12 × 6	1s. 6d. „	Three	One	Four steps below street.
„		168	Borland	12 × 8 × 7	1s. 6d. „	Four	One	
„		82·5	Penman	11 × 6 × 7½	1s. 5d. „	Six	One	
„		154·28	Scott	12 × 12 × 7½	1s. 10d. „	Seven	One	
„		300	Wynn	12 × 10 × 7½	1s. 9d. „	Three	One	
„		412·5	Campbell	15 × 11 × 10	2s. 4d. „	Four	One	
„		780	Finnigan	13 × 12 × 10	1s. 10d. „	Two	One	
„		432	Brannan	16 × 12 × 9	2s. 5d. „	Four	One	
„		351	Hume	13 × 12 × 9	1s. 9d. „	Four	One	
„		216	Gallagher	16 × 12 × 9	2s. 5d. „	Eight	One	
„		275	William Gray	10 × 11 × 7½	1s. 10d. „	Three	One	Earthen floor, and damp.
Brown's Close		344·25	O'Malley	17 × 9 × 9	1s. 9d. „	Four	One	
„		408	Kane	17 × 9 × 8	1s. 7d. „	Three	One	
„		416	Brackin	13 × 8 × 8	1s. 6d. „	Two	One	
„		320	Truman	10 × 8 × 8	1s. 6d. „	Two	One	
„		240	Steven	10 × 9 × 8	1s. 6d. „	Three	One	
„		172·8	Blaikie	12 × 9 × 8	1s. 3d. „	Five	One	
„		432	Laidlaw	12 × 9 × 8	1s. 6d. „	Two	One	
„		249·6	M'Nab	13 × 12 × 8	1s. 8d. „	Five	One	Water from common stre well, no W.
„		208	Stanton	13 × 8 × 8	1s. 6d. „	Four	One	
„		440	Gilhooly	11 × 10 × 8	1s. 6d. „	Two	One	
„		572	Cantley	13 × 11 × 8	1s. 9d. „	Two	One	
„		216	Murphy	9 × 12 × 8	1s. 6d. „	Four	One	
325 Cowgate		540	M'Philip	{9 × 10 / 9 × 10} × 9	1s. 6d. „	Three	Two	
344 Cowgate (Scott's Land)		198	Grady	12 × 11 × 9	1s. 9d. „	Six	One	
295 Cowgate		240	M'Inally	12 × 12 × 10	1s. „	Six	One	Very dark.
„		200	M'Girr	10 × 10 × 10	1s. 10d. „	Five	One, and dark closet	
„		330	Dick	15 × 11 × 10	2s. 2d. „	Five	One	
„		480	Wright	12 × 8 × 10	1s. 6d. „	Two	One	
„		405	M'Farlane	15 × 9 × 9	2s. „	Three	One	
„		270	M'Queenie	15 × 10 × 9	2s. 2d. „	Five	One, and dark closet	
„		288	Murray	12 × 8 × 9	1s. 10d. „	Three	One	
„		297	P. M'Ginn	11 × 9 × 9	1s. 7d. „	Three	One	
289 Cowgate		216	Glass	8 × 9 × 9	2s. 2d. „	Four	One and small recess	
„		216	M. Kirk	12 × 8 × 9	2s. 1d. „	Six	One, and small bed recess	
„		135	Elvin	10 × 9 × 9	2s. 1d. „	Four	One, and small bed recess	
„		193	M'Kenna	11 × 8 × 9	2s. 1d. „	Four	One	
„		158·4	Farrell	11 × 8 × 9	2s. 1d. „	Five	One	
„		280	Sherry	14 × 15 × 8	2s. 1d. „	Six	One	
High School Yards		112	Finnigan	14 × 8 × 8	2s. 2d. „	Eight	One, and dark closet	No Water.
„		325	Burre l.	13 × 10 × 10	1s. 9d. „	Four	One	—
„		247·5	Summons	11 × 9 × 10	1s. 7d. „	Four	—	
„		234	James Dollans	13 × 10 × 9	1s. 9d. „	Five	—	
„		162·5	M'Gill	13 × 10 × 10		Eight	One	
„		243	Scott		1s. 7d. „	Four	One	
„		243	C. Beattie	12 × 9 × 9	1s. 7d. „	Four	One	

* Councillor Macpherson's object being to support his motion by facts as to the condition of these one-roomed houses, the names of the proprietors are meanwhile withheld. While (rightly enough) it is insisted, that the keepers of common lodging-houses shall provide for each sleeper 400 cubic feet of space, it will be found that in the above list instances o where there are only 86 ; 112 ; and 115 cubic feet of space for each person.

Fig. 8.1 The statistics of squalor in St Giles Ward, Edinburgh, 1889 Note the councillor's reticence about the ownership of these slums. (Scottish Record Office.)

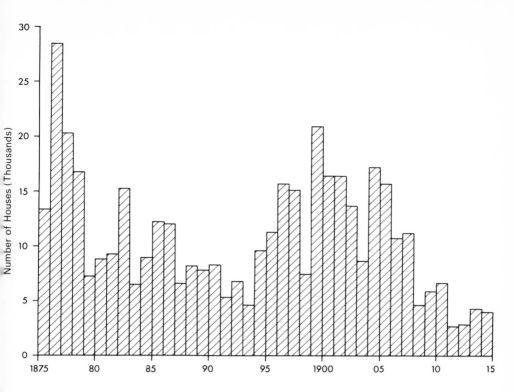

Fig. 8.2 Annual output of houses in Scotland 1875-1915

premises in safe and habitable condition, clean and whitewash insanitary houses, and close any house where a nuisance was 'such as to render the house unfit for human habitation'. This was the first acknowledgement by Parliament that there might be such houses, but they disappeared slowly because officials realized that alternative accommodation might be even worse.[5]

Housing legislation proceeded upon the principle that the responsibility of maintaining houses in proper condition fell upon the owner, and the State only took sufficient powers to compel him to comply. Most of the legislation was a dead letter. The turning point came in 1875 when Sir Richard Cross introduced a new principle in his Artizans' and Labourers' Dwelling Act: instead of singling out individual owners he identified whole areas where houses were so ruinous and congested that nothing short of demolition would solve the problem. Thus in an age of unfettered capitalism Parliament found the wisdom to authorize the State to undertake comprehensive urban renewal, plan the cleared areas and build houses for the working classes. A passion for sanitary purity rather than ideological salvation set Britain upon the path to the socialist city.

Some of Scotland's most populous towns — Glasgow (1866), Edinburgh (1867), Dundee (1871), Greenock (1877), Leith (1880)

159

and Aberdeen (1884) — started improvement schemes, either by local Act or by utilizing Sir Richard Cross's Acts. On the whole the authorities conveniently forgot about the provision of working-class dwellings and concentrated on knocking down slums and widening streets. The policy of not providing alternative housing for those displaced by improvement schemes was self-defeating. The poor were pressed into even smaller areas of greater densities, and any house suitable for subdivision was 'made down'. The creation of the next generation of slums was accepted with some equanimity: 'It is the habit of that class of people not to go into houses of a first class character, but into the nearest houses in that area which they can get. They go to second-hand houses just as they very largely wear second-hand clothes.'[6]

Overcrowding became so bad that Glasgow Corporation attempted to limit the problem by licensing the capacity of all houses of three rooms or less. Power was conferred by the Glasgow Police Act 1866 and a ticket was fixed on each house bearing the number allowed to sleep there. In one year 55,292 'night inspections' of ticketed houses revealed 7,044 over the legal limit, that is, about 13 per cent of these small dwellings housed too many people even by the poor standards of the time. About a third of the overcrowding was due to these one- and two-roomed houses taking lodgers.

City fathers began to explore methods by which they could eradicate slums. They were provided with a model in 1864 when the City of Glasgow Union Railway obtained an Act of Parliament to build a large terminus, St Enoch, and to drive a line through some of the oldest and most crowded areas of the city, clearing away many thousands of insanitary houses. At the same time a group of well-meaning citizens bought up a portion of the worst housing with a view to building model tenements; the task proved beyond them however, and the property was transferred to the Corporation. It was clear that the problem was so vast that concerted effort was needed in the central parts of old Glasgow, and the Corporation launched the biggest urban renewal scheme in nineteenth-century Scotland.

The Improvement Trust, created by the Glasgow Improvement Act 1866, envisaged the acquisition of 36 hectares in the city centre, including the Saltmarket and Bridgegate. The population of 51,000 was living in densely overcrowded and insanitary conditions. Thirty new wide streets were formed and twenty-six streets widened, occupying 9 hectares formerly covered by houses. The Molendinar and Camlachie Burns, two filthy streams which ran through the district, were covered in. Despite all this activity the early years of the Improvement Trust were a complete commercial and social disaster. As the slum areas were compulsorily purchased and cleared, the displaced occupants crowded into the remaining property. Once the new streets were laid out the Trust sold the remaining land. In the depressed conditions of the time, those lots taken up and built upon never yielded sufficient income even to pay the ground rents; the purchasers were driven into bankruptcy and the land and buildings reverted to the Improvement Trust. The Trustees decided in 1888 to start building on their own account, and it can be said that Glasgow then took its first steps towards becoming a socialist city. As the Lord Provost put it,

> After having once again put their hands into the mortar tub, the work of demolition and reconstruction proceeded apace, with the result that practically the whole of the areas scheduled under the Act of 1866 and the surplus lands taken over by the Trustees from the Police Commissioners in 1893 have now [1901] been covered with buildings of a substantial and modern character.[7]

The Improvement Act of 1897 resulted in the eviction of over 3,000 very poor people, but not a single house was built on the grounds that there were plenty of empty houses. In September 1901 the idea of housing one-tenth of Glasgow's population in municipally owned houses was put forward at a 'Conference as to Cheap Dwellings' presided over by the Lord Provost:

> As a matter of fact and experience, the unembodied law of supply and demand has built up all our back lanes, has crowded tenants on one stairhead, and would, if a sterner law than itself had not interfered, have perpetuated these narrow lanes and dark closes and sunless rooms which were the scandal of our social condition . . . I say the cry of the unhoused and the insufficiently housed is one which neither as individual citizens nor as a municipality, and neither as humanitarians nor as Christians, can we afford to neglect.[8]

They had little idea of what they were undertaking, since the Corporation had till then erected only 1,515 houses in four-storey tenements, mainly one-and two-roomed flats. These were let to Corporation employees, shopkeepers, professional men and 'well-to-do' labourers, all carefully selected.

Thus in 1902 Glasgow Corporation began to implement a housing policy, first put forward by Robert Owen in 1827, which advocated the ownership and control of property by the community and its administration for the benefit of all. The Corporation applied for a private Act of Parliament to provide municipal houses for the poorest, especially those displaced by the City Improvements Department or by the Police Department shutting unhealthy dwellings. Opposition was strong among the mercantile and middle-class ratepayers; they foresaw that the Corporation's ambitions would ultimately lead it to be the 'landlords of a large proportion of the labouring population of Glasgow'.[9]

Municipal control did not end with housing, for it had been extended to water supply in 1855, gas in 1869, electricity in 1891, tramways in 1894 and telephones in 1900, as well as ownership of many warehouses and shops. There was even the suggestion of a municipalized milk supply. When D. M. Stevenson, later Lord Provost of the city, attended an International Congress on Workmen's Dwellings (*Habitations à bon marché*) in Paris in 1900 he shocked fellow delegates by his account of the extent of Glasgow's municipal control:

> In the course of the discussion, the impracticability of housing being undertaken by municipalities was emphasised by various speakers. When I pointed out that, so far from being impracticable, it had actually been carried on in Glasgow to an ever-increasing extent, for twenty-nine years, and that the Corporation also supplied water, gas, electricity and tramways, the delegates said that this was nothing short of rank socialism. In Britain it is usually called 'municipal trading'; perhaps 'civic co-operation' would be a better term. It evokes considerable hostility, even in this country, and much has been said and written on the need for placing limits upon it. To my mind the only limit should be the point at which the community ceases to find an adequate supply of disinterested representatives able and willing to carry on public enterprises for the common benefit.[10]

Where Glasgow led, the rest of the country was to follow, but without such clear conviction.

The housing problem was approached only timidly through national legislation because sacrosanct property rights were being violated. Provisions dealing directly or indirectly with the subject of housing were scattered through many statutes, making it difficult for contemporaries to obtain a clear idea of the existing legislation. The statutes included: Housing of the Working Classes Acts 1890, 1900 and 1903; Housing Town Planning, etc. Act 1909; Public Health (Scotland) Act 1897; Burgh Police (Scotland) Acts 1892 and 1903; Local Government (Scotland) Acts 1889, 1894 and 1908; Small Dwellings Acquisition Act 1899; and Housing and Town Planning Acts 1919 and 1923 (Fig. 8.3).

Several improvement schemes were initiated under the Housing of the Working Classes Act 1890. Dr Henry Littlejohn instigated a scheme to rid Edinburgh of its 'chief plague spots of slums', the like of which 'will no longer exist in the city when this scheme has been carried out'. Approximately 2½ hectares were to be demolished in ten areas including Fountainbridge, Potterrow and High School Yards. The choice of areas rested firmly on health statistics: the

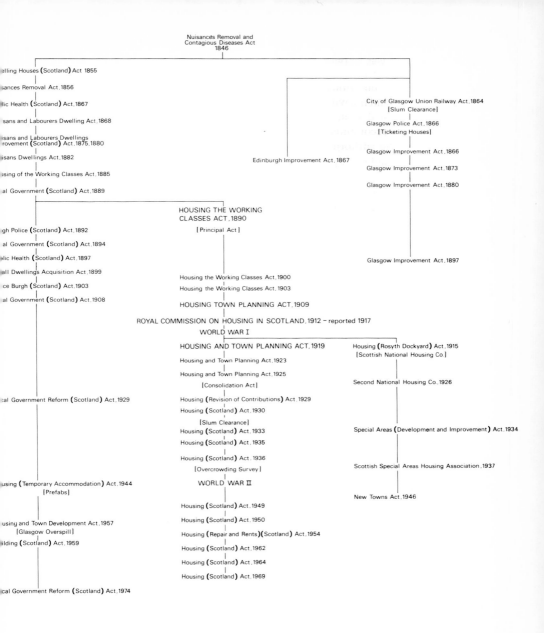

Nuisances Removal and
Contagious Diseases Act
1846

elling Houses (Scotland) Act 1855

sances Removal Act, 1856

lic Health (Scotland) Act, 1867

sans and Labourers Dwelling Act, 1868

isans and Labourers Dwellings
rovement (Scotland) Act, 1875, 1880

isans Dwellings Act, 1882

using of the Working Classes Act, 1885

al Government (Scotland) Act, 1889

gh Police (Scotland) Act, 1892

al Government (Scotland) Act, 1894

lic Health (Scotland) Act, 1897

all Dwellings Acquisition Act, 1899

ce Burgh (Scotland) Act, 1903

al Government (Scotland) Act, 1908

al Government Reform (Scotland) Act, 1929

using (Temporary Accommodation) Act, 1944
[Prefabs]

using and Town Development Act, 1957
[Glasgow Overspill]

ilding (Scotland) Act, 1959

cal Government Reform (Scotland) Act, 1974

Edinburgh Improvement Act, 1867

City of Glasgow Union Railway Act, 1864
[Slum Clearance]

Glasgow Police Act, 1866
[Ticketing Houses]

Glasgow Improvement Act, 1866

Glasgow Improvement Act, 1873

Glasgow Improvement Act, 1880

HOUSING THE WORKING
CLASSES ACT, 1890

[Principal Act]

Glasgow Improvement Act, 1897

Housing the Working Classes Act, 1900

Housing the Working Classes Act, 1903

HOUSING TOWN PLANNING ACT, 1909

ROYAL COMMISSION ON HOUSING IN SCOTLAND, 1912 – reported 1917

WORLD WAR I

HOUSING AND TOWN PLANNING ACT, 1919

Housing and Town Planning Act, 1923

Housing and Town Planning Act, 1925

[Consolidation Act]

Housing (Revision of Contributions) Act, 1929

Housing (Scotland) Act, 1930

[Slum Clearance]

Housing (Scotland) Act, 1933

Housing (Scotland) Act, 1935

Housing (Scotland) Act, 1936

[Overcrowding Survey]

WORLD WAR II

Housing (Scotland) Act, 1949

Housing (Scotland) Act, 1950

Housing (Repair and Rents) (Scotland) Act, 1954

Housing (Scotland) Act, 1962

Housing (Scotland) Act, 1964

Housing (Scotland) Act, 1969

Housing (Rosyth Dockyard) Act, 1915
[Scottish National Housing Co.]

Second National Housing Co, 1926

Special Areas (Development and Improvement) Act, 1934

Scottish Special Areas Housing Association, 1937

New Towns Act, 1946

ig. 8.3 The evolution
f Scotland's housing
gislation

infant death rate was between 125 and 247 per 1,000, the general death rate from 27 to 53 per 1,000, and diseases due to overcrowding and insanitary conditions were rife in the scheduled areas. A few new blocks of tenements with wider streets and new pavements were built in place of the demolished houses. For the rest of the displaced population, new accommodation had to be found in the existing houses nearby. The authorities were certainly aware of the potential problems of this kind of displacement:

> ... one result of the Improvement Scheme of 1867 was the removal of a considerable proportion of the displaced people into the large and unsuitable houses standing on the areas now scheduled as unhealthy. They subdivided these houses, making the long dark lobbies now objected to, and thus rendered them very much more insanitary than they had previously been.[11]

Aberdeen also used the 1890 Act to clean out some 'unhealthy areas' which lay between Exchequer Row and Chapel Lane. Street widening was one of the main reasons for demolition, but again 'they are steep and tortuous, they are the receptacles of filth, they offer facilities for the commission of crime, and the escape of criminals'.[12]

Central government maintained a benevolent control over the emerging mass of housing legislation through the Local Government Board. The creation of standards and the approval of local plans became part of government routine, but conflict between departments was inevitable. The Local Government Board in setting minimum standards found that the Office of Works accepted them 'as establishing a rule of guidance in ... all future housing schemes'.[13] On the other hand, government could advise that minimum legal standards be avoided if necessary; the Burgh Police Act of 1892 provided that the heights of rooms on the ground floor should be at least 2.9m but 'for working classes these heights may be considered too liberal, and burghal local authorities may with advantage consider the discretionary powers afforded by section 39 of the Burgh Police (Scotland) Act 1903 to secure a relaxation of these requirements'.[14] The 'standard house' for the 'poorer working classes' was to include a kitchen, bedroom, scullery, large press (cupboard) for food, water closet and coal cellar. The Local Government Board was most 'zealous for reform in housing schemes and in particular most determined to level Scotland up towards the English standard'. The ideal scheme was on 'garden city lines'. Yet, when the first of the schemes was laid out, geometrical rigidity and economy were the main features:

> Where the houses are built in rows, it is desirable that they should be set back from the street line, so as to allow small gardens or

forecourts to intervene between the houses and the street. . . .
As a rule, the number of houses in a continuous row should not
exceed eight or ten. It is advisable where cottages are erected in
rows to have the gardens placed back to back without any back
street intervening, except in cases where there are no water
closets. Where statutes and byelaws admit it may be desirable to
consider other arrangements of streets and buildings which may
reduce the expenditure on land and street construction. e.g. (1)
the formation of groups of houses on back land, access to the
houses being either from comparatively narrow streets if the
houses are set well back from the street line and if the streets
are not intended to become important thoroughfares . . . portions
might be turfed or planted with trees, and (2) the grouping of a
number of houses round an open space which would serve as a
recreation ground for the occupants of the houses.[15]

Such new landscape as emerged from these regulations was as pre-
dictable as the Acts themselves, for private philanthropy had given
way to state subsidy. A housing estate in Newtongrange, Midlothian,
begun in 1914, was one of the earliest schemes, built for miners in
desperate need of houses. The Newtongrange Building Society
received a government subsidy to provide housing to direct government specification. There emerged houses based on little more than
the traditional room and kitchen with earth closets in a rigid layout
epitomized by the street names: First, Second, Third, Fourth . . .
Streets (Fig. 8.4).

Fig. 8.4 Newtongrange:
The landscape of the
Housing of the Working
Classes Act 1903.
(From a plan in the
Scottish Record
Office.)

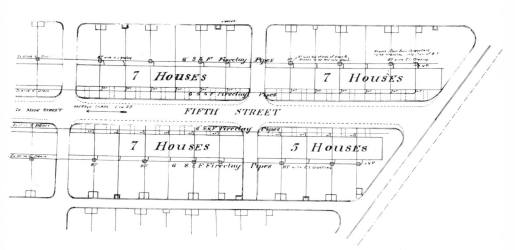

Block Plan

Scale   1' · 33' · 0"

165

John Burn's Town Planning Act of 1909 has been hailed as starting a new age of urban development, but in Scotland there is little evidence to substantiate this. It was the first Act to control the use of land, but was limited to the planning of what was called 'undeveloped land' on the margins of built-up areas. This reflected the current ideas of the centralizing influence of towns and their continued expansion, specifically through coal consuming industries. Furthermore, agricultural land was relatively unimportant because cheap food was flowing in from overseas. Every scheme had to be approved by the Local Government Board which was ill-equipped to handle a situation on this potential scale. As it turned out, not a single local authority town planning scheme submitted to the Board had been passed by 1918. This failure clearly showed the need for codification and strengthening of town planning procedures.

The contribution by the State since the passing of the Housing of the Working Classes Act of 1890 had been woeful: by 1913 eleven towns had, in total, added 1 per cent to their housing stock in the form of local authority houses (Table 2). Sir George McCrae, chairman of the Local Government Board, summed up the general feeling at the Second Conference of the Scottish National Advisory Housing and Town Planning Committee in June 1912:

> The municipal authorities had had a reluctance to put their hands in the mortar tub. It was no lack of public spirit but a fear of the financial burdens which would be involved. If that could not be done on economic lines some other expedient must be tried. Municipalities had departed from economic principles, for they had felt that the clearing of slums and the erection of good dwellings was legitimately a charge on the rates. It was a good investment so far as public health was concerned, but he thought the municipalities were beginning to feel that if that great problem was to be tackled efficiently and effectively some assistance must be rendered by the State (Applause).[16]

Government policy up to the beginning of World War I had remained unambiguous: 'Private enterprise has always been and so far as can be foreseen, will continue to be the main source of the provision of houses for the working classes ... and ... building by Local Authorities will not be required except where private enterprise has failed to provide such houses.'[17]

Investment in property was almost the only method familiar to the small saver. The general practice in those days was for the speculative builder to erect a block of six, twelve or sixteen tenement houses. He made his profit by selling the property to a private investor, often a tradesman, clerk or other worker of modest means, who usually put down one-third of the cost and raised the balance by means of a bond. It has been estimated that as much as 85 per cent

Table 2. Local Authority Housing in Scotland 1890-1913

	Houses built by local authority	Total number of houses in city/burgh
Glasgow	2,199	167,896
Edinburgh	601	74,645
Greenock	214	15,234
Aberdeen	131	36,804
Perth	114	8,300
Leith	84	17,891
Kilmarnock	58	7,513
Clydebank	26	7,363
Oban	24	1,159
Hamilton	23	7,439
Bo'ness	10	2,143
	3,484	346,387

Source: Royal Commission on Housing in Scotland, *Report*, p. 387.

of property in Glasgow was the subject of bonds.[18] In order to meet interest charges and relatively narrow profit margins, property had to be let at all times, for empty houses meant disaster. The building boom of 1900 led many small investors into the property market and, as in most bull property markets, over-supply ultimately burned many fingers. Confidence was severely shaken by some mild proposals contained in the 'People's Budget' of 1909 which promised a token redistribution of wealth. Lloyd George's campaign in support of the measure aroused further apprehension. If profits had been large these measures would have been only minor irritations, but business was in the doldrums. It is clear that the unoccupied houses in Glasgow in 1910 were a more immediate threat to the property investor than any of Lloyd George's pronouncements (Figs. 8.5, 8.6).

By 1914 private enterprise had almost entirely ceased to provide capital to build houses for letting. It was becoming recognized that the provision of working-class houses was impossible on an economic basis and that some form of assistance would be essential. The main reasons for this failure were summed up in the Minority Report of the Royal Commission of 1917:

The rise in the rate of interest and the difficulty of obtaining capital; the increases in building costs; increases in the costs of

167

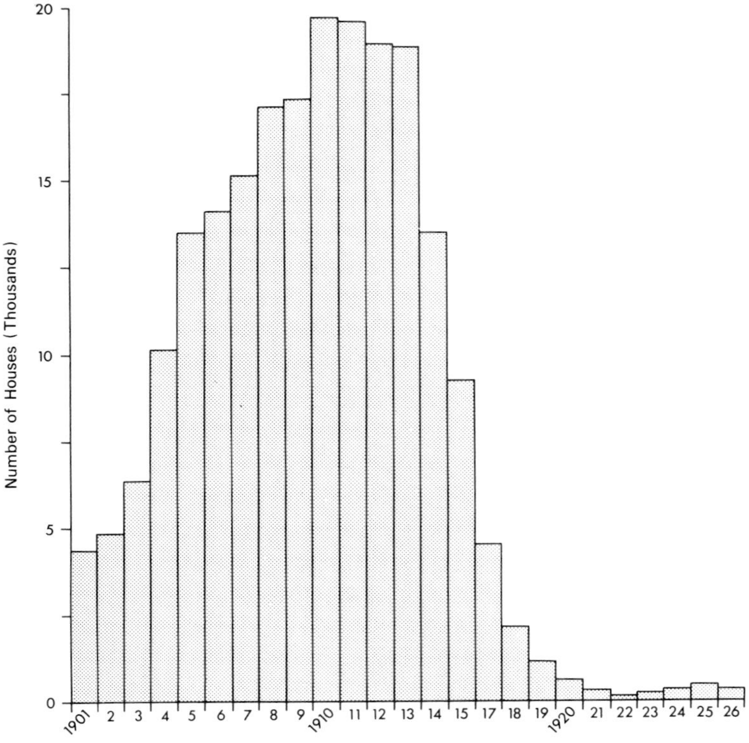

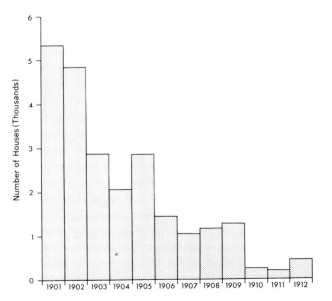

Fig. 8.5 The number of empty houses in Glasgow 1901-1926

Fig. 8.6 The numbers of completed houses in Glasgow: note the decline in completion after the 1901 boom and the catastrophic decline after the Finance Act of 1909. (Royal Commission on Housing in Scotland.)

168

repair and maintenance; the difficulty of securing an economic return on capital; increases in the burden of rates; new taxation and apprehension of further burdens in the future; uncertainty with regard to the intervention of local authorities in house building; the demand on the part of tenants for an improved standard of accommodation.[19]

War brought renewed prosperity to Clydeside's traditional industries and a renewed demand for houses. The introduction of old-age pensions and the National Savings Movement undermined the investment in property that had been a safeguard against old age. There was no other institution, large or small, able to fill the investment void left by the withdrawal of the small investor. Society recognized that the State was the only body capable of channelling funds into housing for the poor. The move was undertaken without ideological commitment and was supported by all political parties, though none appreciated the eventual scale of the commitment. To the Right it was a temporary subsidy that would solve a marginal problem till free enterprise could again take up the responsibility. To the Left it meant better homes and a better life for the urban poor.

Government was pressed by a variety of groups to make plans for the post-war housing. In 1916 the National Housing and Town Planning Council organized a National Congress which expressed itself thus:

This Congress urgently directs the attention of the Government to the critical need for the provision of additional housing for the working classes, and in respect of the national interest and responsibility in the matter urges upon the Government to set aside no less than £20,000,000 to make such advances to Local Authorities and other Agencies as will enable them to provide houses at reasonable rentals having regard to all necessary and equitable circumstances and conditions.[20]

Patriotic appeals, so much in vogue at the time, were used by the National Congress to encourage government to take action:

In responding to the call to serve their country many thousands of men have come from overcrowded dwellings and insanitary slums which are discreditable to us as a nation. We shall not be worthy of these men who, despite their poverty and unwholesome surroundings, are as patriotic as members of the well-to-do classes, if in the years succeeding the war we continue to neglect the conditions under which they live.

The need for munitions and other war materials led to an unprecedented mobilization of industry and in turn to housing problems. The Ministry of Munitions gained considerable expertise in this sphere and showed that government could, if pressed, respond with vigour; for example, they built the village at Gretna, designed by Unwin and Crickmer. Another wartime action, the imposition of rent control in 1915, was to have a longstanding impact in Britain. Rent Restriction Acts were regarded as temporary measures, but successive governments found that they could not return to the days of a free market. The Rent Restriction Act 1915 covered about 85 per cent of working-class houses and the later Acts of 1919 and 1920 extended control to about 98 per cent of all houses in Scotland.[21] The political inadvisability of removing rent control meant that government had to act in order to make good the resulting shortage of private rented accommodation.

Pressure for an inquiry into housing in Scotland arose in part from disquiet over the dreadful conditions found in mining villages. Deputations of miners to the Secretary of State led to the establishment in 1912 of a Royal Commission on Housing in Scotland which reported in 1917. The Commissioners found the existing housing legislation a complicated muddle. When they went on to look at housing generally, they found a situation far worse than the existing statutory provisions admitted to: overcrowded tenements, inadequate sanitation, one-roomed houses, miners' housing, rural housing, the housing of navvies, and much more were all in desperate need of attention. The expressed position of the majority of the Commissioners was that 'the state must at once take steps to make good the housing shortage and to improve housing conditions, and that this can only be done by or through the machinery of the public authorities'. So the pattern was set. While expressing a preference for the cottage or flatted-villa type of house, the Commissioners recommended that: (1) no future tenement should be of more than three storeys including the ground floor; (2) none of the houses entering off a common stair should be back to back; (3) tenements should be arranged in blocks as detached pavilions; (4) there should be sufficient open space for ventilation, and sufficient space in the immediate neighbourhood for (a) children's playgrounds, (b) public bowling greens and gardens, (c) a certain number of private gardens to the houses, and (d) so far as possible a separate bleaching green to each house; (5) there should be no hollow squares; (6) the density should be no more than 77 houses per hectare for three-storey tenements, 58 for double-flatted houses, and 38 for single cottages; and (7) no subdivision of existing tenements should be permitted.

It was now up to the wartime coalition to bring in legislation. A new housing bill was presented, for it not only reflected the political will of all shades of opinion, but also gave the serviceman hope for his future. Society was ready for radical reform. Organized support for the bill came from 300 delegates from all local authorities who met in Edinburgh in February 1918 under the auspices of the

Scottish National Housing and Town Planning Committee. They unanimously recorded that 'politicians generally, local authorities, social reformers are all satisfied and agreed that sweeping reforms are urgently necessary'. Furthermore, they went on to voice harsh criticism of all previous legislation:

> Scottish housing is essentially a matter which should be dealt with for Scotland itself, quite apart from England. Progress in housing matters in Scotland has been materially hindered in many ways in the past as a result of the legislative enactments being based upon English conceptions, English conditions, and English laws. Scotland has a case of its own, a case peculiar to itself and its conditions, and it is believed that its needs can only be suitably and satisfactorily dealt with under a code of laws and provisions conceived with a proper appreciation of its requirements and its circumstances.[22]

Thus the findings of the Royal Commission led directly to the Housing and Town Planning (Scotland) Act of 1919. The scale of the inherited problem was beyond individual, commercial or charitable solution, and only the State could marshall the resources to house the working population. Local authorities were directed to provide and manage housing and to take responsibility for town planning. They were to be the guardians of new standards for the densities of houses, the number of storeys in tenement blocks and the provision of suitable facilities for each house, and to control overcrowding and the subdivision of houses. The Act itself was a consolidation of all the Housing Acts from 1890 and marked the turning point in the responsibility of the State for the provision of homes. The *laissez-faire* Victorians bequeathed massive urban problems to government and local authorities whose world after 1919 was engulfed by economic disaster. Yet throughout the interwar period the authorities tried to provide better houses (Fig. 8.7).

One new and important feature of the Act was the introduction of state subsidies for housing. The Commission's findings formed the basis of the first offer of government financial assistance in 1918, but this was not acceptable to local authorities and a more generous offer was made which became known as the Addison scheme. Under this scheme, which was embodied in the 1919 Act, local authorities were to contribute towards the annual loss on council houses the product of a nominal rate of four-fifths of a penny (in England a penny rate), the remainder of the annual loss being paid by the State. The liability of local authorities under this scheme was limited, whilst that of the Government was unlimited. This revolutionary form of subsidy was considered essential in order to persuade many councils to act, and on these terms most authorities went ahead with schemes. This nominal payment by local authorities

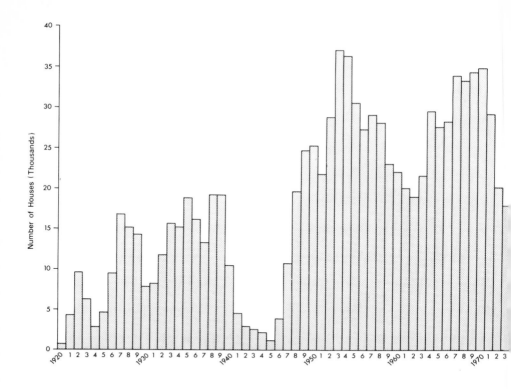

Number of Houses (Thousands)

Fig. 8.7 Annual output of council houses 1920-74

encouraged them to build high-quality housing in the spirit of the 1919 Act, 'the houses to be erected should serve as a model or standard for building by private enterprise in the future'. But progress was uneven and disappointing . Under the Act only 25,540 high-quality houses were produced, and most were let to more prosperous working-class tenants at rents higher than the average wage-earner could afford. It is not surprising that the programme did not do better, for the groundwork had been poorly laid. Local authorities had little experience in this field and snags were encountered immediately. The techniques of the building industry were based on the slowly built but structurally strong stone dwelling. For economy's sake the Government demanded brickwork covered by harling or cement. In 1920 exactly half Scotland's annual production of 144 million bricks went into government housing.[23] The increased demand strained the capacity of the brick industry and led local authorities to bid above the prices fixed by the brick cartel. The result was an uncontrolled increase in local authority housing costs, the average per house rising from £225 pre-war to £959 in 1921, with four-apartment houses exceeding £1,000. In August 1921 the Government decided that no new tenders for houses would be entertained and that house building under the 1919 programme should cease after completion of houses already tendered for. Henceforth government ensured that it exercised close control over housing expenditure and never again entertained an open-ended commitment to build working-class houses.

The proposals in the 1923 Housing Bill amounted to a complete reversal of the policy embodied in the 1919 legislation. This was a United Kingdom bill with an application clause to Scotland, and the Convention of Royal Burghs recorded 'its deep disappointment that . . . the recognition of the essential differences in the housing conditions of England and Scotland was not met in any degree by the government'.[24] An annual subsidy of £6 per house was offered to local authorities as well as grants to private enterprise. There was also a provision for a subsidy (the 50 per cent grant scheme) for the replacement of slums. The effect of the fixed subsidy was catastrophic: building by local authorities practically ceased after the passing of the Housing Act 1923 (the Chamberlain Act). In all, local authorities built 4,022 houses under the Act (excluding 17,025 houses under the 50 per cent scheme which was superseded by the Act of 1930). However, nearly 30,000 private houses were subsidized under this Act. The Government was obliged to pass another housing Act in 1924 (the Wheatley Act) increasing the subsidy to £9 per house for forty years, so that in general the rents charged should not exceed those prevailing before 1914. As a result, 75,000 houses were provided at much lower rents than those charged for houses erected under the 1919 and 1923 Acts. A further 8,000 private houses were built for letting under this Act, mostly in more prosperous districts on the outskirts of Glasgow where higher rents could be charged.

With a fixed subsidy being applied to houses built to specified standards, the price and quality of local authority houses fell rapidly. The cost of the average house was £442 in 1923, dropping to £407 in 1924 and remaining at about this level until World War II. Houses became more uniform and contrasted poorly with those built immediately after 1919.

The period after 1924 was a time of disillusionment in the provision of local authority housing, and economy, not quality, was the criterion. The Housing (Scotland) Act 1925 was merely a consolidation Act, incorporating all housing legislation from 1890. The situation was reviewed in 1928 and it was recommended that the subsidy be reduced to £7 10s, but before this became operative the Government passed in July 1929 the Housing (Revision of Contributions) Act restoring the previous rate of £9. Clearly, government was desperately trying to find the right level of financial support to keep the housing programme going at a controlled rate, but the trickle of houses that was built failed to alleviate urban congestion.

The main object of the 1930 Act was the demolition of slums and the rehousing of displaced slum dwellers, but some of Scotland's most notorious housing estates were the result. Provisions were included for the demolition of all buildings in 'clearance areas', partial demolition in 'improvement areas' and the rehabilitation of individual houses. From this date government policy emphasized economy and housing estates were to be built on the outskirts of towns where land was cheap. The tenement was to be revived in a garden suburb setting.

> The Minister is advised that land can generally be utilised so that from 40 to 60 flats to the acre [96 to 144 per hectare] can readily be planned without congestion. Where the cost of the site be moderate, three-storey flats with a density of 40 to 45 to the acre [96 to 108 per hectare] would be appropriate, but where expensive sites have to be used a density of 60 or more to the acre [144 per hectare] can and should be secured by the erection of blocks of more than three storeys . . . The Government are unable to find any justification in present conditions for a general Exchequer subsidy for ordinary cottage building.[25]

A new Act passed in 1933 reduced the annual housing subsidy to £3 per house for forty years. The local authorities maintained that the subsidy was inadequate and left too heavy a burden on the rates. Sir Godfrey Collins, Secretary of State for Scotland, was well aware of these shortcomings and communicated his fears on 8 November 1934 to Neville Chamberlain, then Chancellor of the Exchequer: 'Our Act of 1933 has completely failed to effect any real measure of decrowding, for the reason that the Exchequer contribution of £3 is much too low to induce authorities to build. The Government cannot risk a repetition of failure.'[26] During the first twenty months that the Act was in force only 1,700 houses were provided under it. The remedy was sought in yet another Bill.

The main purpose of the Housing (Scotland) Act 1935 was, in the words of the Parliamentary Under Secretary of State, 'to stimulate the erection of houses which can be let at rents within the means of people living in overcrowded conditions, who cannot afford to pay ordinary rents'.[27] For the first time overcrowding was statutorily defined and became an offence, 'punishable on summary conviction by a penalty not exceeding £5'. A house was deemed to be overcrowded if sleeping accommodation in separate rooms was not available for occupants of opposite sexes over ten years of age, other than persons living together as husband and wife, or if the total number of persons over that age exceeded 2 in a single apartment, 3 in a house of two rooms, 5 in three rooms, 7½ in four rooms, and 10 in five rooms. An overcrowding survey was instituted which, as we shall see, highlighted Scotland's urban problems. The Exchequer raised the annual subsidy to £6 15s per house for forty years. A secondary object of this Act was to allow local authorities to redevelop overcrowded areas, and more specifically the inner zones of the four cities. 'There is a real case based on industrial and social conditions for the housing of a proportion of the working classes in or near the centre of the town and in which the policy of providing additional houses on the outskirts has so far failed to diminish overcrowding at the centre'.[28] The authority had to define the area on a map and pass a resolution declaring it to be an area of redevelopment. The next stage was the submission of the development plan for the Department of Health's approval.

The hope that Scotland might be cleared of slum houses faded with the realization of the extent of overcrowding. Tens of thousands of houses were needed to relieve this congestion before society could afford to demolish a single slum. Overcrowding throughout Scotland, at a standard of more than three persons to a room, affected 14.9 per cent of the population at the 1931 census compared with 1.5 per cent in England. Beneath these statistics lay not only the pressures of overcrowding, but fear. A survey in Greenock revealed 1,100 sublets and the fact that hundreds of the occupants had not entered their names on the electoral register for fear of eviction.[29] The situation forced the Government to pass the Housing (Scotland) Act in 1936 which required a survey by local authorities of overcrowding levels. The results, published in April 1936, were even worse than had been expected.[30] Over 240,000 or 23.5 per cent of Scotland's houses were overcrowded, and the figure would have been much higher if 28,797 'overcrowded families living in uninhabitable houses' had been included. The comparable figure for England was only 3.8 per cent. The disparity was even worse in the quality of housing, for whilst England and Wales had 4.6 per cent of houses with two rooms or less, 44 per cent of Scottish houses were in this category. In reply to a question in the House of Commons, the Secretary of State for Scotland admitted that although 250,000 new houses would be needed to eliminate this situation, only 12,857 had been built by local authorities in 1937.[31] At that time government thought that Scotland's overcrowding was essentially a city-centre problem. They were sadly mistaken, for it was widespread in a great number of large burghs as well as in the landward areas. In terms of percentage of overcrowded housing, no city had above 30 per cent. The large burghs suffered most, and even four small burghs had over 30 per cent (Table 3).

Following the 1935 Act, an interesting divergence was revealed between west and east Scotland. In Glasgow, an area of high rates, property owners had been vociferous in their opposition. 'The overcrowding clauses in the Bill will subject 90 per cent of the population of Glasgow to inquisitorial inspections by sanitary officials', prophesied the President of the Glasgow Property Owners' and Factors' Association, and he characterized the measure as 'a piece of veiled confiscation and socialism of the purest type'.[32] In areas where rates were low, as in Edinburgh, there was no opposition to

Table 3. Percentage overcrowding in Scotland 1936, showing all towns above 30 per cent. In comparison, none of the four cities reaches this level.

City		Large burgh		Small burgh	
Glasgow	29	Coatbridge	45	Cowdenbeath	40
Dundee	24	Port Glasgow	42	Lochgelly	36
Aberdeen	22	Clydebank	41	Kilsyth	31
Edinburgh	17	Motherwell	40	Renfrew	31
		Hamilton	39		
		Greenock	34		
		Paisley	32		
		Rutherglen	31		

the Act: 'as President of the Edinburgh and District Property Owners' Association, and as an individual, I think the new Bill is a reasonable attempt to provide decent houses for working class people, and as far as we are concerned we welcome it.'[33]

By 1939 municipal estates had become important elements in Scotland's settlement pattern. War brought house building to a halt, but not the formation of plans for a brighter post-war world. Up to World War II the approach to town planning had been through the study of the development of existing urban communities in relation to the evolution of the physical fabric; or the approach had been aesthetic, nostalgic and vaguely medical as in the case of the garden city movement. In 1942 the Department of Health for Scotland decided on a revolutionary approach based on the new techniques developed by sociologists, that of the questionnaire and random sample, to discover the feelings of those who would be directly affected. So new was the idea that the findings of the pioneer American study in this field were not available.[34] The Scottish results, published in 1943, gave considerable insight into people's aspirations:

> Certain difficulties attended asking of questions about the future house and community. To many persons the whole discussion was quite unreal and often our interviewers were greeted with such statements as 'It's no good talking to us about new houses, we have had our name down for one for 10, 15 or 20 years'. So many promises have been made in the past about housing that it was difficult for some people to treat the subject seriously. . . . Discussions about house type were mostly overshadowed by present conditions. . . . The desire to get away from bad tenement conditions was absolutely paramount and it was difficult for

many housewives and some husbands to go the step further to imagine what sort of house they would like to live in. Typical remarks were 'Any house in which we have a door of our own', 'Any house with a bathroom', or 'Anywhere where we do not have to go up more than three flights of stairs'.[35]

City centre dwellers admired the bungalows which proliferated on the outskirts of Scottish towns, but inquiries on the new council estates showed that the poor sound-proofing and insulation of the new houses compared unfavourably with the thick walls and cosiness of the old tenements. Most people wanted to live near their work, and the occupants of new estates complained of the distance from work, shops and pubs. A garden was considered desirable by tenement dwellers, though people on the new estates neglected their gardens. This pioneer work clearly showed that people's lives were dominated by the hope of better housing, but that this was modified by fear of unemployment.

Peace brought renewed demands for housing. During the war years new families had been formed and men returning from the services began looking for homes. Sights had also been raised by wartime experiences — a new age of reform had dawned and people wanted something better than the old room and kitchen. Initially 30,000 temporary houses ('prefabs') were built before a programme of more traditional houses could be started. Government made housing a priority and the remaking of the social geography of the Scottish city was begun.

Of the four cities, Dundee has the highest proportion of public housing: 55.6 per cent in 1970 compared with 25.1 per cent in 1945. In 1970 Dundee had 204 houses in the public sector per 1,000 of total population, compared with 170 in Glasgow, 149 in Aberdeen and 102 in Edinburgh. Much of the urban redevelopment taking place today in Dundee is an attempt to alleviate the consequences of an earlier specialization in the manufacture of coarse heavyweight linens and jute textiles. Before World War I over 60 per cent of Dundee's housing consisted of only one or two rooms. The typical building was a tenement with common access at the rear by a combination of staircases and pletties or platforms. At that time the city had a surplus of housing; even though there was overcrowding, many dwellings stood empty for long periods, and people had an ample choice of houses as is shown by the number of 'flittings' which took place at each removal term. In the inter-war period this situation no longer existed and Dundee was plagued by a shortage of housing.

The story of Dundee's emergence as the leading provider of council housing began in 1917 when the Corporation, with an estimated shortage of 6,000 houses, formulated their post-war housing proposals (Table 4).

Table 4. Dundee's pioneer council house schemes

Fig. 8.8 The numbe
per annum of perm:
dwellings complete(
Dundee in the publi
sector from 1919 tc
1970

Site	Formally approved	Acreage [hectares]		No. of houses
Logie	2 Nov. 1917	21	[8.5]	250
Craigiebank	2 Nov. 1917	80	[32.4]	810
Stirling Park	6 Mar. 1918	9	[3.6]	170
Hospital Park	18 Mar. 1919	10	[4.0]	172
Taybank	18 Mar. 1919	16	[6.5]	204

Sir George McCrae, President of the Local Government Board, cut the first sod of the Logie scheme on 4 July 1919 and thenceforth government and other local authorities looked to its pioneering progress with continuing interest.[36] The scheme embraced the building of 250 houses, 162 of three apartments and 88 of two apartments intended specifically for female workers in the jute trade who often lived alone or in pairs. Far advanced for its time was the adoption of a district heating scheme, the first in Britain, which included a central source of heating and hot water and a communal washhouse. Stirling Park also included a central heating and hot water scheme. Preference for the houses was given to ex-servicemen, especially those who had seen active service. Rents were comparatively high, too high indeed for those of low income. In an attempt to alleviate this problem Robert Fleming, a Dundonian who had made his fortune in the United States, gave £155,000 to the city in 1929 for the building of 496 houses at Fleming Gardens, to be let at low rents. Although many estates were developed northwards from the city centre, only one major one, the Mid Craigie, was built north of the Kingsway, the ring road constructed in the 1920s. It was the largest single inter-war development, exceeding one thousand units. In the twenty years from 1919 to 1939, a total of 7,014 houses was built in Dundee, an average of 351 per annum (Fig. 8.8). Yet setting this against an average annual loss of 241 houses through demolition, the housing stock rose painfully slowly, so that in the immediate post-war years drastic action was required. The 1944 Housing (Temporary Accommodation) Act led to the erection of 1,550 prefabs, some of which lasted nearly thirty years. With the 1950s came a great increase in the construction of houses. Since a large proportion were of the two-storey flatted or cottage type,[37] at fairly low densities, the built-up area of the town saw exceptional expansion, mainly to the north of the Kingsway (Fig 8.9). At the same time the 1952 Development Plan forecast that a fairly high density development would be required in areas close to the city centre, and terraced houses and multi-storey flats of various heights were

Fig. 8.9 Dundee's council housing. Whitfield scheme showing the sharp transition between town and country. (Photo: Aerofilms.)

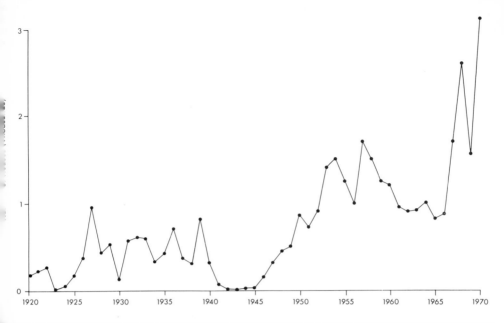

suggested. The results of this policy can be seen in the Comprehensive Redevelopment Areas built in the 1960s.

Glasgow has tackled its housing problems in much the same way as Dundee, differing only in scale. Since World War II Glasgow Corporation has developed estates which could be designated by population alone as towns within a city. Far removed from the centre of the city where the people had their roots, Drumchapel, Pollok, Easterhouse and Castlemilk have been converted from open fields to vast residential areas which until recently lacked every amenity, service and opportunity that is represented by the word 'town'. It is a world in which *graffiti* express the helplessness of urban failure. Teenage gangs brought to national attention planners' and politicians' failure to create more than a one-dimensional solution to Glasgow's housing problem. Publicity brought about the Easterhouse Youth Project, which in turn led to municipal and commercial enterprise in the form of a new multi-function complex including shops, library, sports centre and swimming pool. These amenities provided some relief from urban tensions, but nothing can removed the relative isolation of these peripheral estates.

The seeds of high-rise living in Glasgow can be traced back to early post-war housing schemes at Milton and Barmullock which incorporated some ten-storey blocks. In 1947 several councillors and the city architect visited Marseilles to inspect multi-storey housing and the sight of Le Corbusier's *L'Unité d'Habitation* won converts. However it was not until 1951, with the reduction of multi-storey housing costs through changes in design, that the Corporation decided to build on an experimental basis in the Gorbals. Robert Bruce, the city's Master of Works, warmed to the plan and brought together 'an almost unique combination of designers and "practical men" from whose joint efforts there . . . emerged the solution to economic multi-storey construction'.[38] Thus began a progress which has made Glasgow the foremost exponent of high-rise living in Europe. Approximately 65,000 people, almost equivalent to the population of Greenock, live in some 200 blocks of high flats. These include the highest flats in Britain, the Red Road development, rising 31 storeys over a wasteland of former railbeds. Other Scottish towns followed Glasgow's lead and there is hardly a large burgh withouts its multi-storey block on the *outskirts*. One house in every five built since the end of the war has been in a block of six storeys or more, and in the early seventies this figure rose to one in every three.

The fashion for multi-storey flats reached its peak in the mid-1960s, then rapidly declined as the defects of this type of housing became obvious (Fig. 8.10). Lifts were vulnerable to vandalism and breakdown, loneliness was intensified by the stratification of the building, mothers became housebound and young children were deprived of communal play. High-rise living came to be identified

180

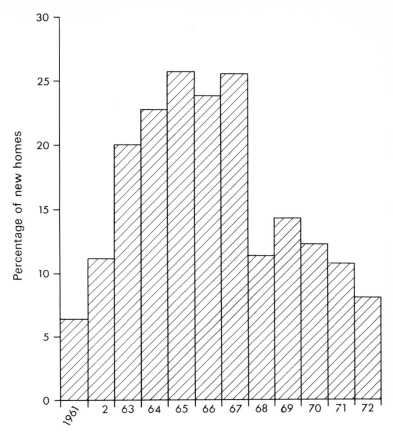

Percentage of new homes

with neurotic living. Glasgow was one of the last cities to operate a policy that had been progressively abandoned throughout Britain. Not enough thought had been given to high-rise living: questions should have been asked. First, what are the social and personal implications? After half a century of condemning the tenement in favour of 'cottage' dwellings, the planners expected people to benefit from thirty storeys. Secondly, what are the long-term costs of maintaining these buildings? Thirdly, if thousands of people are housed in a small area, such as the Red Road development, what is to be done with the large surrounding open spaces? Lastly, what the are fire risks involved, when fire service appliances can reach only to the eighth or ninth storey (30 m)? Britain's best-known architect of high-rise flats, Richard Seifert, who designed some in Glasgow, has gone on record as saying that they are 'socially evil' and have 'created a claustrophobic and depressing environment leading to serious crime, loneliness, unhappiness and mental disturbance'.[39]

181

Glasgow has not been alone in trying to solve its housing problems by building huge peripheral estates. Edinburgh embarked on its biggest single development for two hundred years. The Wester Hailes development occupies a site of 116 hectares, much the same area as the original New Town of Edinburgh, but there the similarity ends. Built for the age of the motor car, and with minimal public transport, the estate provides a car parking space for each household and a central shopping area. In all, it is hoped to house around 18,000 people there, equal to the populations of Galashiels and Selkirk together. An estate of this size gives the impression of a dormitory town without a soul. What do the people do? Work, entertainment and recreational facilities are elsewhere. There is no choice of shops and no secondary school. Where are the nursery schools, tearooms, small sheltered parks, workshops for small craftsmen or repair shops? What life is here for an old person using a free bus pass to escape from the estate, or for a young mother walking her pram or toddler across acres of windy open space?

The lifespan of the average council house is fifty to sixty years, and the earlier estates are nearing the end of that span. Some of the older schemes exhibit all the symptoms of urban decay, but they are aggravated by a lack of the vitality that made the old slums bearable. They are often ugly and suffer from the lack of proper landscaping; cars parked indiscriminately block the inadequate service roads; gardens have become sordid areas of waste ground; the few play spaces, strewn with refuse and broken glass, are unusable; and the dwellings themselves have not kept pace with changing standards. Boarded-up windows of unlet houses are a common sight, whether in the Beechwood estate in Dundee, West Pilton in Edinburgh, or Blackhill in Glasgow. These dead eyes have become a symbol of the low level of community spirit and the endemic vandalism which have reduced these estates to the slums they were designed to eradicate.

Yet one cannot generalize, for many of the older council estates have achieved a maturity that compares well with any private estate of the same age. In Glasgow some of the best and worst estates were built in the inter-war years. Mosspark and Knightswood council estates stand in marked contrast to East Keppochhill and Blackhill. Blackhill is a very sorry place, built in the 1930s to house slum dwellers and anti-social families (Fig. 8.11). Only six shops were included in the scheme, and no cinema, community centre, halls or pubs; van drivers who went into the estate took security guards with them. Since a community centre and a police office with a public telephone were established, gangs and gang fights have disappeared. The community centre is used for a nursery school, further education and sports, but in 1977 there are still no bus services or other amenities.[40] Plans were produced to modernize the Blackhill area, spending about £11,500 per house, but the

182

Fig. 8.11 Glasgow's
disgrace. Blackhill
municipal housing
scheme in 1974.
(Photo: G.B.
Carrington)

project has been dropped and partial demolition has been suggested. For most Scots the name Blackhill means nothing, but it is one part of our country that must shame us all. The landlord, Glasgow District Council, has failed to carry out even rudimentary maintenance — the bleached exterior woodwork testifies to that; the tenants are no better, for contractors working in Blackhill are allowed to charge higher prices to compensate for vandalism *by the people for whom the houses are being modernized.* The policy of demolition for such an area is but a refuge for politicians whose ideals have been exhausted by a callous constituency.

To the visitor, many Scottish towns appear uniform and dull, dominated as they are by council houses whose tenants seem to feel little responsibility for, or pride in the external appearance of their homes. However, this is but a continuation of the Scottish housing tradition. The Scottish tenant, moving from the turf and stone rural hovel of the eighteenth century, through the made-down house to the one and two-roomed tenement of the nineteenth, and finally compulsorily rehoused in a council scheme, in a house chosen and located by some anonymous housing official, has never developed much respect for the fabric of his house. But this is our cultural pattern: Scotland has always been a nation of tenants, and a land-lord, even in the guise of the State, is always a landlord.

The role of council houses in Scotland extends deeply into the fabric of society. If one compares the top and bottom ten burghs of the council house league a clear distinction can be seen between the nineteenth century industrial burghs and the havens of middle-class residential escape (Table 5). That three towns house four-fifths of their population in council houses is a feature unparalleled in the rest of Britain, excluding the new towns. Clearly the constant aim of these and similar towns to keep down their council rents is an act of political reality that cannot be ignored by central government. The council tenant cannot be the bogeyman in Airdrie, Kilsyth, Coatbridge and the like, for he *is* the town (Fig. 8.12).

Table 5. Top and bottom ten burghs of the council house league 1972

	Percentage of council houses		Percentage of council houses
Airdrie	81.57	Galashiels	32.73
Kilsyth	81.30	Edinburgh	30.60
Coatbridge	80.23	Prestwick	29.53
Lochgelly	77.85	Gourock	26.97
Motherwell and Wishaw	74.37	Helensburgh	20.78
		Dunoon	20.16
Port Glasgow	70.33	Largs	18.50
Stevenston	68.08	Bishopbriggs	17.78
Cowdenbeath	65.47	Peebles	15.26
Johnstone	64.05	Bearsden	4.13
Falkirk	62.96		

Source: The Scottish Institute of Municipal Treasurers and Accountants.

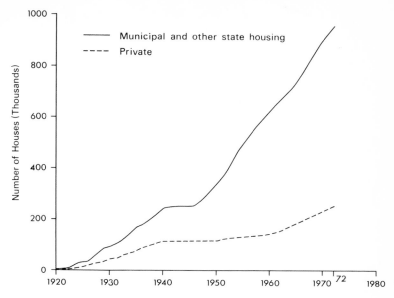

Fig. 8.12 The increasing proportion of council dwellings built in Scotland since the 1919 Housing Act

- —— Municipal and other state housing
- ---- Private

Number of Houses (Thousands)

1000 800 600 400 200 0

1920 1930 1940 1950 1960 1970 72 1980

Notes

1. J. C. Symon, 'The South of Scotland', in *Reports from Assistant Hand-Loom Weavers' Commissioners,* Accounts and papers 1839, XLII, p. 51

2. Report of the Committee 'appointed by the Treasurery to enquire into certain questions connected with the taking of the census', *Parliamentary Papers*, LVIII, 1890, pp. 6-7; one such example was H. D. Littlejohn, *Report on the Sanitary Condition of the City of Edinburgh* (1865).

3. For various viewpoints of this period see A. K. Cairncross, 'Fluctuations in the Glasgow Building Industry', in *Home and Foreign Investment 1870 1923* (Cambridge University Press, 1953); J. Butt, 'Working-Class Housing in Glasgow 1851-1914', in S. D. Chapman (ed.), *The History of Working-Class Housing: A Symposium* (David and Charles, Newton Abbot, 1971).

4. *The Builder*, 26 March 1870, pp. 239-40.

5. E. Gauldie, *Cruel Habitations: A History of Working Class Housing 1780-1919* (Allen and Unwin, London, 1974), pp. 250-3.

6. Brief for owners and occupiers of property in the City of Glasgow, Glasgow Corporation Provisional Order 1902 (SRO British Rail records BR PYB(S)2/72).

7. Glasgow Corporation, *Municipal Enterprises of Glasgow* (1901), p. 38; for a general review see C. M. Allan, 'The Genesis of British Urban Re-development with Special Reference to Glasgow', *Economic History Review,* new series, vol. 18 (1965), pp. 598-613.

8. *Report of Proceedings at the Conference as to Cheap Dwellings* (Glasgow, 1901), p. 2.

9. A. Kay, *The Corporation of Glasgow as Owners of Shops, Tenements and Warehouses* (Glasgow, 1902), p. 13. (SRO BR BYB(S)2/72).

10. City of Glasgow, *Municipal Glasgow: Its Evolution and Enterprises* (Glasgow, 1914), pp. 2-3.

11. Edinburgh Improvement Scheme. Inquiry held by Lt-Col. Bailey in 1893 (SRO DD6/385).

12. City of Aberdeen Improvement Scheme. Local inquiry held by Sheriff Brown (SRO DD6/1058).

13. Memorandum on Housing of the Working Classes Acts, 1890 and 1909 and observations by the Local Government Board for Scotland (SRO DD6/653).

14. Local Government Board, *Memorandum with Respect to the Provision and Arrangements of Houses for the Working Classes* (HMSO, Edinburgh, 1912).

15. Housing of working classes. Newtongrange scheme (SRO DD6/653).

16. Housing and Town Planning Act 1909. Reports of Scottish National Conference on the administration of the Act, 1912 (SRO DD6/264).

17. *Annual Report of Local Government Board 1912-13*, Cmnd 6981, 31, 1913, p. xxxiv.

18. Housing (Scotland) Bill 1934 and Act 1935. Report on property owners (SRO DD6/606).

19. *Report of the Royal Commission on the Housing of the Industrial Population of Scotland Rural and Urban* (HMSO, Edinburgh, 1917).

20. Reports submitted to the Committee of Works and Town Planning of the Scottish National Housing and Town Planning Committee, 1916-7 (SRO DD6/788).

21. Analysis of rent control (SRO DD6/606).

22. Memorandum of Resolutions passed at a conference of local authorities regarding the Report of the Royal Commission on Housing in Scotland, 1918 (SRO DD6/197).

23. Output of bricks: Scottish Office correspondence with Scottish Employers Council for the Clay Industries 1920 (SRO DD6/802).

24. Housing (Scotland) (No. 2) Bill, 1921-3, (SRO DD6/595).

25. Housing (Scotland) Bill, 1934 and Act, 1935 (SRO DD6/604/1).

26. Ibid.

27. *Official Report,* vol. 291, no. 118, col. 945.

28. Papers relating to Housing (Scotland) Bill, 1934 (SRO DD6/604/1).

29. Survey contained in records relating to abatement of overcrowding (SRO DD6/1096, 1097).

30. Department of Health for Scotland, *Housing Overcrowding Survey* (HMSO, Edinburgh, 1036), Cmnd 5171.

31. *Official Report,* vol. 337, no. 130, col. 713.

32. Submissions relating to Housing (Scotland) Bill, 1934 (SRO 6/606). Under the rating system at that time, the owner paid a considerable proportion of the rates. His share of the total rates had to be met out of the rent charged, which consequently inflated the assessed rental on which rates were based. The effect of this 'Catch 22' situation was discussed in the Whitson Report, 1933, paras. 187-92, pp. 73-5.

33. *The Scotsman,* 18 January 1935.

34. *Urban Planning and Public Opinion,* National Survey Research Investigation by Melville C. Branch, jun., Director, The Bureau of Urban Research, Princeton University, Princeton, N.J., 1942.

35. Dennis Chapman, *Wartime Social Survey. The Location of Dwellings in Scottish Towns,* new series, no. 34, September 1943.

36. Memorandum by the Scottish Board of Health on housing shortage and position of housing schemes in various local authorities, 1919 (SRO DD6/671).

37. 'Cottage type' was officially defined in the Glasgow Development Survey as all those houses having a separate entrance to each house, including semi-detached and terraced houses as well as the four-in-a-block type of construction.

38. Press conference by Councillor A. Macpherson Rait, Convener of the Housing Committee, announcing new designs for multi-storey flats, November 1951.

39. *The Observer,* 13 October 1974.

40. *Glasgow Herald,* 21 March 1973.

On 1 September 1974 the feudal suburb appeared to throw off the shackles of eight hundred years of vassaldom, when the redemption of feus became a statutory right. The fundamental principle of the feudal system of land tenure had been that the householder did not acquire land absolutely, but was under obligation to pay his superior a feu duty (an annual sum of money) *in perpetuity*. Furthermore the superior could stipulate the vassal's use of the land, and withhold approval of the plans for any building. Yet the reform contained in the Land Tenure Reform (Scotland) Act was an illusion, for all the feudal restrictions remain and the only benefit was to the superior, who received an immediate lump sum instead of the annual payment in a rapidly depreciating currency. The superior remains such a powerful figure in the vassal's life that the English concept of freehold is still remote.

But in limited circumstances the system had served urban Scotland well. Some areas, like the New Town of Edinburgh, had the aesthetic values of an enlightened age imposed upon them by very strict feu title. The Earl of Moray demanded on his Drumsheugh feu that his architect must approve the building plans, and he took the responsibility for laying out the ornamental gardens. Thus the superior, where he wished, could act as the absolute planning authority. However, one of the great weaknesses of the system was that the superiorities, which were marketable in their own right, gradually fell into the hands of large institutions and the standards demanded by the original superiors were often overlooked for commercial advantage. As a result, large areas of residential housing close to the town centres were taken over and converted to commercial purposes, and obnoxious enterprises were set up which destroyed the quality of the environment. The Town and Country Planning Act 1947 instituted an era of rational planning in which the State concerned itself with environmental standards, and increasingly sophisticated and democratic planning machinery ushered in the end of the feudal superior's power.

The erosion of the absolute authority of the feudal superior began with the Conveyancing and Feudal Reform (Scotland) Act 1970 which allowed the vassal to change the property or its use without the approval of his superior. This Act also led to the setting up of the Lands Tribunal which could vary unduly onerous conditions in the feudal title. The feudal system finally expired on 1 September 1974 when the vassal was enabled to redeem his feu at will, and obliged to do so if the property changed hands. One-third of Scotland's owner-occupiers took immediate opportunity to redeem their feus at Martinmas 11 November 1975.

The story of owner-occupation in Scotland concerns a minority of the population. Many English politicians have come north and preached the sanctity of this tenurial system only to encounter a stunning lack of comprehension on the part of the natives. Land-ownership has always been the prerogative of aristocrat and laird and only in rare instances, such as portioners in Border villages and feuars in burghs of barony, have there been owners of heritable property similar to the English freeholder.

However, there was considerable growth in owner-occupation by the middle classes during the urban expansion of the nineteenth century. Edinburgh's middle class began to reject the communal symmetry of New Town life and was tempted to adopt an English style of secluded living. On 21 July 1827 there appeared an adver-tisement in *The Scotsman*:

GROUND FOR VILLAS

To be feued on the plan which has given such satisfaction near several towns in England, and which is so much required in this neighbourhood. The LANDS of NEWINGTON, within 10 minutes walk of the Tron Church and Lawnmarket by the proposed South Approach. They possess, and will always command extensive views, the best air, access and drainage. They are supplied with water from public pipes, are lighted with gas, and watched by the police; and the neighbourhood is, and must continue to be, very select, common stairs and all public nuisance being specially prohibited. The roads are now laid out, the lodges will be built at the terminations of each, in which gate-keepers, appointed by the present proprietors, will always reside: thus the grounds will be preserved (as in England) exactly similar to a private policy; and the comfort of the inhabitants and the safety of their property will be promoted.

Various sums will be lent, if desired, on security of the houses when built.

The feuing system provided a barrier to home ownership through which few could penetrate. The large landowner could and did exert strong control over the expansion of towns. Edinburgh was surrounded by the lands of three great charitable institutions – Heriot's Hospital Trust (the largest), the Merchant Company and the Trades' Maiden Hospital – and control lay firmly in their hands. Heriot's Trust possessed 644 hectares in a broad arc across the north of the city and they laid down strict controls as to the type and value of dwellings to be erected. Furthermore their differential rates of feus favoured the very rich: for villas £125 to £175 per hectare was demanded, whilst the figure reached £1,200 per hectare for tenements. Thus it was in the offices of these charitable trusts that the geography of nineteenth-century Edinburgh was laid down and it rested on the select committee on Town Holdings in 1891 to expose the selfish nature of their policies:

> 'Then you would hold that owners of town lands, such, for instance, as Heriot's Hospital, like owners of country estates are supposed to do, should manage their estates so that people can live upon them decently, and without having to support too great a burden in the matter of feus' asked the chairman. The reply had a prophetic quality to it. 'I think it is a moral responsibility that rests on every reasonable man who owns land, and it rests on the State to see that citizens of a town are not subject to burdens which really become in many instances intolerable. In Edinburgh it results in a state of overcrowding which should not exist in any well-governed or well-ordered city.'

The inner suburbs of the cities, railway commuter settlements and the more attractive small burghs added villas to their housing stock. Even so, extension of owner-occupation was very limited: even by the end of 1973 only 32.3 per cent of the population were in this category compared with 52 per cent in England and Wales. Why has owner-occupation made such slow progress in Scotland? One may argue that Scotland has even now a less skilled population, lower wage levels (although this has now changed) and a generally lower standard of living, and that owner-occupation is a luxury that Scots have not yet learned to afford, but this explanation alone cannot account for the large discrepancy from the situation south of the Border. Another, and more likely, explanation is purely cultural. Throughout history few Scots have ever owned a home, having migrated from rented cottages in the fermtouns to rented tenements in the industrial cities. Wages were always low and housing standards poor. The gulf between the jute baron in Dundee building his £50,000 mansion in Broughty Ferry and his worker paying £5 per annum in rent must have seemed unbridgeable. Only in the twentieth century have Scots begun to purchase homes on a significant scale. How far this movement will continue is difficult to assess, but on present trends it seems that for the foreseeable future the average Scot will still depend on the State to provide his home.

While houses were built for owner-occupation for the middle classes in the nineteenth century, there existed pockets of home ownership among miners in Leadhills and Larkhall, Lanarkshire, in crofting areas and in fishing communities, particularly on the shores of the Moray Firth. Private enterprise made a particular effort in

Edinburgh to find new forms of housing for artisans. Experiments took many forms: the cottage was compared to the tenement, home ownership was offered in place of economic rents, brick was tested beside stone. The word sanitation had barely been invented before it became fashionable to introduce the improvements associated with it into the model dwelling movement. The Edinburgh Sanitary Association in 1847 had in view

> . . . very soon to promulgate a plan of building a very large establishment of model houses for the working classes, in which it is their intention that even the occupant of one room shall have his closet, where there shall be a sink and a water-closet, with a constant supply of water at high pressure. We have delayed bringing that plan forward until we see what shall be our prospects in regard to this supply of water, for this supply at high pressure, constantly on, and carried into the poorest room, is considered essential to our plan, and essential to the improvement of the health of the town.[1]

The philosophy behind this movement was summed up by George Fox, ninth Lord Kinnaird,

> There is no doubt that a heavy responsibility rests on the owners of property and employers of labour, who are morally bound, whether in town or country districts, to see that those by whom this wealth is created have the means of providing themselves with dwellings where health and decency can be maintained.[2]

His appeal also had a financial aspect for he showed that a return of 6 to 7½ per cent could be expected on capital invested in the building of working-class housing.

Impetus was gained from a model cottage designed by Henry Roberts and displayed under the Prince Consort's patronage at the Great Exhibition in 1851. Results appeared in far-flung places (Fig. 9.1). Mulhouse in France adopted the owner-occupied cottage for its *cité ouvrière* and some of the earliest Scottish examples such as the Colonies in Edinburgh followed the same model.[3]

The model dwelling movement was given statutory backing by the Dwelling Houses (Scotland) Act 1855, it was intended to foster associations for the erection of working-class housing, and it gave rise to the 'Five Per Cent Philanthropy movement'[4] One of the first to show faith by building Rosebank Cottages, Edinburgh, was the railway contractor turned architect James Gowans whose philosophy was summed up in later life, 'Would it not be better if, instead of blaming the poor for a state of matters for which they are scarcely responsible, we exercised our energies in providing them with every facility and every inducement to be cleanly, and in short, give them

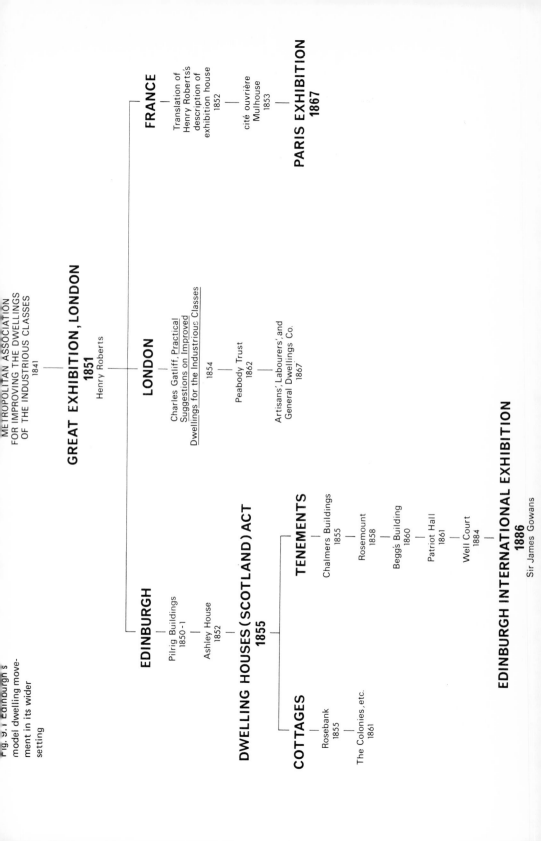

Fig. 9.1 Edinburgh's model dwelling movement in its wider setting

METROPOLITAN ASSOCIATION
FOR IMPROVING THE DWELLINGS
OF THE INDUSTRIOUS CLASSES
1841

GREAT EXHIBITION, LONDON
1851
Henry Roberts

FRANCE

Translation of Henry Roberts's description of exhibition house
1852

cité ouvrière Mulhouse
1853

PARIS EXHIBITION
1867

LONDON

Charles Gatliff, <u>Practical Suggestions on Improved Dwellings for the Industrious Classes</u>
1854

Peabody Trust
1862

Artisans', Labourers' and General Dwellings Co.
1867

EDINBURGH

Pilrig Buildings
1850-1

Ashley House
1852

DWELLING HOUSES (SCOTLAND) ACT
1855

TENEMENTS

Chalmers Buildings
1855

Rosemount
1858

Begg's Building
1860

Patriot Hall
1861

Well Court
1884

COTTAGES

Rosebank
1855

The Colonies, etc.
1861

EDINBURGH INTERNATIONAL EXHIBITION
1886
Sir James Gowans

decent houses and comfortable homes?'[5] The city's large middle-class population had sufficient numbers of pious capitalists to finance several projects, and plenty of architects to take up the challenge.

Several schemes were built in Edinburgh based on the traditional tenement but incorporating such novel ideas as quadrangles and open galleries and the use of brick. Rosemount Buildings in Fountainbridge which houses ninety-six families, incorporated all these features, its red brick decorated with white brick rising over Gowans' Rosebank Cottages. A similar set of buildings for forty-two families, known as Patriot Hall, was built in Stockbridge in 1861.

In 1860 Edinburgh's working classes lived in conditions as bad as any in the United Kingdom. In that year a *Report of a Committee of the Working Classes of Edinburgh, on the Present Overcrowded and Uncomfortable State of their Dwelling Houses* was published. It expressed dissatisfaction with the housing situation, and complained that the buildings which had been modelled on London precedents resembled charity workhouses.[6] To rectify this the Edinburgh Co-operative Building Company was founded in 1861 'to carry on building specially with the view of accommodating all classes of workmen who were desirous of becoming the owner of their own dwellings'. The Co-operative rejected the tenement and adopted the cottage flats pioneered at Rosebank, with a separate entrance to each house. The price range, from £130 to £250, reflected wide differences in size and internal arrangements.[7] The first buildings were erected in Stockbridge and became known as 'The Colonies'. Similar schemes were undertaken on the suburban fringe of Edinburgh at Dalry Road, Abbeyhill, Lochend Road and Fort Street, Leith, and by October 1875 nearly 1,000 houses had been built.[8] By 1885 another 400 houses had been added, but by then the Co-operative had ceased to cater for the working man.

Much of the enthusiasm went out of the model dwelling movement during the 1880s. Professor H.C. Fleeming Jenkin, holder of the first chair of engineering at the University of Edinburgh, published in 1878 a pamphlet entitled *Healthy Homes* which returned to the monumental approach to the rehousing of the poor. His ideas were adopted by John Findlay of *The Scotsman* who engaged Sydney Mitchell in 1884 to design a scheme of working-class houses and a community centre for the Dean Village. Well Court, situated next to a tannery, symbolized the overpowering paternalism of this movement. Not to be outdone, James Gowans wrote a small work, *Model Dwelling Houses*, in a rather hurried attempt to explain and jusify the artisans' dwellings he built for the International Exhibition of Industry, Science and Art held in Edinburgh in 1886. Many of the examples set by this movement were ignored, especially the expensive architectural exuberance. Yet it did bring to the public's notice the housing problems of the poorer classes at a time when the State appeared to be unconcerned. Not all was wasted, however, for Jenkin and Gowans were the driving force behind the foundation in 1878 of the Edinburgh Sanitary Protection Association,[9] which was run on commercial lines by making detailed reports on the sanitary condition of private houses. The Association made Edinburgh's middle class aware of hitherto ignored drainage defects, and was the prototype for similar societies outside Scotland (Fig. 9.2).

No. 2212. **Model Houses for the Working Classes.** [Erected by 36 Firms, and not yet finished.]

Ye Outside.
"You may look—but you mustn't touch."

Ye Inside.
Each occupant of the house has a room to himself (?)

Solo Plumber.	Take equal parts of dust and lime
" I SCAMP the joints, I scamp the drains,	And then you have my mortar.
I am an artful plumber ;	
You'll feel my hand in winter's rains,	" I build my wall with many a trick,
You'll sniff it in the summer.	So shrewd as to astound one ;
	With here and there a rotten brick,
" I dig, I delve, I patch, I pry,	And here and there a sound one."
And lay the pipes so badly	
That even bland surveyors sigh,	*Solo Plumber.*
And tenants chatter madly."	" THE sewer-pipe I love to lay,
	Connecting with the cistern ;
Solo Builder.	And where's the law that dares to say,
" I BUILD my floors on rags and bones,	The tenant should have *his* turn ?"
Or lush-organic matter ;	
Or where the grass in swampy zones	*Finale by the Pair.*
Grows greener, and grows fatter.	" AND GOWANS here, he would restrain
	Our right to scatter fever ;
" My doors are sure to warp in time,	Should this go down, 'tis very plain
My slates let in the water ;	We can't scamp on for ever."

Fig. 9.2 Not everyone held the model tenement movement in respect. This cartoon appeared in Robert Mitchell's lampoon, *Our Own-eries at the Show in the Meadows,* published privately for the Edinburgh International Exhibition of 1886. (By courtesy C. Johnstone.)

There were strong working-class movements for home ownership in Glasgow, Hawick, Dumbarton, Falkirk and Grangemouth, and from time to time in other burghs, mainly in the Central Belt. During the second half of the nineteenth century many houses were no doubt built and paid for outright by means of accumulated savings. Among the middle class generally, a loan was commonly raised on a private mortgage negotiated through a solicitor. The working-class home ownership movement led to the financing and erecting of houses by friendly societies known as 'benefit building societies'. Since these building societies differ considerably from the commercial building society of today, which had its origins primarily in an English movement and is the lineal descendant of the 'permanent' building societies, a word must be said about them. These benefit building societies raised funds by issuing shares to, or taking deposits from their members, they then built a group of houses and

193

sold them to their members who paid off the balance due by annual instalments over a period of up to twenty-five years.[10] The earliest known use of this system was in Kirkcudbright where two building societies were founded in 1808 and 1810.[11] They erected 112 houses before the societies were terminated.

The Grangemouth Co-operative Building and Investment Society Ltd was constituted in 1876 to build houses for the working classes and to lend money to members to purchase their own homes. Between foundation and 1910 the society built 317 houses in the burgh, often whole streets at a time. The Society's first buildings were tenements containing houses of room-and-kitchen, but later, larger houses included a bathroom with hot and cold water. Throughout the Society's history the directors aimed at providing a good type of workingman's house according to the ideas prevailing at the time and each one was sold to an occupying owner as soon as erected. Trouble began in 1906-7 when some new houses remained unsold owing to the depression in the housing market. Many members resigned in 1909 and in the following year building was stopped through 'fear more than the operation of the Finance Act'.[12] By 1920 building costs had trebled, and the society had several acres of undeveloped ground on which it was paying an annual feu-duty of £30. At the same time the State began to build houses to rent to the working classes, the very people the society had been founded to serve. Clearly the moment had come to hand over responsibility to more modern institutions.[13] The activities of the benefit building societies declined for various reasons, primarily from competition from the modern building societies which were prepared to accept deposits from any investor and lend money to non-investors for house purchase. Furthermore, the permanent building society did not involve itself in the process of building or owning property. Permanent building societies began to make progress after 1919, but it will be observed that no substantial use was made of the services of Scottish building societies until about 1929 (Fig. 9.3). Today the building society movement flourishes in Scotland but English incomers dominate the scene, as can be seen by the signs over their offices: Bradford, Cheltenham and Gloucester, Halifax, Huddersfield, Leeds, Leicester, Woolwich. One can question whether this activity reflects a major extension of Scottish home ownership or rather the tapping of Scots saving capacity to transfer the capital to more demanding areas of Britain.

Subsidising the owner-occupier has been a consistent government policy from 1899 when the Small Dwellings Acquisition Act was passed. This enabled local authorities to lend money to a person to acquire the house in which he lived. Although the Act had considerable impact in England it was a dead letter in Scotland with the exception of Bo'ness, where the town council built a tenement block of eight two-apartment houses which were sold to workmen. The

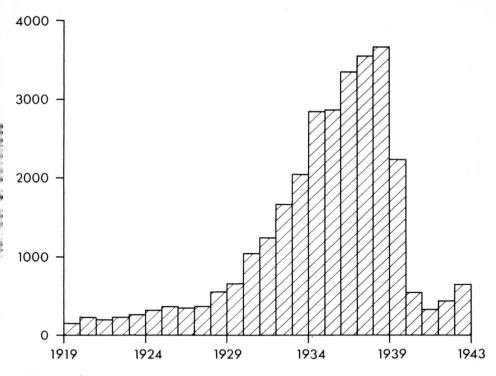

4000 —

3000 —

2000 —

1000 —

0 —

1919   1924   1929   1934   1939   1943

g. 9.3 Number of ıvances made by ːottish building ıcieties in Scotland, ┇19-43. The 16 English ⅃ilding societies ɔerating in Scotland ɹring this period are ɔt included. (Source: ⅂e *Provision of Houses r Owner-Occupation in ∙otland*, HMSO, 1946).

Royal Commission on Housing in Scotland recommended an increased subsidy for building private houses costing less than £600. The Housing Act 1919 in fact raised this limit to £800. Then, in a bout of generosity, the Government passed the Housing (Additional Powers) Act 1919, the only Act under which grants were paid directly to private house owners and, taking advantage of these financial provisions, 2,324 houses were erected. In 1923 the new Housing Act reduced the subsidy but raised the ceiling price to £1,200 and by 1934, when this subsidy was withdrawn, 29,549 houses had been erected. The limit was dropped to £800 in 1935. Clearly, these fluctuations were reflected in the tempo of production and design of houses over this period. Glasgow, in the grip of depression, saw a virtual cessation of building for home ownership. Edinburgh, on the other hand, with its more prosperous economic base, saw a widespread urban sprawl of small bungalows often conveniently priced 'all-in' at £760 (Fig. 9.4). Houses tended to be small in consequence of the subsidy limit but gardens were relatively large because land was cheap. Needless to say, for many urban Scots of the 1930s the bungalow was the ideal, but unfortunately out of reach of the bulk of the population. The inter-war sprawl, so marked in the outer suburbs of London, was kept at bay by the depressed economic conditions of the time.

195

Fig. 9.4 Bungalow land of the 1930s, Duddingston, Edinburgh. (Photo: Aero films.)

Government has devoted considerable energy to tackling Scottish reluctance to purchase a house. Tom Johnston, when Secretary of State in 1944, asked the Scottish Housing Advisory Committee 'to consider and advise on the measures required to encourage the provision of houses for owner-occupation in Scotland'.[14] The general conclusion was that home ownership involved too many liabilities and was inflexible. The question, however, was submerged in the general problem of providing any kind of house in the midst of post-war shortages. Again the problem was raised in October 1967 when studies were launched to examine two aspects of the problem.

The first report published in 1970 made a critical comparison of private house building in England and Scotland with particular reference to cost.[15] It was found that the price of homes, both new and old, coming on the market was higher in Scotland than in England and Wales. The trend since then has not altered and in certain areas of Scotland, such as the north-east, prices have risen much faster.

The second report published in 1972 examined the factors influencing the demand for private housing in Scotland.[16] Five main criteria were isolated: (1) the socio-economic composition of the population showed that there was a weaker demand for owner-occupation in Scotland, especially at the lower end of the scale; (2) mortgage data showed that mortgage holders in Scotland had a higher income than in England and Wales; (3) the public authority tenant who became an owner-occupier tended to have a higher income than other buyers in Scotland; (4) the demand for option mortgages was weaker in Scotland; and (5) the difference in monthly outlay between buying an average priced house and renting a local authority house was greater in Scotland than in England and Wales and was clearly a disincentive to owning a house in Scotland. All these reasons, with the exception of the last, are weak enough to suggest that there may be some deeper cultural reluctance to adopt this form of tenure. The report concluded: 'All these factors suggest the general thesis that there was a lower demand for private housing in Scotland than in England and Wales.' Yes, indeed, but owner occupancy has grown from 29 per cent in 1966 to 33 per cent in 1975 (this is still a long way behind England's 55 per cent).

Other tenurial systems have made little impact. A recent innovation, co-ownership, is still in its infancy in Scotland, with some small developments on vacant plots within towns. Co-ownership combines the advantages of renting with some of the benefits of owner-occuaption, the most important being the repayment of some of the accrued capital value if a member leaves after more than five years. Developments are planned and built by non-profit-making housing societies and fill a vital gap in the provision of unfurnished accommodation where council tenancy or house purchase are either not desired or impossible. The principal sponsor of these societies is the Housing Corporation, a public body which was established under the Housing Act 1964. Its purpose is to encourage and to administer the provision of houses by voluntary societies on a cost rent and co-ownership basis. The Corporation made a modest contribution to the housing needs largely of the mobile middle classes, but high interest rates in the early 1970s virtually extinguished demand for co-ownership. The Housing Corporation was given new powers in the Housing and Planning Bill 1973 and these were enlarged and improved by a new Government in the Housing Act 1974. The Corporation's role is crucial for not only is it promoting the building of new houses but it is also devising new forms of tenure to help people to bridge the gap between renting and owning property.[17]

Scotland's owner-occupied housing stock has been augmented by the sale of privately rented dwellings, a trend which began in the 1950s and accelerated in the 1960s. Furthermore in the slum clearance schemes during this period many privately rented houses were demolished, so that this sector decreased from 25 per cent of

Table 6. Household tenure (in percentage of households) in the four cities 1971

	Aberdeen	Dundee	Edinburgh	Glasgow	Scotland
Owner-occupied	30.4 (31.0)	20.2 (20.3)	46.9 (46.8)	22.1 (22.8)	29.3 (29.5)
Rented, local authority, etc.	48.7 (53.8)	59.6 (68.5)	31.6 (35.6)	53.9 (62.6)	53.5 (59.0)
Rented, private (unfurnished)	13.5 (6.0)	16.4 (7.4)	13.0 (7.0)	19.0 (8.9)	8.7 (3.5)
Rented, private (furnished)	5.2 (7.2)	2.5 (2.8)	5.9 (8.4)	3.3 (4.2)	2.8 (3.4)
Other tenures (tied, etc.)	2.2 (2.0)	1.3 (1.0)	2.6 (2.2)	1.7 (1.5)	5.7 (4.6)

Note: The figures in brackets represent the projected percentage in 1976 if the trends between 1966 and 1971 continue. The conversion of private rented unfurnished accommodation to furnished, however, will probably not be sustained under the impact of the Housing (Security of Tenure) Act, 1974.

the total stock in 1961 to 24 per cent in 1966 and 13 per cent in 1975. The structure of the privately rented sector also changed during this period in response to the 1965 Rent Act. The rate of decline in the number of unfurnished households between 1966 and 1971 was double that during the first half of the decade, but the number of furnished households increased substantially as many landlords furnished their properties to avoid the more restrictive parts of the Act. If this trend is repeated in response to the 1974 Housing Act which embraced furnished accommodation then privately rented property will shortly vanish.

Few council houses have been sold. Labour-controlled councils violently disapproved of the policy and even in areas favourable to the idea there was little response from council tenants — Jedburgh received only one firm inquiry from more than 850 tenants.[18]

The provision of owner-occupied homes has been patchy, both historically and geographically. Owner-occupancy fares better in the east than in the west, in the counties rather than the cities, and in county towns rather than large industrial burghs. Since 1919 1,207,578 permanent houses have been built, 954,540 in the public sector and 253,038 in the private sector. The 1920s saw the addition of 5,000 private dwellings each year, mainly bungalows, often set in ribbon development. Then came the war and a virtual standstill in house building until the late 1950s. Even at its highest in 1972, with all the encouragement of the Government of the day, the rate of private building was only half that of local government building. Glasgow has been a classic case of frigid attitudes towards private ownership; for example, in 1969 only 75 houses for owner-occupancy were built within the city boundary compared with nearly 5,000 council houses.

Yet since 1970 the gap between the numbers of council and private houses built has narrowed considerably (Fig. 9.5). Whilst the numbers of new council houses have decreased, private building has remained steady. In part this reflects the saturation point reached by many councils in the provision of houses, and little more potential demand can be envisaged except for high-quality rented houses. Many, many questions can be raised over the vexed issue of council housing versus owner-occupancy, but one thing is clear — there can be no redistribution of wealth in Scotland, except that accruing to the State, while so few people purchase their own homes. The stark problems of a housing famine have been largely solved: the provision and requirement of houses is just about in balance. That is not to say that everyone has the house he wants nor is it in the place he wishes. In December 1976 the total number of houses was 1,920,000 for a population of 5,206,200 or about 1,740,000 households. Even Glasgow with its long history of housing shortage will have a surplus by 1981 because of its rapid decline in population. With commendable open-mindedness Glasgow District

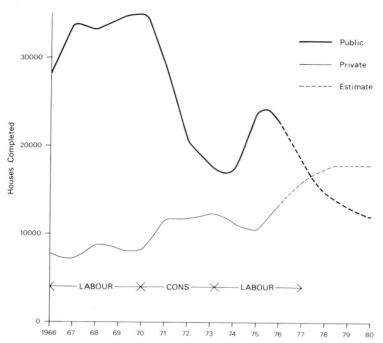

Fig. 9.5 Current trends
public and private hou
building 1963-76

Authority has overturned longstanding policies and sanctioned a survey to see if council tenants want to buy their homes, begun dismantling its direct labour department and released land to private developers which had previously been earmarked for council houses. In the immediate future the responsibility of what tenurial system the Scots want, whether paternalism of the State or vassaldom of owner-occupancy, must lie in their own hands.

Notes

1. *Edinburgh Water-Works Bill. Minutes of Evidence . . .* (Edinburgh, January 1847), p. 103.

2. *Dundee Advertiser*, 30 January 1857, quoted in B. Lenman, C. Lythe and E. Gauldie, *Dundee and Its Textile Industry 1850-1914* (Abertay Historical Society Publication No. 14, Dundee, 1969), p. 81.

3. *Engineering,* vol. 4. 4, 23 August 1867, pp. 145-6.

4. J. N. Tarn, *Five Per Cent Philanthropy: An Account of Housing in Urban Areas between 1840 and 1914* (Cambridge University Press, 1974).

5. Sir James Gowans, *Model Dwelling-Houses* (Edinburgh, 1886) (I am obliged to Mr. Colin Johnstone for bringing my attention to this pamphlet and for a preview of his article on Gowans).

6. H. Gilzean-Reid, *Housing for the People: An Example in Co-operation* (London, n.d.).

7. James Beg, *Happy Homes for Working Men and How to Get Them* (Edinburgh, 1873).

200

8. Minutes of the Edinburgh Cooperative Building Society (SRO GD1/777).

9. H. Macdonald, 'H.D. Littlejohn', unpublished PhD thesis, University of Edinburgh, 1972.

10. *Second Report of the Commissioners on Benefit Building Societies* (HMSO, Edinburgh, 1872), pt. 1. It contains a report by George Culley, Assistant Commissioner, on the development of benefit building socieites in Scotland up to 1871.

11. Revd W. Mackenzie, *The History of Galloway from the Earliest Period to the Present Time* (Kirkcudbright), II, pp. 495-6

12. Papers relating to Housing (Scotland) (No. 2) Bill 1921-3 (SRO DD6/596).

13. Papers relating to Grangemouth Cooperative Building and Investment Society (SRO DD6/675, 681).

14. Department of Health for Scotland, *The Provision of Houses for Owner-Occupation in Scotland, Report by the Scottish Housing Advisory Committee*, Cmnd. 6741 (HMSO, Edinburgh, 1946).

15. N. Sidwell, *The Cost of Private House Building in Scotland: a Report for the Scottish Housing Advisory Committee* (HMSO, Edinburgh, 1970).

16. Scottish Development Department, *The Demand for Private Houses in Scotland: A Report for the Scottish Housing Advisory Committee* (HMSO, Edinburgh, 1972).

17. *Tenth Report of the Housing Corporation for the year ended 31st March 1974* (The Housing Corporation, London).

18. *The Scotsman*, 7 December 1971.

The garden city was really an English concept of urban idealism. There is little to substantiate the underlying romantic philosophy that every man hankers after rustic tranquillity, and the mere subsistence level of Scottish rural life could produce no nostalgia for some half-forgotten idyll. The Scot's mental transformation from cottar to urban man was complete and the English compromise of the garden city, or more rightly suburb, was rarely relevant to Scottish urban problems.

The making of docile urban man was one of the aims of the founders of eighteenth-century planned villages. Robert Owen believed that the construction of an ideal settlement in ideal surroundings would create the desired product and he introduced this philosophy into the industrial scene (Fig. 10.1). Utopian settlements of his were planted in the North American prairies to spread the gospel of community life; while back in Britain, Owen's writings inspired Minter Morgan and James Silk Buckingham to develop ideas in social engineering. Morgan believed that man would be the better for living in a village or an open part of a large town rather than in the congestion of alley and wynd. Buckingham's model of an ideal city, called Victoria, was published in 1849. Later town planning schemes used some of his ideas, such as his emphasis on low densities, zoning, ample space for gardens, and 'social balance'.[1]

The publication in 1898 of Ebenezer Howard's *Tomorrow* (retitled *Garden Cities of Tomorrow* in 1902) stimulated men's minds as have few books in this century. It is a short book, written without evangelical fervour. Yet from it sprang government legislation, the professional town planners and towns themselves, not only in Britain but across the world, all conforming to his vision. The essence of Howard's theory lay in the ideal of a balanced community of 50,000 people. Man had to earn his living through his industrial skills and was to be rewarded by escape to his cottage and garden. In order to achieve this no more than 27 houses per hectare should be built. Given this limitation, and with the need for extensive open spaces and green belts to surround this self-supporting community, universal application of the theory was obviously impossible.

The Fabian Society took up the cause and in 1900 organized a conference and issued a number of pamphlets including Raymond Unwin's *Cottage Plans and Common Sense*. Thereafter Unwin, with Barry Parker, designed Letchworth, the first garden city which did much to convince people of the soundness of these ideas.

At this time two new inventions, the electric grid and the motor

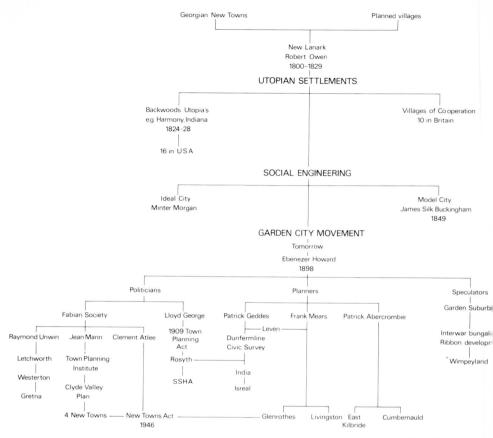

Fig. 10.1 The search for Utopia

car, were about to free men from the old locational restraints. The electric grid allowed industries to be sited away from coalfields and near their markets, and so began a steady drain of work and people to south-east England where rising prosperity was stimulating extensive building — the suburban sprawl. Ribbon development and the new breed of commuters were not really a problem in Scotland, which lay in the trough of depression. Howard's ideas were hailed by many as a means of reversing the excessive urbanization of Britain's society. They did not see that this idealized semi-rural alternative would result merely in urban man spreading his blight further afield. The garden city movement basked in the success of Letchworth, the product of the First Garden City Ltd. Whilst its idyllic design was taken as the reason for its success, it is improbable that any development just off the Great North Road, 54 km from London, would have failed in those inter-war years. Would the results have been the same if Letchworth had been built 54 km from Newcastle or Glasgow?

Another stimulus to town planning ideas came from a band of vigorous apostles led by Patrick Geddes, who has been justly described as the father of town planning. His urban experience developed from a boyhood in Perth, in Dundee where he was Professor of botany from 1888 to 1919, and in Edinburgh. Geddes was many years ahead of his time in laying stress on the need for a civic exhibition and a permanent centre for civic studies in every town, foreshadowing the now increasingly fashionable idea of public participation. In the Outlook Tower in Edinburgh he set up his own exhibition, which formed the basis of his great Cities and Town Planning Exhibition held in Edinburgh in 1910, London, Belfast and Dublin in 1911 and Madras in 1915. It is hard to measure the catalytic effect of the ideas of such men as Ebenezer Howard and Patrick Geddes, for their inspiration percolated to every corner of urban society. 'It was in 1898 or 1899 that, as a very young student,' wrote Sir Frank Mears towards the end of a distinguished career in planning, 'I bought a little paper covered book called *To-morrow*, the work of an unknown shorthand writer called Ebenezer Howard . . . A few years later I came under the influence of Professor Geddes in his Outlook Tower.'[2] In 1913 Geddes and Mears together planned a garden suburb to the north of Leven in Fife but the venture came to naught.[3] This movement had a humdrum beginning but later Mears was to influence the foundation of two garden cities.

The garden suburb idea was forced on Scotland by the rearmament programme prior to World War I. Government demanded new housing for workers who were being transferred from English bases. In June 1910 the Scottish Garden Suburb Company was incorporated. Unfortunately the name had little to do with the company's concern to provide houses as cheaply as possible for Admiralty workers being moved from Woolwich to the new torpedo factory at Gourock and the whole scheme soon dissolved in bitter litigation between the professional men and the speculators.[4]

A more substantial scheme on the other side of the country properly introduced the new ideas into Scotland. In 1910 the Admiralty proposed the building of a new town at Rosyth on garden city lines, in conjunction with the projected naval dockyard. Much was at stake, for government prestige had become closely linked for the first time with a town planning venture. Failure could jeopardize the success of the town planning movement itself, as a letter from the Secretary of State for Scotland indicated:

No doubt it is very much in the interest of the Government as a whole that we should see that the principles of town planning, which we have carried into law, should if possible be successfully applied in the case of Rosyth. The town furnishes an early and signal instance of the situation which the Act of 1909 was designed to meet, and the same Government which passed the Act is responsible for the creation of the new community. The steps taken at Rosyth will therefore be keenly watched by municipalities and by the public generally, and a successful application of town planning principles will not only be of the highest value to the community directly concerned, but will afford an example of powerful influence over other Scottish cities where the old system, or lack of system, has produced deplorable results.[5]

Dunfermline was to play a significant part in the evolution of town planning into an accepted discipline. Patrick Geddes was commissioned in 1903 by the Carnegie Trust to prepare a 'civic survey' of the burgh.[6] Although its recommendations were not acted upon, the people of Dunfermline were conditioned to the new planning ideas. Houses for a sudden influx of 1,200 workers at the Rosyth Naval Dockyard could not be found in the housing stock in the nearby burghs of Dunfermline and Inverkeithing. Dunfermline town council took up the challenge and put forward a town planning scheme for the agricultural land stretching southwards which they described as 'land well adapted for the laying out of a new town under modern conditions'.[7] The sheer size of Dunfermline's proposal caused amazement in early planning circles. For the first time a municipality was trying to plan on a massive scale and the council wanted to make sure that no part of the area should become the 'happy hunting ground of the jerrybuilder'.[8]

The council turned for guidance to their English counterparts. The Town Planning Committee made a tour of northern England to see schemes at Barrow-in-Furness, Liverpool, Manchester and Birmingham. They returned 'with enlarged conceptions of real town planning',[9] and a Birmingham town planner, J. Wilkes, was seconded to the burgh. A road plan was prepared including roadside verges to allow for road widening to accommodate future traffic growth, a feature which would figure prominently in inter-war planning. All this activity gave the Local Government Board for Scotland the confidence to authorize preparation of the first town planning scheme in Scotland.[10]

In the meantime it had been suggested that the Admiralty should hold a competition on the lines of one recently conducted by King's College, Cambridge, for their Ruislip Estate. But the Lords of the Admiralty did not take into account local feelings, especially those of the burgh of Dunfermline, for the whole issue had become an emotional matter. While work on the dockyard progressed and war loomed on the horizon the garden city languished. No department would take responsibility for the planning process nor dare to let Dunfermline have its head. Research conducted by the Garden Cities and Town Planning Association (Edinburgh Branch) at Chatham and Devonport dockyards revealed differences in ideas about urban living. The English workman would not entertain the thought of living in a tenement, he had to have his cottage and garden. This coincided with the current ideas for a new urban/rural utopia. If war had not intervened the debate would have been long and bitter; as it was, government was pressed into its first experiment in large-scale town planning.[11]

The Admiralty asked Dunfermline council to develop a town of 128 hectares within which the Admiralty would feu 110 hectares to the Scottish National Housing Company Ltd to erect 3,000 houses within six years. Notwithstanding the pressures of war, the burgh, local landowners and the tramway company fell out with the Admiralty and by May 1915 the Government resorted to severe action to bulldoze the measure through Parliament so that at least 150 dwellings would be ready for the arrival of the first dockyard workers only four months later. Whilst the houses were being hurriedly erected locals visited the site and found it incredible that people were actually going to live in these brick structures.

The Housing (Rosyth Dockyard) Act 1915 was passed and the way was open to start the new town. The result was far more radical than anyone expected, for the normal Scottish building acts and by-laws which favoured tenement construction were suspended, enabling dwellings of the 'garden city cottage type' to be erected. Ultimately 1,872 houses were built at Rosyth by the company, which was finally wound up in 1969 and its properties conveyed to the SSHA.

While Rosyth was being made a test case for garden city living in Scotland the first bricks and mortar were being laid just outside Glasgow at Westerton on the Garscube estate, about 9 km by rail from the city. In 1911 the Glasgow Garden Suburb Tenants Company Ltd was registered to build 200 to 300 dwellings. Raymond Unwin, who was commissioned to design the scheme, had seen that in most cases the resources to create garden cities would not be forthcoming, and that more modest suburbs on garden city lines would be a more practical proposition. Traditional stone was rejected in favour of bricks and roughcast. The streets were lit by gas, for there were aesthetic objections to overhead supplies and the Clyde Valley Electric Power Company refused to put in underground lines. When the official party arrived by train on 19 April 1913 for the laying of the foundation stone, they found that the North British Railway Company had obligingly added the words 'Garden Suburb' to the station nameboard.[12]

The promoters had no doubt about their market. The original subscribers were the new technocrats of the twentieth century whose steady employment made them attractive tenants: half were employed by the Post Office in supervisory positions and the rest were mostly skilled tradesmen. The distribution of their home addresses reveals that they already lived in better-quality tenemental districts (Fig 10.2). Clearly these were economically mobile people making an additional geographical step to a new way of urban living. The promoters promised residential escape with a third-class annual season ticket of £3.50 and an annual rent of about £20. Unfortunately war interrupted the promoters' plans and only forty houses stand as a memorial to the first garden suburb started in Scotland.

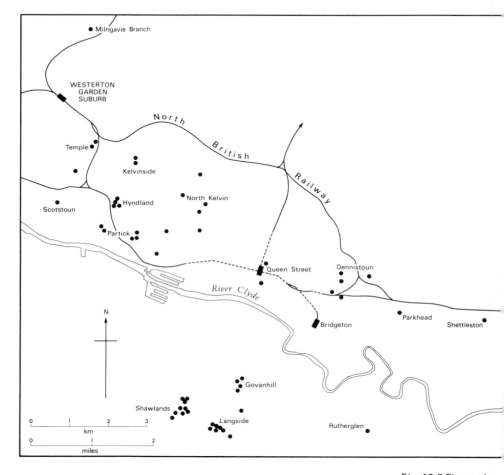

Fig. 10.2 Places of origin of Westerton tenants 1911 (in the better tenemental area of Glasgow)

The term 'garden suburb' was used widely by speculative builders to give their projects a modern image. Several such schemes were planned in Scotland just before the First World War. One of the first was designed by Robert Maclauren, secretary of the Glasgow and West of Scotland Garden City Association and built at King's Park, Stirling. A rather far-fetched feuing plan for the Duke of Portland's lands at Barassie was floated as the Garden Suburb of Troon, 'the feuars will be the well-to-do middle classes whose main recreation is golf and gardening'. At ten houses to the hectare some 200 houses were planned, but the scheme fell through. Concern for returning servicemen after World War I led to the founding of the Scottish Veterans' Garden City Association. From its foundation in 1915 under the presidency of the Earl of Wemyss, the Association had the ear of the very highest in the land.[13] The title was somewhat misleading for the Association concentrated on building small communities of homes in congenial surroundings and in 1973 still administered 666 cottages throughout the country.

Reference must be made to the speculative dream of Gilbert Lang, a Glasgow solicitor. He created the Third Garden City Ltd (the first two being Letchworth and Welwyn Garden Cities) with visions of accommodating 40,000 inhabitants around Killearn, 28 km north of Glasgow. The scheme was presented in 1924 to a sceptical public:

> The proposal is that the Garden City proper should be limited to an ultimate population of 40,000, that a belt of land extending to 1,000-1,500 acres [405-608 hectares] should surround it, restricted to small holdings, allotments and market gardens. The small holdings would have a ready market in Glasgow for an added food supply and they would also have a growing local market and would prosper.[14]

His brand of rural fundamentalism was evident in a letter to the press: '. . . intensive manual cultivation of the land is suited to our circumstances'.[15] No more was heard of this or any other proposal, for the economic collapse of the late twenties prevented the creation of garden cities in Scotland through private enterprise. The Government did its best to stimulate action by empowering the Scottish Board of Health in the Town Planning (Scotland) Act 1925, to purchase on behalf of a local authority or an association whose objects included the promotion, formation or management of garden cities, land to be developed as a garden city (the term included garden suburb or garden village).

Rosyth remained the main example of the pioneer planners' experiments with garden cities and it was left to the post-war Labour Government to implement Howard's ideas with sufficient thoroughness to test their application to the Scottish scene. Experience of the one-class dormitory suburb of the inter-war years left a feeling of revulsion in planners' minds. Baillie Jean Mann of Glasgow, who had been instrumental in setting up the Scottish branch of the Town and Country Planning Association, dismissed the results of inter-war house building as being largely unplanned, 'resulting in a nation of bus-catchers and strap-hangers'. She suggested in 1941 that at least four new towns would be necessary for Scotland after the war and urged that the many mistakes made in the past should be avoided by adequate preparation during the war.[16] New Towns were to become as precious to Labour ideologists in the 1940s as comprehensive schools are today. Central to the ideology was the concept of the 'balanced community'. It was hoped that New Towns would recruit inhabitants from all social classes in proportions similar to the national population. People would not be forced to live cheek-by-jowl, rather in groups of 100 to 300 families, and their social mixing would occur at the shops, community centres, churches and schools. All felt it was a unique opportunity to create a brave new world.

By the end of the war it was felt that up to eight new towns would be required in central Scotland. The Clyde Valley Regional Plan proposed the establishment of four new towns at Cumbernauld, East Kilbride, Bishopton and Houston to cater for approximately 250,000 people who would be dispersed mainly from the Glasgow area. The existing population of Glasgow and its immediate periphery was about 1,250,000 so that the proposal envisaged the redistribution of approximately 20 per cent of that population. This sounded an exceptionally high proportion to English ears, particularly in comparison with the corresponding proposals for London (see below page 214). However, 52 per cent of all houses in Glasgow had two rooms or less and one house in three was overcrowded even by the comparatively low standards set by the 1935 Housing Act. In several wards of central Glasgow the proportion of houses of two rooms or less was as high as 80 per cent and the housing density in the central areas ranged up to 300 houses or 1,680 persons to the hectare. This alone would have made it impracticable to redistribute the population within the existing city boundaries. With all these considerations in mind the Clyde Valley Committee decided that new towns were essential.

On the suggestion of Tom Johnston, the Secretary of State, the local planning authorities in the Central and South East Region agreed in September 1943 to set up a Regional Planning Advisory Committee. The Committee appointed Sir Frank Mears to survey, report and make plans for the development of the region, which embraced Loch Katrine and the Trossachs and, at one point near Milngavie, came within two miles of the built-up area of Glasgow. Regional boundaries hardly reflected geographical reality. Unlike its counterpart in the Clyde Valley the Committee was faced with no single overpowering problem and so was able to cover a much wider field. From the beginning the Committee felt that great harm would result if the application of standardized planning methods were attempted:

> Under Scottish conditions all planning schemes, if they are to be successful, must be directed so that the land may be used in the best way to promote a variety of conditions and occupations under which the traditional way of Scottish life may be maintained.[17]

The whole tone of east coast development was optimistic, for the planner had more scope for creative expansion than his counterpart in the west. The Report of the Scottish Coalfields Committee in December 1944 predicted the decline of the central coalfield but the expansion of those around the Firth of Forth. The proposed new coalmines led Frank Mears to project four new towns at Woodside, Cardenden and Kennoway in Fife, and in the Dalkeith area in Midlothian. Each would have a target population of 10,000-15,000 and they would therefore be much smaller than the four new towns proposed for Clydeside. His plans, however, did not impress Edinburgh which was not beset by the problems faced in Glasgow. Indeed, Edinburgh's danger was of choking on complacency: 'Edinburgh is a Capital City', declared a town council memorandum, 'it is not a competitor of any other City. It does not seek to model itself upon any other city. It wants to be what it has been, but only more so'.[18]

Edinburgh town council set up an Advisory Committee on City Development which reported in 1943 that the proper solution was to create 'relatively self-contained communities in suitable places on the outskirts within the existing boundaries, and the encouragement of the growth of similar communities adjacent to existing centres of population outside the city boundaries'.[19] The Committee was adamantly opposed to the creation of new towns around Edinburgh. Sir Patrick Abercrombie prepared a detailed strategy embodying many of the Committee's suggestions, which was published in a sumptuous volume in 1948.[20]

On a national scale, the New Towns Committee under the chairmanship of Lord Reith recommended that the decision on the situation and boundaries of a new town must rest finally with the Government. The site acquired should include the whole of the built-up area and a surrounding green belt of appropriate depth, the Government having powers of compulsory purchase on behalf of the town development agency. Each development corporation would be responsible directly to the Secretary of State. The New Towns Act 1946 was one of the first major bills passed by the newly elected Labour Government and to save parliamentary time it was framed on a United Kingdom basis. A long and complicated Scottish application clause, requiring the issue of two White Papers, was made imperative by the differences in the legal systems, terminology, local authority administration and previous legislation. Government was now actively creating substantial towns on green-field sites which would give a new way of life to millions of people. The Act was the culmination of a long campaign waged by town planners and social philosophers who were convinced of the need to move people into the utopian environment of the garden city.

A new era started with the designation of East Kilbride in 1948. The new town was planned to meet Howard's ideals. Its target population was 50,000 at a maximum overall density of 36 houses to the hectare, and the typical housing layout was to be 29 two-storey terraced houses to a hectare of residential area. The same characteristics were envisaged for Glenrothes, and together they became Scotland's Mark I new towns.[21] In the *Clyde Valley Plan* the old village of East Kilbride was selected as one of four sites suitable for planting a new town. While rehousing people from Glasgow was the primary reason for the establishment of this new town, in many ways it grew up independently from its massive neighbour. From the start East Kilbride was successful in attracting industry from the south of England and the Midlands and some American firms set up their first European ventures there after the war. An aspiring tenant was obliged first to find a job in the town and this method of selecting tenants has been followed throughout the town's existence. East Kilbride steadfastly avoided becoming a reception area for Glasgow's overspill and thus in 1955 only 48 per cent of the town's tenants originated in that city. Government at this time was anxious that the new town should take the maximum number of overspill families and to this end was willing to compromise with the garden city ideal, demanding that housing densities should be at the highest possible levels. It was hoped in 1956 that the new town would house 3,000 overspill families but the Development Corporation declared that claims by incoming industry were such that no houses would be available for Glasgow's housing needs in the near future. In 1957 government introduced new subsidies for taking overspill families and through the years the proportion of tenants coming from Glasgow has risen to about 60 per cent. The migrants from Glasgow's tenements encountered an alien environment in East Kilbride. They found six 'neighbourhoods', each with its shopping centre, local shops, schools, churches and recreational areas, separated by looped district roads radiating from the town centre to the housing and industrial areas. For many the shock of living in a new town brought on the malady of 'new town blues'. But with time and the transition from a pioneer to a fully developed town, newcomers have found a thriving community which for a short period enjoyed political independence. Recently the town has received commercial acceptance with the opening of several national multiple stores. Thus in thirty years the green fields of East Kilbride have become a fully fledged town, a landscape tribute to Ebenezer Howard and his disciples.

In August 1946 Joseph Westwood, Secretary of State for Scotland, announced the Cabinet's approval to build a new town between Cowdenbeath and Lochgelly in central Fife. 'This new town', he said, recalling his Fabian origins, 'is the fulfilment of a dream of mine some forty years ago, and it will be, I hope, the blueprint of its type in Scotland.'[22] The plans for the town, which was never named, though Westwood was suggested, incorporated ideas such as a central supply of hot water, swimming bath and local theatre and the town itself was to make the 'Forth road bridge inevitable'.[23] A few days later came the first indication of a second new town in Fife to serve new mining developments in east Fife. Whilst a new town at Lochgelly fell through, the second site, first suggested by Frank Mears, was considered. The Department of Health for Scotland's 1946 report announced that Glenrothes was to be created for the new mining population as a balanced community which would be 'a complete breakaway from the outmoded conception of a mining village'. Between 1946 and 1948 Department officials debated the boundaries of the new town and in particular tried to persuade the burghs of Leslie and Markinch to come within the designated area. Independence prevailed and the new town was designated on a green-field site, in 1948, with a target population of 50,000. As at East Kilbride, several facets of garden city planning were adopted: low density housing of 30 houses per hectare, an encircling green belt, and the neighbourhood principle (Fig. 10.3).

ig. 10.3 Glenrothes om the air 3lenrothes Development Corporation.)

Throughout the 1950s, the Glenrothes development programme was related directly to the manpower needs of the National Coal Board. As early as 1951, however, the Development Corporation had been notified that the Board's manpower estimates had been revised downwards to such an extent that the population of Glenrothes was unlikely to exceed 18,000 within 25 years.[24] Future expansion was thus in doubt and there was serious consideration of the possibility of confining the new town to the south of the River Leven with a possible target population of only 23,000. The construction programme was reduced to a dangerously low level for it was impossible to prepare detailed plans for such necessities as the town centre and the school system while uncertainty continued. The turning point came in 1962 when the ill-fated Rothes Colliery was closed and Glenrothes could no longer be regarded as a super mining community. The change of plan was used as an opportunity to attract industry, offer better facilities, give assistance to Glasgow overspill and, most important of all, fix the target population at 55,000.

The overspill problems facing Glasgow and London were of roughly similar magnitude, about half a million people in each city, but the ramifications in housing and finance were substantially greater in Glasgow and the Clyde Valley. However, the solution was undertaken in a very disparate manner and to Glasgow's detriment. By 1954 no fewer than eight new towns were being established round London under the New Towns Act, but only one, East Kilbride, for Glasgow and the Clyde Valley. In population terms the disparity was stark: the English new towns had absorbed 320,400 people compared to 45,000 at East Kilbride. At this time Glenrothes had not yet entered the overspill field and pressure mounted to force government to create another new town for Glasgow's needs.

Cumbernauld had been one of the new town sites put forward in the Clyde Valley Plan of 1946. Pressure for overspill provision led the Clyde Valley Regional Advisory Committee to revive this suggestion in August 1953. Cumbernauld was thus the first Scottish new town intended to cater almost exclusively for one authority. The brief to the Development Corporation called for a balanced community of 50,000 persons, up to 80 per cent of whom were to be attracted from Glasgow, with appropriate provision for industry, housing, social, commercial and recreational facilities. By the time Cumbernauld was designated several of the principles of the Mark I new towns were being challenged. Target populations were being raised to 70,000 or more; higher densities were being proposed which effectively destroyed any garden city approach. Finally the universal ownership of the motor car was recognized. The outcome was the Mark II new town which in many ways was a replica of the new Glasgow with tenements and flyovers but on a hilltop setting.

The decision to build Cumbernauld's town centre on the top of a hill, with the whole of the residential area grouped closely around it and extending down the slopes, gave an opportunity to build a unique town. On the broad scale the model was undoubtedly the hilltop town of Provence, but the housing areas themselves owe a great deal to Scottish vernacular architecture. No separate neighbourhoods were proposed in the original plan, for the whole of the 50,000 population was to live within a kilometre of the town centre and be linked to it by a network of footpaths safely segregated from the roads. It was virtually the resurrection of the old Scottish burgh. The town centre rising grey like a dreadnought on the hilltop is one of the most spectacular features of the town. It is a huge multi-deck structure containing covered parking, shops, offices, civic and residential areas. Cumbernauld emerged as a truly Scottish application of Howard's principles, rejecting the rustic idealism but embracing the concept of the creation of a viable urban community. Already the town has a mystique which attracts worldwide attention. Planners from all over the world come to study its unique features: complete segregation of car and pedestrian, for example, has led to the lowest road accident rate in Britain. Probably the most important moment of international recognition came in 1967 with a prize for community architecture awarded by Reynolds Metals Company of America in a competition whose entries ranged from Tapiola in Finland to Brazilia.

Livingston new town was the outcome of continuing pressure to house Glasgow's overspill for by 1960 it was evident that a new town was needed outside the Clyde Valley. The Scottish Development Department mounted detailed studies of the few potential locations for a large new town in central Scotland and in 1962 a site was chosen at Livingston, straddling the boundary between Midlothian and West Lothian. As the designation order of the Secretary of State puts it,

'. . . a new town here would offer the possibility not merely of helping solve Glasgow's housing problem but also of using overspill constructively to create a new focus of industrial activity in the central belt of Scotland, linking the west with the centres of expansion in the Forth basin, and at the same time revitalising with modern industries an area hitherto overdependent on coal and shale.'[25]

While the provision of overspill housing was the main reason for building Livingston, the new town was given a strategic role in revitalizing the declining regional economy of West Lothian. The town became a central pivot of growth policy in the Central Scotland Plan (see Chapter 11 for details) and a special regional plan for an area of 200 sq. km around the new town was drawn up under the title of the *Lothians Regional Plan*. Thus it was intended that Livingston should become the largest new town in Scotland and the new regional centre for over a quarter of a million people. Experience gained in the Marks I and II new towns led to the evolution of ideas that emerged as the Mark III version at Livingston. Some of Howard's ideas were given a fresh airing but on the whole the sheer size of Livingston precluded his ideal of the small self-sufficient community and indeed the regional dimension was the antithesis of Howard's ideals. The use of systems building has given the town a uniformity which has considerable links with Georgian concepts of new town symmetry and the later Scottish townscape of tenements (Fig. 10.4). The key decision was to build the town centre astride the River Almond in the centre of the area. Following Cumbernauld's example some 40,000 people will live close to the town centre. The rest of the population will live in three residential districts with their own service centres some three kilometres from the town centre and divided by a grid of major roads into roughly equal-sized districts for about 10,000 people. The road pattern, though not as elaborate as Cumbernauld's, has also been built to serve universal car ownership.

As an overspill town for Glasgow, Livingston has not been a success. As a new regional centre the town has yet to prove itself, for Edinburgh still dominates the region. However, Livingston gave a much needed boost to the region's economy especially as its rise coincided with the death of the shale industry. The future can only be successful, for the new town occupies a position of maximum accessibility to the population of Scotland by excellent road, air and (potentially) rail services. Of all the towns in Scotland Livingston has the greatest potential population catchment within 100 km, amounting to 4,139,000 people.[26]

Ultimately, it is clear that the garden city concept of Howard and its even more doctrinaire interpretation by later exponents, have been modified by cultural, political and economic pressures. Yet Howard's fundamental principles — limitation of numbers and area, growth by colonization, variety and sufficiency of economic opportunities and social advantages, and the control of the land in the public interest — have been followed.

The designation of Irvine new town in November 1966 marked a complete break from the garden city concept and green-field location. The new town incorporated the two old burghs of Irvine and Kilwinning, together with a number of surrounding villages and smaller communities. This meant that the designated area of 50 sq. km included a population of around 40,000 with a well-established commercial and industrial structure. In many ways this complexity has been a disadvantage and growth has been slow because much of the development land was owned by the Ministry of Defence, the Board of Trade, British Rail and the South of Scotland Electricity Board. Some progress has been made, especially in the planning obsessions of the 1960s — roads, 'pedestrianized' shopping and recreation. Two new approach road systems and the by-pass have been completed in order to isolate the old town centre for pedestrians. A new shopping complex has been built, spanning the River Irvine. The pent-up energies of car-bound urban man have been catered for by the building of a leisure centre with ice rink, indoor bowling greens, the vast games hall, the swimming pools, etc.

Irvine was Britain's first coastal new town and the deep water available in the Clyde has created a long-term viability which was not entirely foreseen when the plan was launched. At Hunterston some 22.5 km north of the town the British Steel Corporation has three projects underway, an iron ore and coal terminal which can handle ships up to 300,000 tonnes, two direct reduction (ore pelletizing) plants producing 800,000 tonnes of iron a year and an electric arc furnace with associated continuous casting plant. But this is only the beginning of the steel era at Hunterston. By the second half of the 1980s the British Steel Corporation envisage a massive integrated steelworks producing up to 5 million tonnes a year of liquid steel from a battery of basic oxygen furnaces. Other developments include the Clyde Port Authority's container port, a government-sponsored concrete oil platform yard and two nuclear power stations. It is not hard to foresee Hunterston as Scotland's main marine terminal. Thus it may happen that Irvine will be to the twenty-first century, what Glasgow was to the nineteenth.

Finally, brief mention must be made of Stonehouse which lies 30 km south of Glasgow close to excellent road communications in the Clyde valley. A proposal for designation was published in September 1972 and East Kilbride Development Corporation was made responsible for formulating a master plan and then developing the new town. Building started in August 1975 of the sixteen advance factories and a thousand houses scheduled to be completed by 1977. The inauspicious inauguration of Stonehouse reflected the disquiet as to the feasibility of yet more new town development to solve Scotland's economic ills. Clearly, any industry attracted to Stonehouse would have been at the expense of the other five new towns still working towards their planned targets. Government was committed by a programme of advance factories to help the towns of Lanarkshire, such as Cambuslang, affected by the closure of steelworks to make a bid to attract replacement industry. Furthermore, the rapid voluntary migration from Glasgow and a dramatic fall in demographic projections undermined even the overspill and housing function of Stonehouse. Indeed the situation was sufficiently serious for West of Scotland planners to recommend a ten-year moratorium in Stonehouse's development. For a time their advice was ignored for government-sponsored new towns have a momentum of their own. But two days after the keys were handed over to Stonehouse's first tenants the Government cancelled the project on 12 May 1976. Already Stonehouse has become a mere footnote in the history of town planning.

The Secretary of State has made it clear that new towns are to remain centrally controlled by the Scottish Office.[27] He has also given priority to the development of the five new towns as centres of economic growth and has relegated the provision of overspill housing to a secondary function. Even so it can be assumed that the existing new towns will receive virtually all the estimated 166,000 overspill population from urban redevelopment in the period 1971-81. By 1981 Cumbernauld, East Kilbride and Glenrothes should have achieved their target populations and Irvine and Livingston should do so by 1991 (Table 7).

The garden suburb movement remains alive in the developers' hands. In areas favoured by economic growth garden suburbs are still being built. On the shores of the Firth of Forth 3.2 km east of Inverkeithing lies the private enterprise new town of Dalgety Bay. The town was built in consequence of the opening of the Forth road bridge, for its declared function was to cater for affluent Edinburgh commuters as well as Fife-based industrial managers. Its plans call for a population of some 10,000 people in an area of 52 hectares.[28] After a decade in existence Dalgety Bay remains a suburb rather than a town, but a strong community nonetheless. Yet their idyllic refuge has been shattered by the prospect of an oil terminal on their doorstep. A self-contained community at Westhill, Skene, is being privately developed as a garden suburb of Aberdeen. This project has some affinity with the private enterprise garden suburbs of the eastern seaboard of the United States such as Reston in Virginia. Westhill is designed to accommodate an eventual population of about 10,000 mostly in 'executive residences'. A golf club with squash courts and sauna baths will be an integral part of the development and residents will have 'special membership facilities'. An area for light industry and warehousing is planned on the edge of the estate to provide 'a certain amount of local employment without detriment to the residential environment'.[29]

Table 7. Progress of the Scottish new towns

Name	Starting date	Site area (hectares)	Population Target	By 1975
East Kilbride	1947	4,151	100,000	71,200
Glenrothes	1948	2,292	75,000	31,400
Cumbernauld	1956	1,660	70,000	41,200
Livingston	1962	2,677	100,000	21,900
Irvine	1968		116,000	48,500
Stonehouse	1975	cancelled 1976		
Total				214,200

Had the garden city movement remained thirled to the concept of the new town, the success of East Kilbride and its successors would have been a major tribute to the idealism of Ebenezer Howard. Unfortunately the garden city philosophy and the problems of urban development and redevelopment became inexorably mixed in the inter-war period. Without any central direction, the three became merged and the outcome was seen in ribbon development of private homes and the peripheral council estate. The landscape of tiny bungalows on large plots, or neo-tenements set in vast green spaces was the product of the age. The smoky journey by bus to and from work has become an integral part of the lives of many urban dwellers, and the remote dormitory suburb a nightly prison. Man has escaped the congestion of burgh life at the cost of losing all the variety that it offered. Dozens of pubs have been replaced by one;

the multitude of shops has been exchanged for the shuttered shopping centre; and the crowded street has given way to the planners' green, but now muddy, verge.

NOTES

1. Asa Briggs, *Victorian Cities* (Penguin, Harmondsworth, 1968), p. 73.

2. Paper read by F. C. Mears at the Town and Country Planning Association Annual Conference in Edinburgh, September 1945.

3. The plan for this scheme is in Durie House, Fife.

4. Court of Session process Knox *v.* The Scottish Garden Suburb Co. (SRO CS251/442).

5. Letter from Lord Pentland to Reginald McKenna MP, 17 February 1910 (SRO DD12/502).

6. P. Geddes, *City Development. A study of Parks, Gardens and Culture Institutes*, Report to the Carnegie Dunfermline Trust, 1904.

7. Report of Dunfermline Burgh town planning scheme 1912 (SRO DD12/167).

8. *Glasgow Herald*, 19 June 1912.

9. *The Scotsman*, 29 April 1912.

10. *The Edinburgh Gazette*, 29 May 1912; for the town planning inquiry see SRO DD12/167.

11. Various Development Department records in the SRO deal with the development and building of Rosyth. Report on Dunfermline Town Planning scheme (DD6/264); Rosyth proposed new town on garden city lines (DD12/501, 502); and Rosyth housing for Admiralty workers (DD6/426-57).

12. British Rail records (SRO BR NBR/8/1356).

13. Correspondence relating to the financial assistance given to the Scottish Veterans' Garden City Association 1919 (SRO DD6/781).

14. British Rail records (SRO BR LNE/8/410).

15. *Glasgow Herald*, 30 July 1924.

16. An address given by Jean Mann at the Town Planning Conference, Largs, September 1941.

17. Sir Frank C. Mears, *Central and South-East Scotland Regional Planning Advisory Committee* (Draft report, Edinburgh, July 1946). p. 2. Later published as *A Regional Survey and Plan for Central and South-East Scotland* (Edinburgh, 1948).

18. Reports of Central and South-East of Scotland Regional Planning Advisory Committee (SRO DD12/36).

19. *Advisory Committee on City Development (Edinburgh) Report* (Edinburgh Corporation, 1943).

20. P. Abercrombie and D. Plumstead, *A Civic Survey and Plan for Edinburgh* (Oliver and Boyd, Edinburgh, 1949).

21. P. D. McGovern, 'The New Towns of Scotland', *Scottish Geographical Magazine*, vol. 84 (1968), pp. 29-44.

22. *Glasgow Herald*, 31 August 1946.

23. *The Scotsman*, 31 August 1946.

24. P. J. Smith, 'Glenrothes: Some Geographical Aspects of New Town Development', *Scottish Geographical Magazine*, vol. 83 (1967), pp. 17-28.

25. Quoted by D. Diamond, 'Urban Change in Mid-Scotland', *Scottish Geographical Magazine*, vol. 78 (1962), pp. 150-1.

26. Isobel M. L. Robertson, 'Scottish Population Distribution: Implications for Locational Decisions', *Transactions of the Institute of British Geographers*, no. 63 (November 1974), pp. 111-24.

27. Scottish Office, *Consultation Document on Scotland's New Towns*, 31 January 1975.

28. D. R. Macgregor, 'A Survey of the Social and Economic Effects of the Forth Road Bridge with Particular Reference to the County of Fife', *Scottish Geographical Magazine*, vol. 82 (1966), pp. 78-92.

29. *The Scotsman*, 15 July 1972.

The sheer scale of urban society in the twentieth century and the scars inflicted while reaching this magnitude created conditions which only a national government could rectify. During World War II the role of government in modern society was scrutinized: the whole community, through the Government, accepted the responsibility of ensuring that all citizens enjoyed a minimum standard of living. In the narrow area of town and country planning, this commitment had been mapped out by three bodies which acted as pressure groups (Fig. 11.1). The Town and Country Planning Association, which incorporated the older Garden Cities and Town Planning Association, aimed at the establishment of garden cities and satellite towns and the provision of green belts around towns. Secondly, the Town Planning Institute trained planners and established professional standards. Lastly, the Scottish National Housing and Town Planning Council was more directly associated with Scottish local authority administration. Few groups have been as successful as these, for all that they advocated, and more, has entered the statute book and has given rise to much of our present-day urban landscape.

Like so many other British institutions, urban planning evolved over a long period. Under the Burgh Police (Scotland) Acts 1892 and 1903, town councils were given planning powers relating to the widening and improvement of existing streets, the formation of new streets, the fixing of building lines and street widths, and the control of open space around tenements. New by-laws prescribed building methods, housing densities and building heights, and in addition, controlled certain land uses such as the keeping of pigs in towns. Overall control was haphazard and lacked a central philosophy but, as we have seen, the rise of the garden city movement, the birth of the planning profession and the spread of statutory control, especially in housing, forced society to re-evaluate its ideas about urban living.

The provisions of the Housing, Town Planning, etc. Act 1909 for the first time laid an obligation on all sanitary authorities to consider the production of a town planning scheme for land in and around the areas under their control. The Act laid down that a town planning scheme might be made in respect of any land which was being, or seemed likely to be, developed, with the object of securing proper sanitary conditions, amenity and convenience. A local authority could prepare a town planning scheme only when the Local Government Board was satisfied that there was a *prima facie* case for a scheme. Thereafter, a scheme could have effect only with the

Board's approval and after a draft of the Board's order had been laid before Parliament.[1]

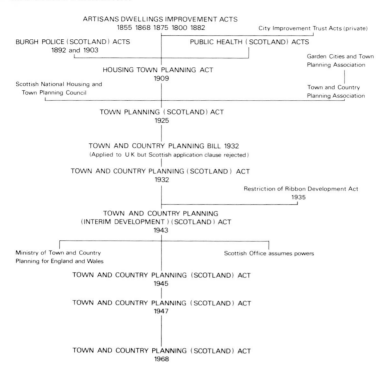

Fig. 11.1 The evolutic of town planning legislation

The need to secure physical planning brought the question of land prices and betterment (the increased capital value due to development) to the fore. Lloyd George made it amply clear who, in his opinion, created the increased value:

> The growth in value, more especially of urban sites, is due to no expenditure of capital or thought on the part of the ground owner, but entirely owing to the energy and enterprise of the community. . . . It is undoubtedly one of the worst evils of our present system of land tenure that instead of reaping the benefit of the common endeavour of its citizens a community has always to pay a heavy penalty to its ground landlords for putting up the value of their land.[2]

The local authority was given the right to a betterment levy from any developer to the extent of one-half of the increase in property value due to his development. This section of the Act produced a great furore and had to bear the blame for the collapse of the building industry after 1910. This belief can be called into question (see chapter 10), but it is clear that many local authorities were deterred from embarking on planning by the financial provisions of the Act, which required them to pay compensation if they prevented private development. Some of the deficiencies of the 1909 Act were made good in the 1919 Act. The laborious preliminary procedures were greatly simplified and the town council of every burgh with a population of over 20,000 was obliged to prepare within three years a scheme for any land within their authority which could be developed. Although the Town Planning (Scotland) Act 1925 was primarily a consolidation Act, some significant innovations were included. The Scottish Board of Health was empowered to authorize a town planning scheme for preserving the character of any property of special architectural, historic or artistic interest.

The inclusion in UK Bills of numerous special Scottish application provisions made Scottish legislation highly confusing and at times almost unintelligible. This difficulty arose in the 1932 Town and Country Planning Act, where the Scottish Application Clause was so long and detailed that Parliament ordered the Scottish applications to be presented as a separate Act. Since 1925 there has been separate planning legislation, apart from minor provisions and amendments and the New Towns Act 1946. The Town and Country Planning (Scotland) Act 1932 provided a new and enlarged framework for planning, with more detailed machinery and increased safeguards. The system based on the Act of 1932 had afforded some control of development but its administration had been unwieldy and its effects mainly negative. Planning powers had been vested in the county councils, the town councils of large burghs and, at their own insistence, the small burghs of St Andrews and Thurso. The main defects of the planning codes were sufficient to nullify any possible benefits. Procedures for preparation of schemes were cumbersome; the schemes themselves were too local and too rigid; setting up and amending were lengthy procedures; and the developers were not bound to obtain permission. Local authorities had no power to carry out public development of land, and between 1909 and 1932 they had been required to pay compensation if they prevented private development. Effective planning control was thus financially impossible.

The need for an even wider national planning system was accepted by three major and complementary inquiry bodies, the Barlow Commission and the Scott and Uthwatt Committees, which had all reported by 1940.

Early in 1943 a Ministry of Town and Country Planning was established for England and Wales, while the same duties, without the elegant title, were laid on the Scottish office in Edinburgh. In 1943 Parliament passed the Town and Country Planning (Interim Development) (Scotland) Act which, for the first time, brought all land under planning control. The difficulties faced by post-war society were deep-seated. The housing shortage remained and had indeed increased through destruction by air raids, lack of mainten-ance and cessation of building. Heavy industry was vulnerable to post-war slump and there was a desperate need to re-locate modern industries away from south-east England. Again, the regeneration of small burghs and coastal communities was advocated to stop the drift from country to town. The problems were so diverse, their solutions so interconnected, that the wartime Government took action to create statute, institution and system to make post-war Scotland a planned community.

Planning procedures were consolidated in the Town and Country Planning (Scotland) Act 1947 which has since become the main guide for urban development in Scotland. Although the 1947 Act strengthened planning and introduced important changes in method, its aims were not fundamentally different from those of the 1932 Act. Each planning authority was to prepare a development plan by July 1951 and make periodic revision. No development was to take place without permission and wide powers were conferred to acquire and develop land. Finally, power was given for the preservation and improvement of amenities by the removal of non-conforming build-ing, the stopping of non-conforming uses, the control of advertise-ment, and the preservation of trees and of buildings of special archi-tectural or historic interest. Whilst few people of all political persua-sions offered serious criticisms of the principles underlying these planning provisions, the financial provisions relating to compensa-tion and betterment values encountered strong opposition and were repealed after a change of government in 1951. The Conservative Party's slogan was 'set the people free'. Urban development, how-ever, is still covered by two of the three basic principles of the 1947 Act. The planning system introduced by the Act remains virtually untouched; planning control still operates and the development plan system was not changed for twenty years. Development plans are based on a basic map, a comprehensive development area map, a designation map, a special road map and a programme map. Clearly, within the framework each planning authority is afforded consider-able opportunity to shape its own destiny. By April 1954 twenty-eight plans had been lodged with the Secretary of State, although only those of Hamilton, Greenock, Paisley, Perth, Motherwell and Wishaw had been approved.

Glasgow's development plan was held up in the current dispute with the Government about overspill. However, all the essential post-war features of planned Glasgow had been laid down and it is worth examining the plan to assess the success or, as some would prefer, the level of impact of that document. The objectives of the City of Glasgow Development Plan were clearly stated in the Plan-ning Committee minutes of 8 April 1948:

   ... to plan the city on a community area basis consisting of an inner core and 19 such areas, each of these areas consisting of approximately 5 neighbourhood units (each neighbourhood unit having an average population of 10,000 persons) and that each community area be planned in accordance with the following principles:

(a) to provide physical conditions conducive to the safety of the citizens by the proper location of houses, schools, public buildings, shops, etc., so as to combine accessibility thereto and adequate safety against road dangers;

(b) to create conditions in which the health of the citizens would be fully safeguarded by the grouping of buildings of a like kind, the adequate provision of open spaces and the proper design and orientation of buildings;

(c) to provide the fullest possible measure of amenity and convenience; and

(d) to ensure that each community area would comprise a representative cross-section of the population of the city.

Implicit in the plan was a bias against new towns; for example, the population of the five neighbourhood units making up a community area conveniently totalled 50,000, the proposed size for new towns. One does not have to look far for the author of this document. The post-war map of Glasgow is a reflection of the strong personality of the city's Master of Works and City Engineer, Robert Bruce, for he believed Glasgow could solve her population problem without overspill. He furthered the policy of building large estates on the edge of the city and encouraged the adoption of multi-storey flats because of lowered costs. He was a pioneer of traffic segregation and envisaged the Inner Ring Road and the Clyde Tunnel. For good or ill Mr Bruce was the man who remade the face of Glasgow.[3]

The Clyde Valley Regional Planning Advisory Committee

A wide range of urban problems persisted throughout Clydeside, and their solution was retarded by the large number of local authorities involved. The Clyde Valley Regional Planning Advisory Committee, composed of the local planning authorities in Lanarkshire, Dunbartonshire and Renfrewshire, had been set up in 1927 'to prepare a scheme dealing with the particular features of planning within the area'. In practice its work was mainly confined to considering the line of road communications in the area and in 1929 it produced a report on roads, which was adopted by all the local authorities concerned, followed in 1932 by a report on open spaces. In 1938 the Committee was revived to re-examine regional road plans in the light of changes since the initial report, and especially the passing of the Restriction of Ribbon Development Act 1935.[4]

In November 1942, with the outcome of the war still uncertain, men began to plan for peace. The war had brought a widening of outlook, and the planners no longer concentrated simply on the need for improvement of the road system but rather took a broader view of the Clyde Valley problems, many of which demanded a regional solution.[5] There was the enormous burden of siting and building some 500,000 houses in an area of exceptional housing densities; the task of regenerating and diversifying industry to cushion the effects of decline in the traditional basic industries; and the question of future exploitation of coal reserves and preservation of agricultural land. In the urban areas, the approach to these difficulties required a continuous review of public services such as transport, water and drainage, open spaces and recreational facilities. Co-ordination was also required between such specialized agencies as the Scottish Housing Advisory Committee, the Scottish Coalfields Committee and the Scottish Council on Industry. The Old Committee was therefore again reconstituted in 1943, with representatives from the main urban areas and the five counties, and was empowered to draw up an outline plan for the region which could form a basis for the statutory planning schemes of individual local authorities.

The work of the 1943 Committee ended, for practical purposes, with the publication of *The Clyde Valley Regional Plan 1946*, prepared for the Committee by Sir Patrick Abercrombie and Mr (later Sir) Robert Matthew. The authors stated that they had had certain considerations in mind when making their proposals for remedying 'this acute congestion of housing and industry':

1. The topographical difficulties surrounding the central urban area, and limited opportunity for future expansion of the built-up areas.

2. The maintenance of individuality and character of the separate towns and main communities with a planned system of open spaces.

3. The preservation of first-class agricultural land immediately surrounding the built-up areas.

4. The necessity for planning the movement of people and the distribution of housing in relation to industry and employment.

5. The unbalanced development of the Central Midlands of Scotland in relation to the whole of Scotland.

Over 500,000 people in Glasgow and about half of Greenock's 80,000 population needed to be rehoused. It was suggested that half of Glasgow's overspill population should be rehoused in 'planned communities' on the outskirts of the city and that the remainder should be absorbed in new towns at Cumbernauld, East Kilbride,

Bishopton and Houston.

In 1948 a conference of planning authorities was held in Glasgow but its only outcome was a working party of technical officials who would meet from time to time to discuss mutual problems. Basically each authority wanted to develop its own plan to meet the 1951 statutory deadline. In 1951 Glasgow Corporation initiated the revival of the Advisory Committee under a provision of the Town and Country (Scotland) Act 1947 that any two or more local planning authorities might, with approval of the Secretary of State, establish a joint advisory committee to advise them on the preparation of development plans. The new terms of reference were 'to review from time to time the facts set out and the recommendations contained in the Clyde Valley Regional Plan 1946 [and] to advise on measures required for further implementation or modification of the plan'. Behind this review lay the growing realization that Glasgow simply could not provide adequate living space for its population. The time had come for all parties to reassess the need for overspill.

Although the 1946 Clyde Valley Report had established otherwise, Glasgow Corporation asserted its ability to provide all the necessary housing within the city bounds and, indeed, went on record with a minute in 1946, which was not formally revoked until 1953, declaring that there was no overspill problem. The Corporation had even opposed the new town projected at East Kilbride. This attitude was symbolized by the reliance the Corporation placed on its own direct labour department to carry out the house building programme. The submission of the city's Development Plan in 1952 marked the end of this self-deception for it showed that only 43,000 house sites were left in the city. For a time the Corporation hoped that a straightforward extension of city boundaries would provide a solution, but soon realized that this would be inadequate. Already there was a model for dealing with overspill in the Town Development Act 1952 which applied to London. Yet central government, appalled by the financial implications, was reluctant to pass similar legislation for Scotland and delegated responsibility to the Clyde Valley Advisory Committee. In August 1953 this committee felt that a partial solution lay in the immediate establishment of a second new town at Cumbernauld, to be reinforced by a planned policy for re-allocation of population and industry similar to that embodied in the English Town Development Act. Later the committee re-opened the question of developing Houston in Renfrewshire but the Government felt that a third new town in the Clyde Valley was impracticable at that time.

Considerable apprehension was felt in the burghs of the region during the deliberations by the Advisory Committee. None of them wanted to become a dormitory for Glasgow; most had employment problems and therefore were against the movement of people without a parallel movement of industry. Financial obligation was another vexed question. Government felt that the problem was Glasgow's and that Glasgow should pay; and although the receiving authorities realized that Glasgow alone could not afford to foot the bill, they were reluctant to share the costs. A change in government policy became apparent with the designation of Cumbernauld as a new town late in 1955, but this was not enough and pressure was maintained for a Scottish Overspill Act.

Glasgow's congestion in 1956 was unparalleled in the United Kingdom: 700,000 people were living in the centre of the city, an area of 7.7 sq. km at an average density of over 900 people per hectare, with 12,000 people huddled together in one area of 7 hectares. Housing standards in these areas were unbelievably low: 43 per cent of all houses in the city were of one or two rooms, compared with only 5 per cent in London and 2.5 per cent on Merseyside; 30 per cent of Glasgow's families shared toilets compared with 2.6 per cent in London and 1.1 per cent on Merseyside. Furthermore it was estimated that by 1959 all Glasgow's housing sites would have been used and homes would then have to be found outside the city, not only for those without their own home but also for those displaced by redevelopment of the congested central areas. Ultimately it would be necessary to provide homes outside the city for 300,000 people. The Housing and Town Development Act 1957 contained overspill provisions similar to those of the earlier English Act. Glasgow Corporation was recognized by the Secretary of State as the sole 'exporting authority', which might meet its overspill housing needs in three ways. The Corporation might build houses outside the city boundaries (under powers contained in the Housing (Scotland) Act 1950); arrangements might be made for another local authority or new town development corporation to provide houses under an 'overspill agreement'; or houses might be provided elsewhere by the Scottish Special Housing Association. A scheme of town development grants for industry, shopping centres and other social requirements as well as the extension of water and sewerage services was added, to induce the receiving authorities to take large numbers of people.

Other burghs in the Clyde Valley suffered from the preoccupation given to Glasgow's overspill. Kirkintilloch, for example, agreed to house between 1,000 and 2,000 families but their reservations clearly indicated that the process was viewed with disquiet. The sewage works and water supplies were already overburdened, a situation common to nearly all the potential receiving authorities. A good housing mix was needed, including houses at higher rents and private development. The town council insisted it should have some say in the type of tenants to be received, who would be mixed with existing tenants to encourage their integration in the community. Finally, while Kirkintilloch was resigned to remain a dormitory area for

Glasgow it reserved the right to attract new light industry. Milngavie offered to build 400 houses, but with the same reservations. Hamilton, struggling with its own housing problems, reluctantly agreed to build 1,090 houses on condition that a private development and burgh extension were approved. Ratepayers were safeguarded by their councils, for without exception it was insisted that no additional rate burden should be imposed.

The first overspill agreements were signed before March 1959 by Haddington, Kirkintilloch, Grangemouth, Hamilton, Johnstone and Irvine, and forty more authorities had indicated their interest in accommodating Glasgow families. The target was for 3,000 families to leave the city for the reception areas each year, but only 2,000 did so and only half this number had been living in acutely overcrowded conditions. New towns, with houses and jobs waiting, took the majority of the overspill population (Fig 11.2). Of the rest, those areas within commuting distance of Glasgow received the majority of families. A further 3,500 families left Glasgow each year of their own accord.

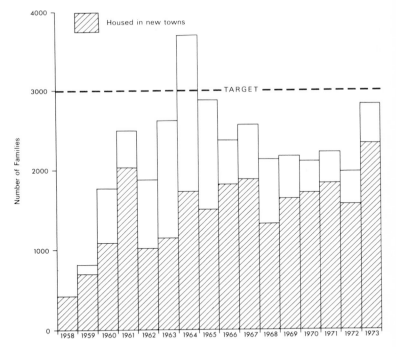

Fig. 11.2 Glasgow's overspill. Numbers of families re-housed in reception areas. Note the heavy reliance on new towns. (Source: *Housing Return for Scotland*, HMSO 1966, 1974.)

Why has overspill not been more successful? Basically because Glasgow's industries did not migrate, they died, and many of the reception areas were themselves in poor economic health. The overspill programme can only be a short-term palliative for, while crude densities may be reduced, the old, the unskilled and the underprivileged are left behind. Clearly, Glasgow must not allow herself to become the urban equivalent of a crofting parish.

Comprehensive Redevelopment

In 1948 nearly 20 per cent of the population of Scotland was housed within a 7.7 sq. km area of central Glasgow. The Corporation had halted slum clearance to maintain the number of houses in the city, and the only tenements that came down were those that fell down. During the emergency of the post-war years the Corporation regarded as habitable those properties that, just before the war, it had been anxious to condemn as obsolete, over-used, inadequate, and ill-maintained. In a housing stock of 285,000 houses, the single-end and room-and-end dominated. By 1948 a policy emerged involving demolition of whole districts; Garngad, Gorbals, Govan, Hutchesontown, Roystonhill and Townhead were considered suitable for comprehensive redevelopment (Table 8).

Table 8. The structure of Glasgow's housing 1948.

House size	Number	Per cent
One apartment	34,937	12.2
Two apartments	110,276	38.6
Three apartments	79,273	27.7
Four apartments	38,329	13.4
Five apartments and over	23,062	8.1
	285,877	100.0

Glasgow Corporation embarked in the 1950s on a massive urban renewal programme which was intended to result in the wholesale reconstruction of twenty-nine Comprehensive Development Areas. The Gorbals, with all its myth and misery, was to be a prestigious example of what could be achieved. Each scheme, however, involved a massive displacement of population and less than half could be rehoused in the area after redevelopment. Not only people were displaced. Many industries sited in or near the city centre felt their existence threatened: 'In the majority of congested areas it is impossible to carry out essential redevelopment without physically disturbing firms ... such firms cannot all be resettled in Glasgow and a proportion will have to secure accommodation outside the city in areas where the overspill families will themselves be housed'.[6] In fact this did not happen, for in the period 1958-68 most firms disturbed by comprehensive redevelopment were relocated within the city boundary and there was little industrial overspill.[7] Many of the older industries simply vanished from the scene.

Between 1955 and 1972 some 268,000 dwellings were demolished in the process of slum clearance. It might be assumed that at this rate little sub-standard property would be left standing. Unfortunately the 1971 census revealed that intolerable conditions still abound in Scotland's central urban areas; and Glasgow is in the grip of a 'cycle of deprivation' from which the city has been unable to escape. For almost all the criteria of deprivation, Glasgow compares badly even with other British cities which are in themselves far from ideal (Table 9).[8] Of the 21 factors isolated, Glasgow ranks first in 14 categories and fills second place in the rest with only one exception, the number of inhabitants over the age of 64. Glasgow is very clearly revealed as a deprived city in the realm of housing. Despite continuous house building and a drop in the city's population of 8 per cent in 5 years, the numbers of Glaswegians living in overcrowded houses leaped in a decade from 187,890 to 226,902. Only 4 of the 37 municipal wards had under 10 per cent of the population living in overcrowded conditions, but in 5 wards the figure was over 40 per cent. It is especially perturbing that relatively new housing estates, such as Easterhouse, appear in the statistics for overcrowding. Low-quality housing is also reflected in the poor health standards of Glaswegians. High unemployment has led to a massive migration from the conurbation, which in turn has produced an imbalance in the age structure of the population, with a relatively high percentage of retired persons.[9]

One of the most significant features apparent in the 1971 census returns is that many of the Corporation's housing estates exhibit the highest levels of multiple deprivation. A report by the community minister of Easterhouse states unequivocably, 'in matters of disadvantage, Scotland is always worse than England, Glasgow is always worse than the rest of Scotland, and Easterhouse, Barlanark and Garthamlock are among the worst-hit areas of Glasgow'.[10] In listing their priorities, the inhabitants of these districts put first, 'wanting out', and particularly 'wanting out of Easterhouse'. Of 42.9 per cent of the 14,078 householders in Easterhouse, Barlanark and Garthamlock who expressed this view in 1972, 34.4 per cent were in Easterhouse. In the case of particularly bad streets or areas the dissatisfaction rose to 90 per cent.

Clearly government is well aware of the situation and has taken the initiative in implementing programmes at various levels.[11] Individual deprivation has been ameliorated by programmes in which subsidies and social work have been the main tools. Urban aid programmes have assisted in alleviating special problems particularly in the older inner city zones, for example grants have been made to enable nursery schools and youth and community centres to be

Table 9. Comparative statistics of urban conditions in Scottish and selected English cities

	Glasgow	Aberdeen	Dundee	Edinburgh	Birmingham	Liverpool	Manchester	Scotland	Great Britain
Population									
Population 1961 (enumerated)	1,055,017	185,390	182,978	468,361	1,110,683	745,750	661,791	5,179,344	51,283,892
1971 (enumerated pop)	896,958	182,006	182,084	453,422	1,013,366	606,834	541,468	5,227,422	53,821,364
Net change 1961-71	− 158,059	− 3,384	− 894	− 14,939	− 97,317	− 138,916	− 120,323	+ 48,362	+ 2,537,472
% change p.a. 1961-71	− 1.5	− 0.2	− 0.1	− 0.3	− 0.91	− 2.04	− 1.99	+ 0.1	+ 0.5
Age Structure									
% under 15 (1970) (a)	27.5	23.4	26.6	23.8	23.7	24.4	23.4	26.2	22
% 15-64 (1970) (b)	59.4	63.0	61.0	62.1	64.5	62.7	63.7	61.7	65
% over 64 (1970) (c)	13.1	13.5	12.5	14.1	11.9	12.9	12.9	12.1	13
Dependancy ratio 1970*	683	586	641	610	552	563	570	621	538
Housing Conditions									
% of population at over 1.5 persons per room	11.8	4.0	5.2	4.9	5.6	5.3	4.5	5.4	1.6
% of households of: 1-3 rooms	45.9	36.4	37.6	33.1	12.0	10.6	9.9	27.9	11.8
Over 7 rooms	1.9	4.9	4.1	6.3	3.5	6.2	4.2	3.0	4.8
% of households lacking hot water tap	23.8	15.1	22.5	10.5	17.5	20.2	13.0	12.4	12.5
% Lacking bath	32.7	31.3	32.4	20.2	18.6	25.6	19.5	20.0	15.4
% Lacking exclusive use of WC	17.8	30.8	17.9	6.2	11.1	7.7	6.9	11.2	8.1
% of multi-dwelling buildings**	88.7	59.4	66.9	70.4	11.0	13.8	10.0	51.7	14.4
% of owner-occupied dwellings	20.1	29.4	18.7	47.3	39.9	29.8	34.2	28.2	46.7
Morbidity etc.									
Deaths per 1,000 population all causes (1969)	13.3	12.5	12.3	12.9	11.6	12.3	12.7	12.3	11.9
Tuberculosis	0.09	0.02	0.01	0.02	0.03	0.03	0.04	0.03	0.04
Bronchitis	0.84	0.50	0.55	0.56	0.74	0.69	1.20	0.56	0.68
Live Births per 1,000 population	18.8	14.1	16.9	14.8	17.5	16.6	16.8	17.4	16.4
Infant mortality per 1,000 live births	27	17	20	22	21	20	29	21	18
Economic Grouping									
% males professionals, managers and employers	8.7	14.0	11.1	17.3	10.2	9.3	10.7	13.2	15.1
% males intermediate and junior non-manual and semi-and unskilled manual workers	48.0	46.7	46.8	45.0	44.2	52.1	46.7	45.7	43.3
Unemployment June 1971	6.5	3.2	6.7	5.6	3.3	5.5	3.1	5.6	3.2
	(Glasgow City)	(Aberdeen Inverurie and Stonehaven)	(Dundee City)	(Edinburgh and Lothians)					

* Dependancy ratio: the number of persons under 15 (a) and those over 64 (c) per 1,000 persons aged 15-64 (b).

added to schools. Lately the Government has pioneered an environmental approach in areas which feel neglected and isolated. Inter-war council housing estates are being renovated in the hope that the spruced-up houses and surroundings will give the tenants a renewed sense of community.

Yet the scale of central government initiative has reached such a level that one questions whether there is any need for local government at all. Tweedbank, Stonehouse and the East End of Glasgow have been the result of decisions made in the Scottish Office. The last of these decisions reveals the Secretary of State displaying scant respect for the capacity of Strathclyde or Glasgow to rescue themselves from a largely self-inflicted urban decay. 'Physically shocking', 'like going through a bombarded city' and 'dreadful' were some of the comments made by delegates from the European Parliament at the sight of the East End of Glasgow in 1976.[12] They were observing 1,400 hectares of wasteland which had formerly contained much of Clydeside's heavy industry, an area which stretches from the East End to Shettleston and Dalmarnock. As recently as 1961, 140,000 people lived there, now only 55,000 are left. The scale of the problem is so great that central government has taken over the responsibility for its regeneration. The East End Project or GEAR (Glasgow Eastern Areas Renewal) has a budget of £120 million, a target of eight years to bring about the transformation and a radical new organization to by-pass the older authorities. The Scottish Development Agency, founded in 1975 with an environmental and job creating remit, was given overall responsibility for rejuvenation of the East End. The SSHA is to provide most of the houses to fit the plans drawn up by the planning team of the defunct Stonehouse. The local authority's contribution is largely restricted to Strathclyde's provision of infrastructural services. Glasgow District hopes to reap the benefit. It is a daunting challenge for the area is suffering from *planning dementia*, a species of planning blight, a condition which is the result of earlier notions of planning which themselves have created more problems than they have solved and thus demand even greater efforts by planners to solve the problems. . . . Already people closely involved predict failure for the project for it resembles too closely the 'single-solution' planning philosophy of the past.

Planned society has done much to lift people out of appalling housing conditions, but there are obviously still many lessons to learn. Short cuts like large peripheral estates or tower blocks have not yielded the same return as the carefully planned and nurtured new towns. The question could be posed as to whether local authorities or central government should take responsibility for the situation. It may be that the time is coming when the planning and building of houses should be done by a central authority and only the management delegated to district level. As it is, over the last forty years central government has become increasingly involved in economic and physical planning and the provision of houses has become central to its plans.

Central Government Housing

Central Government did its utmost to avoid direct responsibility for housing but inevitably it drifted into the business. The exigencies of war led to the founding in 1914 of the Scottish National Housing Company and to the creation of Rosyth (see Chapter 10 for the details of this development). In 1926, when the construction of local authority houses was flagging, the Second National Housing Company was formed to construct 2,500 so-called steel houses, mainly in the Glasgow area (these houses were wood-framed with a thin steel plate as an outer covering).[13]

Owing to severe unemployment, large areas of industrial Scotland were scheduled under the Special Areas (Development and Improvement) Act 1934. 'Since taking office as Secretary of State for Scotland', wrote Walter Elliot in a memorandum to the Cabinet in January 1937, 'I have been deeply impressed by the deplorable condition of Scottish housing but also by the recent falling off in the rate of housing progress.'[14] It was decided that Scotland should be treated as one unit in the matter of housing. Nothing more insensitive could have been proposed to local authorities, yet it was achieved with their co-operation. A Third National Housing Company was proposed which would draw on the experience of the First and Second National Housing Companies. Finally, in May 1937 the Minister of Health suggested that the Commission of Special Areas should set up a housing association.

The Scottish Special Areas Housing Association (SSHA — Areas was dropped from the title in 1939) was modelled upon the North Eastern Housing Association which was building houses around Tyneside and Durham, but unlike its counterpart, the Association was subject to restrictions which led it into novel fields of house construction. At a time of chronic unemployment it is ironic that Scotland suffered from a severe shortage of building workers, especially bricklayers. In order not to lure these men from employment with local authorities, the Association was confined to non-traditional methods and materials such as poured concrete and timber. The local authorities were suspicious of both the political implications and the technical soundness of this new body, but prejudice was overcome and by 1938 5,000 houses were under construction by these methods in nine burghs and six counties in the Special Areas. Experience gained in Amsterdam and the Hague in the use of foamed slag was also incorporated into the Scottish programme. Demonstration timber houses were built by the Swedish Government in Carntyne in Glasgow and the Association erected two at Carfin near Motherwell which were inspected by King George VI during his tour of the Scottish Special Areas in May 1938. Throughout that year the timber house controversy raged and brought out some of the contradictory attitudes held at the time:

> Mr Maxton: As the people of Scotland could be housed in good solid granite and sandstone 100 years ago, will the right hon. Gentleman see to it that he does not descend to this inferior substitute now?
> Mr. Colville: I understood that the hon. Member's colleague a few moments ago wanted me to investigate every method which would help the housing conditions in Glasgow.
> Mr. Maxton: I hope that the right hon. Gentleman will not understand that he is expected to start jerry building.[15]

As early as 1938 the original terms of reference of the Association were found wanting. As new industry was directed to places outside the Special Areas, such as a torpedo factory to Alexandria and aircraft manufacture to a new industrial estate at Hillington, it was clear that houses would have to be built in anticipation of need. With the coming of war, the old problems of the Special Areas were temporarily forgotten. In the immediate post-war years non-traditional housing was again examined, justified now by a shortage of construction materials and the need for speed. Timber was in short supply and in any case cost precious foreign currency, so the timber house was abandoned.* Government explored methods of using more concrete and speeding up building by mass production. In order to monitor the quality of the new materials, a branch of the Building Research Station was established at East Kilbride. Apart from this innovative role, the SSHA also built traditional houses; between 1945 and October 1975, a total of 84,352 houses were built in its name. This is no mean achievement when set against the 46,035 houses built in Scottish new towns over the same period.[16]

In its first thirty years the Association built 45,000 houses for local authorities under the General Needs programme. Its role began to change in the 1950s when high standard housing was seen as a key feature in attracting new industry. Under the Economic Expansion programme, a further 24,000 new houses were built for essential workers, such as at the Corpach paper mills near Fort William, Rootes (later Chrysler) car factory at Linwood, and in South Queensferry for people moving from Bedford with their factory.

The responsibility for much of the housing for North Sea oil workers will fall on the Association's shoulders. Houses are being built at Dingwall (200), Evanton (70), Milton of Kildary (180)

*After some 2,500 dwellings were erected in various parts of the country.

and Tain (100). In Shetland the Association is building nearly 300 homes, using prefabricated Norwegian timber buildings. Work has recently begun on 1,000 homes at Tweedbank to house the population for expanding Border industry. The need for housing for Glasgow overspill has led to the building of 5,000 houses at Erskine, one of the largest projects undertaken by the Association. All this activity is financed by the Scottish Development Department. A map of its present and future development shows that the SSHA is going to be fully engaged in eastern Scotland, and that the old problem areas are being left to the local authorities (Fig. 11.3).

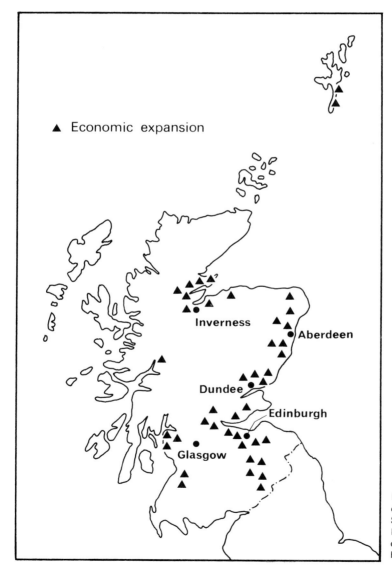

▲ Economic expansion

Inverness

Aberdeen

Dundee

Edinburgh

Glasgow

Fig. 11.3 The east coast expansion of the Scottish Special Housing Association's current and future housing strategy

At this crucial moment in Scotland's economic development it is important that a national housing strategy is maintained, for in their parochial structure the new districts are ill-equipped for this important task.

Economic Change and Urban Development

Today's urban developments can be traced from the massive economic transition of the last two decades, and under the impact of oil the pace of change is accelerating. The death throes of the old Scots economy made many headlines during the 1950s and '60s — geological exhaustion closed the pits, shipyards on the Upper Clyde became vacant sites, foundry after foundry ceased production, proud locomotive works built their last steam engine, the shale oil industry died without a requiem, famous names in Edinburgh's printing industry vanished into oblivion after business mergers, and the aroma of Kirkcaldy's linoleum became a nostalgic memory.

The awful lesson of the depression had shown the vulnerability of Scotland's industrial base: iron and steel, heavy engineering and textiles were the products of the age of steam. Recognition of this obsolescence had come when the Special Areas Act of 1934 led to the setting up of publicly sponsored industrial estates, including Hillington just outside Glasgow, but progress was very slow (Fig. 11.4). In July 1937 the Government resorted to a Royal Commission

> To inquire into the causes which have influenced the present geographical distribution of the industrial population of Great Britain and the probable direction of any change in that distribution in the future; to consider what social, economic or strategical disadvantages arise from the concentration of industries or of the industrial population in large towns or in particular areas of the country; and to report what remedial measures if any should be taken in the national interest.

The outcome was the Barlow Report, a landmark in regional thinking published in 1940, which recommended the redevelopment of congested urban areas by the dispersal of industries and industrial population to other parts of the country. Throughout the report was the explicit acceptance of government control and direction of private industry as a means of securing a balanced pattern of regional growth. War came and revived the heavy industries, but the inevitable decline was merely postponed. In February 1942 Tom Johnston, mindful of the need for Scotland to have a proper share of industry, set up the Scottish Council on Industry. An independent and highly authoritative body, its general purpose was

237

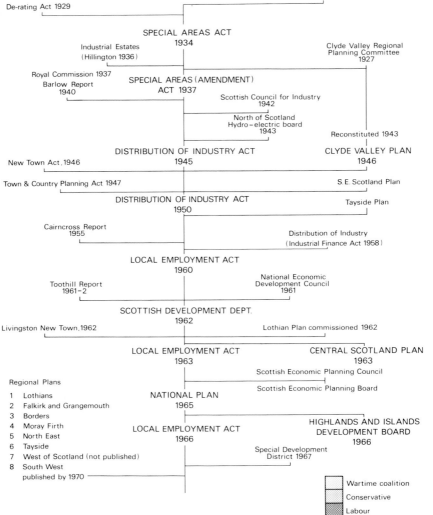

Fig. 11.4 The evoluti█
of government inter-
vention in Scotland's
economy

and still is to safeguard, stimulate and assist Scottish industrial development.

As war ended it was clearly recognized that the problems of the depressed areas could not be overcome without coordinated control over development of prosperous areas like south-east England. The Distribution of Industry Act 1945 was passed designating Development Areas (largely the old Special Areas) which were to receive preferential treatment. Economic development and town and country planning were integrated through the introduction of the Industrial Development Certificate. Similarly the New Towns Act 1946 not only provided overspill housing but, as at East Kilbride, became a focus for new industrial growth. The good intentions of these early post-war years became a casualty of the economic crisis in the autumn of 1947 and did not recover until 1950 with the passing of the second Distribution of Industry Act. The success of the Conservatives at the general election of 1951 introduced a new era of total indifference to regional economic planning.

Throughout the 1950s Scottish development programmes were run down in response to government policy of restricting public investment: housing, roads, power stations, schools and hospitals were included in the cuts. Relief, when given, was usually in the form of an isolated project in an unemployment blackspot. Government saw the malady but merely tinkered with it. Fatally, Motherwell received only half a steel mill, the other half going to South Wales, a decision which could be justified for only the shortest-sighted political reasons. The motor industry was coerced into building factories at Bathgate and Linwood. A paper mill was established at Fort William to use the highland forests, but local roads were so bad that it was cheaper to import pulp from Canada. Government economic policy came under fire and criticism culminated in the *Report on Local Development in Scotland* (the Cairncross Report). Its findings were in direct contradiction to government policy, which concentrated financial assistance in Development Areas (i.e. old industrial areas with high unemployment), right up to the Local Employment Act 1960. For example, the only agency which built factories to let was the government-financed Scottish Industrial Estates Ltd and it could build only in Development Areas. This policy, made within the framework of the Distribution of Industry Act 1945, was warping the economy of Scotland by forcing new industry into old, run-down urban areas and starving more promising areas of economic development. Professor A.K. Cairncross advocated that the whole of Scotland should be treated as a Development Area.[17] He saw clearly that long-term growth would only come from the use of optimum locations or 'growing points' and not from attempting to rescue nineteenth-century obsolescence. Government failed completely to grasp the implications of Cairncross's arguments and decisively rejected the Report, asserting that Scotland's industrial well-being depended on 'her great basic industries' and that the amount of assistance the Government could give was 'really marginal'.[18] The almost total collapse of these very industries led to a complete reversal of government policy a few years later.

The bankruptcy of policy and the inadequacy of local government structures led the Conservative Party to adopt a planning philosophy. Like many late converts, the Party was more radical in its new position than older adherents to planning ideals. The Toothill Report, commissioned in 1961 by a Conservative Secretary of State and published a year later, recommended that there should be a concentrated programme of public investment in the infrastructure — housing, water supplies, energy production and communications — to attract modern industry. In the same year the Government created the National Economic Development Council which propounded a policy for regional growth incorporating a large social content. The Government set up a programme of regional studies concentrating upon the north of England and Scotland. So by 1962 Scotland was well prepared for planning growth: Toothill had been published, the Lothian Plan had been started, Livingston had just been accepted as a new town, and most important of all, the Scottish Development Department (SDD) had been founded. Up to this time there had been no Scottish economic planning machinery and each decision had been made on a pragmatic basis, often in response to economic conditions in southern England. At best, from the time of the Town and Country Planning Act 1947 the Secretary of State had regarded himself as an arbiter between various vested interests, and it was the weaknesses of these interests that ultimately forced him to adopt a more active role. The local authorities lacked the skills and drive to tackle problems within their own province. The problems, such as Glasgow's overspill, spread over local boundaries and the record of co-operation between authorities was very poor. In 1962 the Scottish Development Department was given twelve months to produce the Central Scotland Plan, at the same time the Scottish Development Group was set up to encourage participation by authorities such as the Ministry of Power and the Board of Trade, so that unity of purpose would replace destructive competition.

In November 1963, with the publication of the White Paper, *Central Scotland: A Programme for Development and Growth*, areas of growth rather than areas in decline were officially recognized as profitable fields for government financial aid (Fig. 11.5). There were several different types of growth areas. The new towns, with a proved record and plenty of reserve capacity to expand, were a natural choice; already they were building houses for all income groups, and they were encouraged to prepare industrial sites, which were not allowed elsewhere at that time. Irvine and Grangemouth were identified as areas where suitable sites for housing and industry could be obtained. Lastly, areas of old industrialization in north Lanarkshire and central Fife were identified, for they had some industrial potential though with little prospect of any large-scale housing. The new towns (including Irvine and Stonehouse which post-date the plan) thus gave a nucleus to six of the eight growth areas, the others being the Vale of Leven and Falkirk/Grangemouth. In the Vale of Leven little has been attempted, but Falkirk/Grangemouth has developed into the fulcrum for Scotland's economic future. The importance of the success of this plan cannot

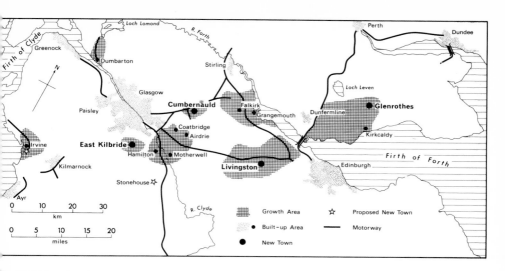

be overstressed, for its implementation in the second half of the 1960s rescued government from the grave consequences of the collapse of the older industries.

The Central Scotland Plan was a novel document at the time of publication. Skilfully drafted and with no unnecessary detail, the overall sweep of the plan ignored local authority boundaries, regional concepts and the three cities, giving it a simplicity that made it a powerful tool in public education.[19] The Plan had a favourable reception and gained quick government approval. Implementation, especially of the road programme, was also rapid. In this sphere the date of publication was fortunate, for the need for an expanded road programme was established by the acceptance of the motor car as the universal form of conveyance. Central Scotland was lucky in that the plans *seemed* to be ready. In fact, the roads appearing on the Central Scotland Plan had little justification in a United Kingdom context for the *pro rata* expenditure on Scottish roads was much higher than in the south. Detailed studies to give the Plan more depth were commissioned; a study on Livingston was published in 1966, the same consultants were immediately commissioned to develop a plan for Falkirk/Grangemouth and two transport studies focusing on Glasgow and Edinburgh were commissioned to tie the whole together. Many of the objectives of the Central Scotland Plan have been achieved and it is a tribute to the foresight of the strategists of the early 1960s that the Central Belt will play a significant, perhaps even a crucial role in the oil economy of the future.[20]

With nearly thirty years' experience of planning controls, perhaps it is time for us to ask whether they have brought lasting benefit to urban dwellers. Fortunes have been made or lost when a change of land use has first been pinpointed on a development plan; individuals have found that rights of property are not sacrosanct; when objectors have been successful they have sometimes seen victory signed away by the Secretary of State; an urban ring road on a development map can create a swathe of planning blight. On the other hand, planning has saved us from the ugly uncontrolled urban sprawl, ribbon development and haphazard land use which scar the United States, West Germany and other countries.

The modern planning movement had it genesis in the garden city movement which was committed to the concept of the ideal town. This became an inherent weakness, as only development on a greenfield site could satisfy the criteria. Little thought was given to creating a worthwhile environment in existing towns except perhaps to consign their centres to comprehensive redevelopment. Dispersal of communities and the blighting effects of clearance were seen as minor evils when set against the benefits of improved housing standards. While only the run-down inner-city zones were involved in large-scale demolition, the policy continued unchecked; but when better-quality houses still occupied by the middle class came under attack, such as during Edinburgh's ring road controversy, reaction was immediate and voluble. It became obvious, too, that the gap-site, the hallmark of comprehensive development, produced long-term planning blight. Not even the bombs of World War II wrought as much damage as did the demolisher's hammer. Society at first did not question what was happening, because the utopian plans provided a glimpse of a new, happy world of gleaming concrete, glass and steel, rising high above citizen's heads. Disenchantment came with experience, for the new developments contributed little to the everyday life of the cities: urban motorways, new office blocks, an expanded university or college, new shopping centres and more parking sites left the centre dead at night. As more people pushed through congested streets during two short rush hours each day, the planners were confirmed in their belief that the old towns were uninhabitable. Their answer was to knock down even more houses to build ideal roads. The madness had to stop — but not before most major cities in Britain were demolishing houses faster than they could be replaced. Experience, too, began to accumulate from the new towns and peripheral housing estates. Human beings were far more fragile than had been suspected: when transplanted to open fields they wilted and succumbed to a new disease, 'new town blues'. Likewise, the demolition of the 'no mean city' reputation of the Gorbals saw the transfer of the image to a new generation in estates such as Easterhouse. Molly Weir's account of life in Glasgow's slums between the wars shows less social stress than is found in many present-day council estates.[21] Recently, questions have been raised about the enormous cost of a policy of total clearance. When council houses, as in the Dumbiedykes scheme in Edinburgh, cost £15,000 per unit in 1970 (the average cost of a comparable private dwelling in that year was around £5,000), justification is hard to find. By 1975 the Government was driven, mainly as a result of the extravagance of several London boroughs, to stop comprehensive redevelopment, and local authorities were directed to undertake a thorough review of their policy for older dwellings.[22] The idea of growth for growth's sake has now been buried and society is faced with important decisions which will have a profound effect on Scotland's urban future.

Notes

1. The Town Planning Procedure Regulations (Scotland) 1911, made by the Local Government Board in accordance with the provisions of the 1909 Act, laid down the procedure to be adopted by local authorities in the process of preparation and submission of schemes.

2. Department of the Environment, *Land,* Cmnd. 5730 (HMSO, London, 1974), p. 1, quoting the *Official Report,* 29 April 1909, vol. IV, col. 532.

3. R. Miller, 'The New Face of Glasgow', *Scottish Geographical Magazine,* vol. 86, (1970), pp. 5-15.

4. Reports of the Clyde Valley Regional Advisory Committee (SRO DD12/94).

5. General reconstruction of Clyde Valley Regional Advisory Committee (SRO DD1 2/92).

6. Glasgow Corporation, *Industry on the move,* (1959).

7. R. A. Henderson, 'Industrial Overspill from Glasgow 1958-1968', *Urban Studies,* vol. I (1974), pp.61-79; G. C. Cameron and K. M. Johnson, 'Comprehensive Urban Renewal and Industrial Location — the Glasgow Case', in J. B. Cullingworth and S. Orr (eds.), *Regional and Urban Studies* (Allen and Unwin, London, 1969).

8. Scottish Development Department, *Summary Report of An Investigation to Identify Areas of Multiple Deprivation in Glasgow City* (CPRU Working Paper No. 7, March 1973).

9. Glasgow Corporation, *Areas of Need in Glasgow: Development Plan Review* (Planning Department, June 1972).

10. Revd R. Ferguson, *Community Action: A Working Handbook for Groups in Easterhouse, Barlanark and Garthamlock* (January 1975), p. 7.

11. *Council House Communities — a Policy for Progress.* Report of the Sub-Committee on Amenity and Social Character of Local Authority Housing Schemes, 1970.

12. *The Scotsman,* 22 September 1976.

13. Second Scottish National Housing Co., 1925 (SRO DD6/243).

14. Papers relating to the establishment of the SSHA (SRO DD6/1131).

15. *Official Report,* 28 June 1938, vol. 337, no. 136, col. 1679.

16. Scottish Development Department, *Housing Return for Scotland 30 September 1974* (HMSO, Edinburgh, 1974), table 1.

17. A. K. Cairncross, *The Scottish Economy* (Department of Social and Economic Research, Glasgow, 1954).

18. *The Scotsman,* 5 August 1953 and the *Official Report,* 9 February 1954, col. 974.

19. Scottish Development Department, *Central Scotland: A Programme for Development and Growth,* Cmnd. 2188 (HMSO, Edinburgh, November 1963).

20. C. J. Robertson, 'New Industries and New Towns in Scotland's Industrial Growth', *Scottish Geographical Magazine,* vol. 80, (1964), pp. 114-23.

21. M. Weir, *Shoes Were for Sunday* (Hutchinson, London, 1970) and her sequel *Best Foot Forward* (Hutchinson, London, 1972).

243

22. Department of the Environment, *Housing Act 1974: Renewal Strategies*, Circular 13/75, January 1975.

The independence of 201 burghs ended with the implementation of the Local Government Act on 16 May 1975, and with it the heritage of centuries. Half these burghs were in existence when James VI went south to London to take up the unified crown and the future site of Jamestown, the first permanent English settlement on the other side of the Atlantic, was still a swampy meadow. Scottish burghs were flourishing then, and even today in an age of 'bigness' the burghs show great powers of survival. About 20 per cent of Scotland's population live in small burghs. Amid the national preoccupation with urban problems and their legislative solutions the vitality of these small communities has often been forgotten.[1]

In recent years those small burghs which lie in a rural rather than an industrial milieu have, at best, been stagnating, while government policy has been virtually to ignore these small towns. In the Town and Country Planning and the Distribution of Industry Acts, legislation was almost entirely urban and approached problems from the viewpoint of the industrial rather than the rural town. Basically both Acts assumed that urban areas must continue to grow but that their growth should be better planned. Small burghs have rarely faced problems of congestion or extensive obsolescence of domestic or industrial fabric, for these burghs are essentially part of the countryside and provide limited services for those who live and work there. This is especially true, as we shall see, of the small burghs in the two areas north and south of the Central Belt. Their schools and colleges give an excellent education; their shops often stock a range of goods more imposing than the facades imply; doctors, dentists and solicitors practice within their bounds.[2]

The survival of the small burghs has depended on agricultural prosperity and this has often proved too uncertain to sustain even a static population. The drift from small burghs in post-war years has been largely due to the failure of their narrow economic base to give opportunity to their young people. Eventually the European experience was followed and small-scale factories set up in country towns.

Size alone does not give an accurate picture of the vitality and nature of the burghs; it would be strange if it did, since burghs occur in a wide range of geographical situations and differ much in resources and functions. The small isolated burghs of the Islands contrast markedly with the industrial towns of the Central Belt; the textile towns of the Borders are quite different from the country towns of Galloway. Of all the distinctions that exist between burghs in Scotland, the most significant is that between the burghs lying within and without the Industrial Lowlands. Those that lie within the Lowlands benefit from the presence of the three cities, coal-fields, and the main concentration of industry, and are served by a dense network of communications. The focus of activity of the burghs outside this zone is the land. The 1961 census revealed that 65 of the 92 burghs in the Industrial Lowlands had increasing populations, while in the outlying areas 63 of the 101 burghs recorded a decrease. This difference is also reflected in the absolute size of burgh populations in the two contrasting areas. Today 25 burghs in the Industrial Lowlands exceed 20,000, whereas only three in the outlying areas — Dumfries, Inverness, Perth — exceed this modest figure.

Before 1961, burghs in the outlying areas suffered from a high rate of emigration, a discouraging situation in view of all the money that had been invested in agriculture, forestry, fishing and hydroelectric development since World War II. The situation during the decade 1961-71 showed a marked improvement and a new prosperity is encouraging people to stay in their small towns. Where single large industries have been established, as at Fort William, Invergordon and Thurso, new life has been injected; oil is having the same effect on east coast burghs as far north as Lerwick.

How does one measure the success or failure of a burgh? Absolute increase or decrease of population may be taken as a rough index, but even an increase may conceal a potentially difficult situation. One measure, and in many ways the most important, is whether the burgh can retain its young folk after they have left school — a 2.2 per cent natural increase of the general population means a living community which is giving a home to its young people.

After a long period of decline the Border burghs are displaying renewed confidence. Although recent population figures show a slight drop in Hawick, Melrose and Selkirk, the remaining towns prosper (Table 10). At the same time the landward areas continue to lose population. In essence, both these developments reflect healthy economic trends, although not without side effects. The increasing productivity of the Border farms has brought a decline of the labour force which in many ways puts the survival of the rural community in jeopardy. On the other hand, Border towns suffer from a chronic shortage of labour which could not be relieved without a substantial increase in the number of houses. These problems were apparent in 1966 when the Central Borders Plan was commissioned. The publication of this project brought out all the inbred tensions of the region.[3] Newtown St Boswells was identified as the area with the greatest long-term potential growth and recommended for major expansion, a recommendation which united all the oppostion. Yet it had centrality and ample land for industry and housing, and lay astride the main road bisecting the region. The grandiose concept died but the obvious advantages of

Table 10. Border burghs. Demographic trends 1951-71 showing a revival of towns in the decade 1961-71 and the Registrar General's estimate for 1974.

| Town | Population | | | Percentage increase/decrease per annum | |
	1961	1971	1974	1951-61	1961-71
Hawick	16,342	16,499	16,378	- 0.31	+ 0.05
Galashiels	12,393	12,551	12,788	- 0.10	+ 0.19
Peebles	5,505	5,934	6,064	- 0.80	+ 0.59
Selkirk	5,697	5,753	5,628	- 0.34	+ 0.11
Kelso	4,069	4,915	4,957	- 0.37	+ 2.03
Jedburgh	3,726	3,910	3,917	- 1.12	+ 0.61
Eyemouth	2,188	2,573	2,797	- 0.48	+ 1.59
Innerleithen	2,319	2,230	2,304	- 0.26	- 0.36
Melrose	2,119	2,235	2,181	- 0.06	+ 0.24
Duns	1,964	1,811	1,902	- 0.98	- 0.38
Coldstream	1,245	1,315	1,429	- 0.54	+ 0.42
Lauder	630	622	637	- 0.42	

St Boswells led to its selection as the regional administrative centre.

Galashiels, already the second town by size in the Borders, is on the point of considerable growth through government intervention, though the site is geographically restricted and development sites are scarce. Two large new housing schemes, Langlees and Tweedbank, have been built by the Scottish Special Housing Association, but these have created a linear settlement which extends 5 or 6 km from the centre of the town, thus depriving their inhabitants of easy access to services.[4]

Kelso and Galashiels have similar population structures, with a noticeable lack of younger workers (Fig. 12.1). Until recently the lack of jobs and houses forced many young people to seek a livelihood elsewhere. Recently Kelso has begun to grow again, due mainly to the diversification of industry on a very successful industrial estate. It is a pleasant town with space for expansion and evident potential for attracting industry, but its population is still too small to justify the establishment of higher order retail services. Kelso clearly illustrates two basic, related handicaps of the Borders region: the population is modest in number and the burgh is so near others that their potential spheres of influence overlap.

The weakness of urban links in the Borders is well illustrated by an examination of the only public transport in the region, the bus system. Borders bus services are characterized by a strong orientation towards Edinburgh, reflecting the dependence of the region on the city for many business, social, educational, shopping, enter-

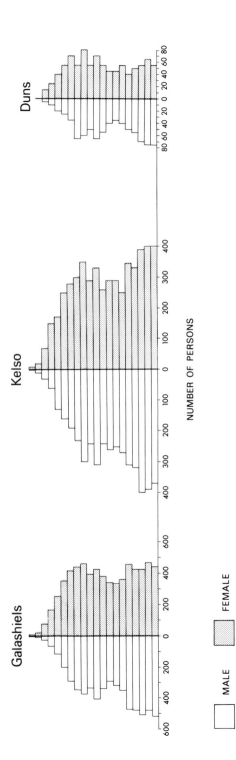

Fig. 12.1 Population pyramids of Galashiels, Kelso and Duns showing a demographic imbalance reflecting heavy migration from the burghs of the economically active age groups. (After Macgregor 1974.)

tainment and long-distance transport facilities. There are only three direct buses daily from Kelso to Galashiels, the main shopping centre within the region; there is none from Hawick to Newtown St Boswells, the new regional authority centre, nor to Duns, the former administrative centre of Berwickshire, nor to Berwick-upon-Tweed, the railhead for the region on the Edinburgh to London line. Indeed, Edinburgh has a greater number of bus links with Border towns than any town within the region itself, with Galashiels following a fairly close second and Hawick a poor third.

Decline was registered between 1961 and 1971 in three Border towns. A mill closure in Innerleithen dealt a fatal blow to this essentially industrial town. Duns relied principally on its role as the administrative centre of Berwickshire to maintain its viability, but even this function did not stem a slow decline which could turn into a torrent with the emergence of the new Borders Region. Finally, the royal burgh of Lauder, the smallest town in the Borders, has shown a decrease in population at every census this century except 1921, but new houses and an extended primary school have now reversed this trend.

The long-term future for the Borders is somewhat gloomy. A recent report on the region summarized the relative remoteness of the area and its towns from the mainstream of modern life: 'The region has no airports, ports, motorways, dual carriageways or railway stations; no university, polytechnic or government training centre, no major defence establishments; not even a prison.'[5] Above all, the report suggests, the region's 98,000 people and their problems are overlooked because they are not crammed into the centre of a big city. There has been a tendency

> . . . to notice the problems of inner cities because of the sheer numbers of people involved, the mass movements of vehicles and people, and the concentration of poor housing and social problems . . . In comparison, the dispersed nature of many of the problems in the Borders and the relatively small numbers of people affected, make them less noticeable.

In many ways Galloway is the forgotten corner of Scotland. Agriculture prospers in the neat countryside with its whitewashed farmhouses, large forests clothe the marginal areas and no single distinctive problem manifests itself. Yet the population declines. Dumfriesshire, Wigtownshire and the Stewartry of Kirkcudbright all lost population in the decade 1961-71 and the burghs reflect this trend. Unlike the Borders with their intensity of burgh identity, Galloway's burghs have little influence over their surrounding region.

Dumfries derives its strength from a varied industrial base including food processing, chemicals, iron founding and rubber manufacture, and all the evidence points to a prosperous future. Annan too possesses good growth potential. Lockerbie is one of the few small burghs in the south-west whose economy is sufficiently diversified to thrive.[6] In the last decade there has been a shift in dependence from agricultural processing to more general light industries and services for the traffic on the main road from England. The by-pass has brought relief from thundering congestion and the town prospers as a small regional centre. Further north Moffat, isolated among the Tweedsmuir Hills, has lost much of its residential holiday business and prospers mainly as a tourist stopping place.

Peripheral burghs such as Sanquhar and Langholm continue to decline, and Lochmaben is static. The closure of Sanquhar's coal-mines and brickworks led to a decrease in population that has proved hard to stop in spite of advance factories at the edge of the town. Langholm, a small and fairly isolated settlement only 11 km from the English border, is a textile town and farming centre similar to Jedburgh and Selkirk in the eastern Borders; decline has persisted throughout this century and shows no sign of stopping.

In Wigtownshire only Stranraer has maintained population growth. In spite of its isolated position in the Rhinns of Galloway the port has prospered as a railway base and latterly as a roll-on/roll-off ferry terminal on the shortest sea route to Ireland. It is also the main agricultural centre for Wigtownshire and as such possesses a major Milk Marketing Board creamery. A new industrial estate to the south of the town has widened industrial opportunity. Two small burghs — Wigtown and Whithorn — continue their perceptible decline. Wigtown, the county town, is but a shadow of its former self, whose spacious square recalls its regional importance in the nineteenth century. Whithorn, although of great historical interest, is now no more than a small service settlement for the southern part of The Machars. Newton Stewart functions as a service centre for the farms in the Cree Valley, but suffers from too narrow an economic base and a resulting high rate of migration of young people.

The Stewartry is doing little better, for between 1961 and 1971 its five burghs — Castle Douglas, Dalbeattie, Gatehouse, Kirkcudbright and New Galloway — added less than five hundred to their combined populations. Castle Douglas is an important rural service town with, for its size, one of the finest selection of shops of any small burgh in Scotland. It has good hotels and an important cattle market as well as many professional services, yet there is little work for its young people. Dalbeattie is rather a plain working town, in no way comparable to Castle Douglas for amenities. It has lost both the railway and harbour which led to its growth a century ago, but has recently begun to prosper as a result of its granite quarry, a new factory and the considerable tourist potential of the area. Kirkcudbright, a spacious town with a useful range of shops, hotels, banks and other county town services, is also a town in which time has stood still and even the tourist industry is largely undeveloped. Gatehouse-of-Fleet and New Galloway are no more than large villages; indeed New Galloway, with a population of 344 in 1971, retained its position as Scotland's smallest burgh.

In the light of the evidence one is forced to conclude that Galloway contains a larger number of burghs than is consistent with today's economic and social conditions. With local government reform the smaller burghs lost their burgh identity and became no more than villages. Ageing populations will bring increased tranquillity to much of this region, interrupted only by the influx of summer visitors.

North of the industrial belt the burgh populations showed a uniform trend towards stagnation and decline up to 1961. The past decade has seen this consistency vanish under a welter of economic and geographic change. Government has taken over the responsibility for reviving the slumbering regions: the Highlands and Islands Development Board has made valiant efforts to retain population within its area. Planning reports have poured from consultants' pens and computers, mapping out new visions of an expanding society. The steering of industry by government carrot-and-stick created a new science of industrial location, but on the whole government action led to minimal change. Re-evaluation of resources has had a far bigger impact. Fishing became prosperous in response to the world-wide protein shortage, but over-fishing and the European Economic Community's fishing policy have created little confidence in the future of this industry. Oil has been found in the North Sea and deep water has become a valuable asset.

The small burghs along the rich farmlands south of the Highland line have not grown much during the past hundred years. Alyth, Brechin, Coupar Angus, Crieff, Inverbervie, Doune, Laurencekirk and Montrose recorded decreases in their population over the decade 1961-71, a process which for several of these towns had been going on since the turn of the century. Alyth is an ancient textile town which is in an advanced state of decay. It has an elderly population, its shops and local services are rather poor in contrast to Blairgowrie, only five miles away. Brechin and Coupar Angus are small agricultural service centres whose populations have been static throughout this century. The importance of Coupar Angus to the farms of southern Strathmore has been drastically reduced since road replaced rail in the movement of agricultural produce. Crieff no longer attracts either the wealthy or retired and in the future should be concerned with the attraction of small-scale industry rather than with the established hotel industry and boarding school. To the east of the region, Inverbervie is a small, exposed settlement on the coast which has had to face consistent loss of its young people, and Laurencekirk, an eighteenth-century planned village, has remained in effect a village; both seem doomed to decline.

The ancient town of Montrose, distinctive both for its architecture and its unusual location at the mouth of the South Esk River, illustrates that new oil service facilities do not necessarily quickly bring back lost population. The town suffered unemployment of nearly 7 per cent (fluctuating between 270-400 people) before the new development, which has provided only 50-100 jobs, and the population has declined since 1971.

Several small burghs have become centres of private residential building. Dunblane has grown at an enormous rate as a dormitory for industrial centres such as Grangemouth, Falkirk and Stirling. Similarly, Monifieth provides private housing so lacking in Dundee. Callander, a planned village that grew as a Victorian holiday centre, is another residential town of this type (Fig. 12.2). Kirriemuir, only 27 km from Dundee and 8 km from Forfar and with an elderly population, faced an uncertain future but is now reviving, with a population increase of nearly 700 in a decade. In Abernethy, another very small burgh which was declining until 1961, new houses have been built for commuters and it appears that its main role will be as a modest suburb of Perth.

The North-East is a prime example of how unexpected change can solve old problems and bring new ones in its wake. The area is characterized by a plethora of burghs and villages which serve a small farming and forestry community, while along the coast a number of small harbours serve the fishing industry and generate a little coastal traffic. When Professor Gaskin and his team from Aberdeen produced their *Report and Development Plan for North East Scotland* in 1969 there was no thought of an oil boom.[7] Standing head and shoulders above the region is Aberdeen, which has acted as a magnet for the population of the smaller centres. To a greater or lesser extent the city provides educational, medical, research, manufacturing and service facilities. Gaskin suggested that this pull will continue, though Elgin forms an important sub-centre with links to Inverness. Peterhead and Fraserburgh are sufficiently isolated to form important service centres in Buchan. There were various suggestions in the Development Plan for small local growth points, mainly to arrest decline rather than to boost population; the survey envisaged growth in engineering, in research which was already very well based in and around Aberdeen, and in provision for campers and caravanners. Five years after the Report, the main problem is that of accommodating the frantic growth caused by the oil boom. Pressure for housing in Aberdeen has extended far beyond the city bounds; Banchory, Ellon, Inverurie and Stonehaven are commuter towns for the oilmen. Banchory has a good climate and a beautiful situation, whose nearness to Aberdeen makes it an inevitable dormitory settlement. Ellon, too, is an attractive small town in which new private housing schemes are springing up to the south of the River Ythan. Inverurie presents a different picture, for the

closure of the railway workshops in 1970 caused economic depression although the longer-term effects were less than envisaged. Stonehaven was another town with an ageing population and no industry apart from declining tourism. All these towns are under pressure to provide houses for the Aberdeen oil workers.

Peterhead has become a classic boom town for good geographical reasons. It was erected a burgh of barony in 1587 and since then its fortunes have been wrested from the sea, becoming the second fishing port in Scotland in 1970 when the seine-net fleet moved there from Aberdeen as a result of pressure from oil developments. The Harbour of Refuge, which was started by Act of Parliament in 1886 and only completed in 1958, is one of the most valuable anchorages on the east coast and Peterhead, at the most easterly point of the Scottish mainland, has the shortest steaming time to the Forties field. Natural gas from the Frigg gas field will come ashore at St Fergus, a few kilometres north of Peterhead, where it will be purified before entering the national grid at an annual rate equivalent to 60 million tonnes of crude oil. Peterhead has become a major servicing centre for the North Sea industry and much permanent employment is being generated. Some of the other employment will be cyclical in nature; about 1,000 men are employed for five years in

253

the construction of the gas plant. It has been estimated that 3,000 jobs directly related to the oil industry and a further 2,580 indirectly will have been created by 1981. During the period 1971-6 about 1,500 jobs will be available in the construction industry, tailing off considerably towards the end of the decade.[8] In addition to this, but difficult to quantify, is the multiplier effect of work being created right through Peterhead's economy. Current estimates indicate that approximately 12,000 more people will be living in Buchan by 1981. Peterhead's transformation from a fishing centre to a key strategic centre for North Sea industry in five years will strain both community and urban fabric.[9]

Westwards along the Moray Firth beyond Banff, the small fishing burghs of Portsoy, Cullen, Portnockie, Findochty, Lossiemouth and Branderburgh, and Burghead were still declining during 1961-71. In contrast Buckie and Macduff have resisted population decline by maintaining their harbours, and have become the main operational fishing centres. The inland burghs of Aberlour, Ballater, Huntly, Dufftown, Forres, Grantown-on-Spey and Keith showed the same tendency to decline. In these areas much of the North East Report holds good, not only for the burghs but also for the landward areas. The situation for those outside direct contact with the oil boom is even more serious than a decade ago. Then, people drifted out of the region; now they are being pulled towards Aberdeen. The traditional occupations of farming and fishing depend on continuity which can no longer be guaranteed. Already half the region's population lives within 25 km of Aberdeen and one can only predict an intensification of this trend.

While the North East is an area of closely situated burghs, the Highlands and Islands region is the complete reverse. The few burghs, ranging in size from Inverness with 34,655 to Cromarty with only 514 inhabitants, tend to dominate their sparsely populated hinterlands. For their livelihood the population depends upon varying combinations of administration, agriculture, fishing, tourism and industry. Despite differences, the burghs have one thing in common: all are located within what is, both geographically and economically, the most marginal area in Britain. For decades most Highland burghs have survived as stepping stones to emigration, for their landward populations have been falling rapidly and in the period 1931-61 the proportion of total population living in burghs in this area grew from 22 to 30 per cent.

The Dornoch Firth area has so far been only marginally affected by oil developments. There has been some small increase in migration in search of oil-related jobs, and in commuter traffic to such jobs. The Jack Holmes Planning Group reported to the Highlands and Islands Development Board in 1968 that the Nairn to Tain growth area could accommodate a potential population of 250,000.[10] In 1972 the Ross and Cromarty Planning Officer proposed that, as part of that growth, a new town of 80,000 people be designated at Lamington, just south of Tain.

The University of Edinburgh's Dornoch Study, published in 1973, pinpoints some of the problems and possible development points. Of the 10,000 people in the Dornoch area, half live in the five main settlements — Tain, Golspie, Bonar/Ardgay, Lairg and Dornoch. Each of these villages is an important local service centre, though only Tain, a thriving small burgh with people coming many miles to shop, has any wider regional significance. The future of these villages and the associated smaller villages and hamlets, with their high proportion of elderly people, is bound up with future improvements of local facilities. With the exception of Tain and Lairg, steep slopes inland restrict suitable house building space so that any extensions to the villages must continue the present pattern of linear settlement. At Lairg suitable building land is available, and the survey suggests that this nodal point should concentrate on improving and increasing tourist facilities.

In the early 1950s Caithness stood out as the only Highland county with a growing population. One project alone, the atomic energy plan at Dounreay, made this possible. Houses were built at Thurso, and new secondary schools at Thurso and Halkirk. The incomers were highly skilled scientific workers who played an active part in the community. Thurso has been used to illustrate the success of the growth point philosophy, but can also show the vulnerability of prosperity based on a single project, especially one subject to the vagaries of the atomic energy industry. Wick has been affected by this development, though to a lesser extent; its functions as county town, shopping centre, fishing harbour and airport have all been boosted, and the successful rise of Caithness Glass broadened the town's industrial base.

Fort William had been a small service centre with an allied distilling industry, but the opening of an aluminium smelting plant in 1929 transformed it into an industrial town.[11] Large-scale afforestation in the Great Glen led to government backing for a pulp mill at Corpach; tourism, based on the motor car, has given a further boost to local incomes. Oban thrives as a holiday resort, with road and rail links southward and steamers to the Isles. Although all seems well, there are doubts about the future, for failure to widen the economic base has led to a loss of young people from the town.

The holiday resorts around the Clyde estuary face many problems. Populations have dwindled since World War II and at best these burghs will become holiday villages. The growth of Dunoon, for example, was based upon the Clyde steamer service which provided a fast regular passage for middle-class commuters to Glasgow. Their substantial villas were converted during the 1930s into boarding houses catering mainly for Scottish holidaymakers. Today the town cannot compete with package holidays to the sunny Mediterranean and it has one of the most elderly populations in Scotland. Only the American servicemen from a nearby base provide the customers for the older service industries.

Off the main lines of communication, Campbeltown, Cromarty, Dornoch, Inveraray, Lochgilphead and Tobermory were still (1961-71) losing population. Campbeltown suffers from its comparative isolation. The burgh reached the peak of its prosperity between 1880 and 1910 as a centre for fishing, whisky distilling and coal-mining. Hopes have been raised by the granting of planning permission for a petro-chemical refinery, but the project has languished. Luckily its small boat building yard prospers. Because of Campbeltown's isolation it will probably not decline to a local service centre like Tarbert at the other end of the Mull of Kintyre. Cromarty, Inveraray and Lochgilphead are really villages whose urban importance has long since vanished. Dornoch, the former county town of Sutherland, survives because of its administrative function and tourism. Tobermory, the only significant service centre on the island of Mull, has lost much of its will to survive and is now down to 600 people after a hundred years of continuous decline. What can society do to help an attractive place like this, suffering from isolation and with no real economic advantages in a twentieth-century world?

In contrast to their landward areas, the burghs of the northern isles have been growing. Kirkwall is an ancient burgh of great charm and warmth which serves a stable and prosperous agricultural community and a steady tourist trade. Prior to 1972 there was little evidence that Orkney would attract oil-related development, but since then the oil pipeline from Piper and Claymore fields has been laid to the wartime anchorage at Scapa Flow and an oil terminal built on the island of Flotta. Stromness, a small attractive town which cannot compete with Kirkwall, recorded a falling population from 1931 to 1961. The trend has been reversed and the population has grown from 1,523 (1961) to 1,681 (1974) and should continue to do so with the introduction in 1975 of the new drive-on/drive-off ferries which have replaced conventional vessels at Kirkwall. Lerwick, the most northerly town of Britain, has a slightly decrepit air but the island spirit of the Shetlanders had begun to reverse the decline of opportunity and population in the second half of the 1960s. Fishing, handicrafts, small-scale manufactures, knitwear and tourism have brought real prosperity. Now oil has come in a big way and Shetlanders are very unsure about the future. Lerwick is going to grow and the suburbanization process will spill out to Scalloway and even as far as Weisdale. In the Outer Hebrides, Stornoway has grown at the expense of the landward population. Whilst the fishing remains prosperous and export markets demand Hebridean tweed all will be well.

A completely new trend can be identified in the development of

Table 11. Burghs in decline 1971-4

Decrease in population between 1971 and 1974

Strathclyde			Fife		
L	Greenock	2514		Buckhaven and Methil	694
L	Clydebank	1685	L	Kirkcaldy	427
L	Motherwell	1533		Lochgelly	337
L	Coatbridge	1399		Cowdenbeath	278
L	Paisley	1378		Burntisland	153
L	Hamilton	1153		Leven	97
L	Rutherglen	1115		Leslie	78
	Dunoon	781		St Monance	71
	Prestwick	403		Elie	54
	Stevenston	300		Tayport	41
L	Port Glasgow	271		Kilrenny	41
	Rothesay	170		Auchtermuchty	27
	Largs	158		Culross	21
	Oban	107		Crail	19
	Saltcoats	105		Cupar	13
	Darvel	67			
	Lochgilphead	34			
	Millport	7			

Central			Lothian	
L	Falkirk	810	Bathgate	125
	Alloa	715	Cockenzie	58
	Grangemouth	327	East Linton	34
L	Stirling	131	Loanhead	27

Borders/Galloway		Highlands and Islands	
Selkirk	125	Kingussie	50
Hawick	61	Thurso	15
Wigtown	56	Cromarty	11
Melrose	54	Tobermory	4
Whithorn	22		
Gatehouse	13		
New Galloway	6		

Grampian		Tayside	
Macduff	64	Pitlochry	143
Keith	35	Montrose	66
Dufftown	17	Brechin	13
Findochty	7		

L = large burgh

Note: The large decline in the large burghs of the central belt contrasts strongly with the stability of the rural and upland regions. Note burghs with growing populations are not shown.

burghs during the years 1971 to 1974.[12]

The Lowland burghs are now declining: of fifty-nine burghs with a diminished population, two-thirds lie within the industrial Lowlands (Table 11). Specifically, eleven Lowland large burghs declined out of the national total of twenty-one. Fifteen of Fife's twenty-five burghs declined in population during this short period.

At a stroke, local government reform removed political independence from the burghs discussed in this chapter. What cannot be taken away is the sense of community created by the small scale of these settlements. In a world which recognizes strength and size, the burghs often pass unnoticed, though within their bounds lies a communal heritage which cannot be reproduced within the city or new town. The small burghs' roots lie in the countryside, though all too often their role has been to prepare the young for their first steps towards the city.

Notes

1. I am grateful to D. R. Macgregor for stimulating my interest in this subject and for allowing access to his unpublished research, 'The Small Burgh 1951-61'.

2. For an example of functional analysis of four small burghs, Aberfeldy, Biggar, Dingwall and Pitlochry, see Joy Tivy, 'Four Small Scottish Burghs', *Scottish Geographical Magazine* vol. 77 (1961), pp. 148-64.

3. Scottish Development Department, *The Central Borders. A Plan for Expansion*, 2 vols. (HMSO, Edinburgh, 1968).

4. D. R. Macgregor (ed.), *The Borders Region* (Department of Geography, University of Edinburgh, March 1974).

5. Scottish Border Local Authorities Joint Committee, *The Borders Region, 1975* (Newton St Boswells, Roxburghshire, 1975).

6. Scottish Development Department, *A strategy for South-West Scotland* (HMSO, Edinburgh, 1970).

7. Scottish Development Department, *North East Scotland: A survey of Its Development Potential* (HMSO, Edinburgh 1969).

8. Planning Department Aberdeen County Council, *Buchan: The Next Decade* (April 1973); and *Peterhead '73* (September 1973).

9. J. Francis and N. Swan, *Scotland's Pipedream: A Study of the Growth of Peterhead in Response to the Demands of the North Sea Oil and Gas Industry* (Church of Scotland Home Board, January 1974).

10. Jack Holmes Planning Group, *The Moray Firth — a Plan for Growth* (Inverness, 1968). For the latest analysis of this area see J. S. Smith, 'Development and Rural Conservation in Easter Ross', *Scottish Geographical Magazine*, vol. 90 (1974), pp. 42-56.

11. D. Turnoch, 'Lochaber: West Highland Growth Point,' *Scottish Geographical Magazine*, vol. 82 (1969), pp. 17-28.

12. Registrar General of Scotland, *Annual Estimates of the Population of Scotland 1974* (HMSO, Edinburgh, 1975).

The City region is a complex and subtle entity, made up of the entire range of diverse activities that link town and country. Towns have always had a sphere of influence which Professor Smailes has called the urban field.[1] City regions reflect not so much the dominant influence of town over country but rather their integration in daily life. Towns have been making large inroads into the countryside for about two hundred years: the New Town of Edinburgh, as we have seen, marked the start of this trend. It was continued with the complex growth and interrelationships of the industrial city, which left the old burgh with its limited function in a backwater. It was not just a regional influence but a physical spread of housing, industry and services in places like Glasgow that led Patrick Geddes to coin the word conurbation. The vast extent of the conurbations, the outcome of uncontrolled growth, left a legacy of problems that could not be solved by the fragmented political bodies of the day. To Geddes the conurbation was 'a new heptarchy, which has been growing up naturally, yet almost unconsciously to politicians, beneath our existing, our traditional political and administrative network.'[2]

Geddes took the concept of the conurbation a step further by suggesting the term 'city region', which he closely identified with a second industrial revolution based on electricity, aluminium and intensive lines of communication. Regional planning ideas emerged from the writings of Patrick Geddes and Lewis Mumford because they recognized the waste of the overgrown, tangled city and the careless use of peripheral land. They saw the interrelationship between town and country, the needs of the one served by the other. The effects of a town do not end at its boundary but exist right up to a zone in which another town holds sway. Indeed, because of the hierarchical nature of settlement, the picture is more complicated, for these spheres of influence are superimposed on each other. Ultimately the largest settlement in a region, the city, dominates.

Two elements that should give the region its cohesion − lines of communication and political structure − have evolved in patterns showing few regional characteristics. Competition between different forms of transport has usually left each one too impoverished to work efficiently. The Greater Glasgow region, more than any other city region in Scotland, exemplifies the difficulties of creating a rational regional transport policy. In 1949 the Inglis Report on Transport in Glasgow and the Clyde Valley recommended the setting up of a coordinated transport authority and the replacement of the city's tramcars by electric trains on the suburban railways. The same recommendations were reiterated in the Halcrow Report in 1954. Electric trains started service in November 1960 but, after many teething troubles, were withdrawn until October 1961. Notwithstanding this unhappy start, suburban electrification in the Greater Glasgow area proved to be increasingly popular and was extended from Glasgow to Gourock and Wemyss Bay in June 1967. Passenger journeys after electrification increased by over 100 per cent on the three lines.[3]

The arrival of the 'Blue Trains' at Wemyss Bay coincided with the publication of *The Greater Glasgow Transportation Study,* one of the many surveys that evolved from conurbation studies developed in the United States in the 1950s, and which recommended a massive investment in electrification. So far, few of its proposals have been implemented and only then in conjunction with the main line electrification programme, but current plans include the electrification of the Central low level lines to join up the two separate networks. The passenger transport system in the 2,000 sq. km of the Greater Glasgow region is now organized into the Greater Glasgow Passenger Transport Executive and the existence of the ready-made electrified regional links should give Strathclyde Region the best coordinated transport system outside London.

Predictions towards 1990 indicated that the bus will decline relative to rail and that the private motor car will dominate in the overall increase in traffic (Fig. 13.1). Armed with this information, planners continued the remodelling of Scotland's cities to accommodate the car. The planning of an urban motorway is an emotive subject for it seems that the basic rule is to lay a line through working-class districts, conveniently labelled slums, and leave the land of villas severely alone. Each of the four cities has grappled with the problem differently. Aberdeen has used the legacy of late eighteenth-century roads and later ring roads and has no grandiose plan for road construction. Dundee has been able to combine a major road improvement programme with a comprehensive redevelopment scheme and the building of approaches to the Tay Road Bridge. With maximum publicity, Edinburgh succeeded in not building an inner ring road and allowed plans for an outer by-pass to lapse. Glasgow has undertaken the most ambitious scheme in Scotland, and probably in Britain, which even in its half-finished state has markedly reduced congestion on the city's streets and has permitted the successful pedestrianization of Buchanan Street. The cost has been high, for many houses have been demolished and their former occupants driven to outlying corporation estates. For economic reasons, there is little chance of the remaining road plans being carried out, so at least Glasgow Green will be saved from becoming a replica of Birmingham's Spaghetti Junction. Robert Bruce, Master of Works and City Engineer, drew up in 1948 the

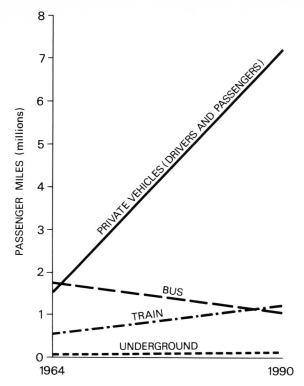

Fig. 13.1 Projection of annual travel volume in the *Greater Glasgow Transportation Study* (1967) showing the expected growth in the use of cars

lines of the Inner Ring Road, along which few properties were deemed to have a 'long life'. Bruce was well ahead of his time in insisting on the principle of total segregation of traffic. He also realized that the four bridgeheads were among the worst bottle-necks in the city and proposed a new bridge in conjunction with the Inner Ring Road and a tunnel to the west of the city: both have been built. The impact of these massive road developments has totally changed the use of land in central Glasgow, where whole residential areas have been replaced by commercial and institutional buildings (Fig. 13.2). Glasgow has moved a long way towards having a dead city centre. In many ways the road programme met the objectives laid down in Buchanan's classic work, *Traffic in Towns*. Now society is learning that free-flowing traffic is not in itself the solution, but merely leads to the greater problem of city centre parking. An ironic contradiction arises in Glasgow, where the num-ber of parking places is being reduced while the capacity to fill them has increased.

The solution of urban problems by new forms of transport has been a recurrent theme throughout the twentieth century. H.G. Wells, in *Anticipations*, insisted that the ever-increasing congestion of great cities could only be relieved by rapid transit systems, but

261

Fig. 13.2 Kingston Bridge and Glasgow's inner ring road and redevelopment area north of the River Clyde (Photo: R. Ralston Ltd.)

the search for such systems has had little success. Futuristic schemes, such as the Kearney High-Speed Railway system (1908) and Charles Boot's Railplane (1930s), were canvassed in terms of their ability to reduce slums by making distant areas available for working-class housing.[4] Boot's ideas were translated into an experimental track over the LNER's Milngavie branch. His vision came to nothing for it presupposed a mass housing movement with very cheap land and houses, and these conditions were hard to find in the depressed inter-war years. Wells may ultimately be proved right. Since his prediction the motor car has dominated other forms of urban transport, but traffic congestion, environmental damage and fuel scarcity are turning the thoughts of policy makers back to rapid transit schemes. It may not be long before progressive politicians will be advocating the reintroduction of the tram.

Political systems do not have the same competitive flexibility as transport systems, but when reform does take place it has to last for several decades. During the years immediately preceding local government reform in 1929, the piecemeal evolution of Scottish local government failed to master the growing problems of the conurbation. Numerous anomalies were inherited from the burghs' original constitutions: Renfrew, a royal burgh with a population of 13,000, had all the functions of local government, whereas Motherwell and Wishaw, a police burgh of 69,000 people, relied on Lanarkshire County Council for many of its local services. Furthermore, there were many authorities administering very small areas. The whole system was scrutinized by the Royal Commission on Local Government between 1924 and 1927, and this led to the Local Government Reform (Scotland) Act 1929.[5]

The Act swept away parish councils and education authorities, greatly reduced the powers of the smaller burghs but enhanced the powers of county councils (Table 12). Large burghs, that is those with 20,000 persons and over, retained most of their old powers and took over some of the powers which had previously belonged to parish councils. The four cities became single-tier authorities. An immediate problem created by this reorganization was friction between the small burghs and the county councils which in many cases were dominated by the rural faction. After four years' experience of working the Act, the Convention of Royal Burghs concluded that:

The general consensus of opinion expressed provides ample evidence that the Act has not in point of fact effected material improvement in the administration of local government in Scotland; on the contrary, local administration is in many respects less efficient than before, and the Act has led to increased expenditure in practically every important department of municipal activity. It has in certain areas created friction and disagreement, and in certain aspects has given ground for legitimate complaint.[6]

In September 1936 small burghs inundated the Secretary of State with requests for an inquiry into the working of the 1929 Act; three years later a further request for a Royal Commission was turned down, and again in 1943.[7] The need for a regional approach, especially in planning, was finally recognized by central government when three regional advisory plans were commissioned during the war to cover the Clyde Basin, Central and South East Scotland and the Tay Valley (Fig. 13.3). Although without statutory powers of implementation, these regional plans have served, in varying degrees,

Table 12. Local government reform in the twentieth century

	Pre-1929	1929-1975	Post-1975
Regional Councils	—	—	9
District Councils	—	—	49
All-purpose Island Authorities	—	—	3
Community Councils	—	—	?
City Councils	—	4	Abolished
County Councils	33	31	Abolished
Large Burghs	—	19-21	Abolished
Small Burghs	—	173-176	Abolished
Town Councils	201	Abolished	—
District (landward) Councils	—	199-198	Abolished
District Committees	98	Abolished	—
Standing Joint Committees	33	Abolished	—
Commissioners of Supply	33	Abolished	—
Parish Councils	869	Abolished	—
Education Authorities	37	Abolished	—
District Boards of Control	27	Abolished	—
Distress Committees	9	Abolished	—

as broad frameworks for the local development plans.

The declared purpose of the 1929 Act was to strengthen local government to fit it for a greater measure of devolution. Increasingly this was shown to be unworkable, for central government continued to create *ad hoc* statutory authorities, or alternatively transferred functions from local to central authorities. An example of the former was the creation of the Special Areas Commission which included the Special Areas Housing Association, and of the latter the Trunk Roads Act 1937 which transferred responsibility in this field to the Ministry of Transport.

Local authorities had to combine to fulfil the functions demanded of them. Police forces were amalgamated to meet the changing character of crime. Before 1939, every burgh had the power to provide its own fire brigade, but ultimately eleven forces provided fire cover for the whole of Scotland. The spatial nature of sewage, water purification and water supply projects forced councils to co-operate. The Water (Scotland) Act 1967 established a new administrative structure for the water service in Scotland whereby the functions of 200 local water boards were transferred to 13 regional water boards, with a water development board to co-ordinate their activities. Ultimately these different bodies contributed to regional confusion, for rarely did their administrative boundaries coincide (Fig. 13.4).

Fig. 13.3 Post-war
regional surveys

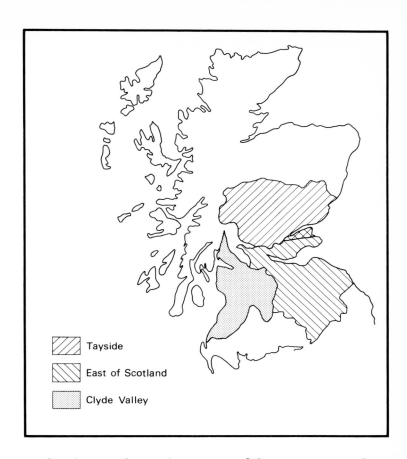

Tayside

East of Scotland

Clyde Valley

After the war, planning became one of the most important functions of local government for the public demanded action to solve
traffic problems, improve living conditions, attract industry, clear up
dereliction and provide for increased leisure. Yet the distinction
between urban and rural areas remained. The lack of regional planning could cause considerable uncertainty for smaller authorities
overshadowed by a larger neighbour:

> The main forces operating on the future of East Lothian are
> largely outside both the knowledge and control of the Local
> Planning Authority. For instance it is foolish merely to plan for
> the natural increase of a small burgh like North Berwick when
> the main quandary is the number of people moving out of Edin-
> burgh. The post-war Regional Advisory Plan for Central and
> South East Scotland provided no estimate or framework to guide
> us as Edinburgh was not part of the study. However now Edin-
> burgh's Development Plan Review states that there will be an
> overspill of between 15,500 and 38,000 people and the Corpora-
> tion has indicated its willingness to participate in Regional

265

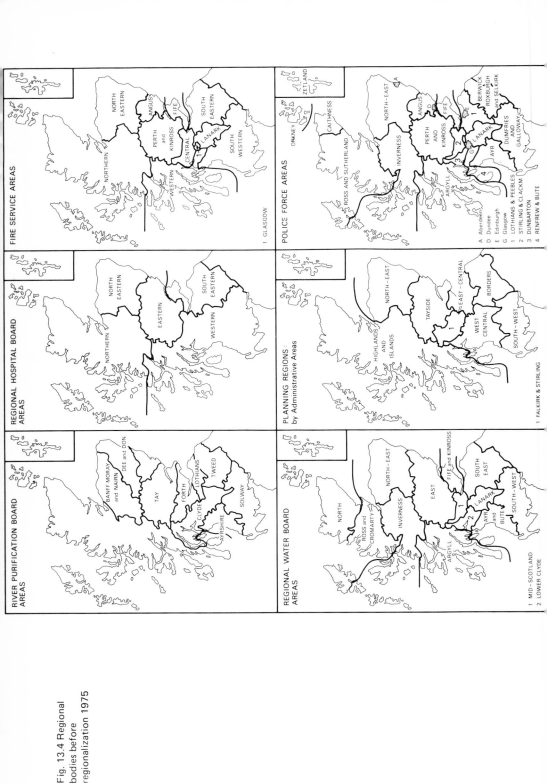

Fig. 13.4 Regional
bodies before
regionalization 1975

RIVER PURIFICATION BOARD AREAS

BANFF MORAY and NAIRN
DEE and DON
TAY
FORTH
CLYDE
LOTHIANS
TWEED
AYRSHIRE
SOLWAY

REGIONAL HOSPITAL BOARD AREAS

NORTHERN
NORTH EASTERN
EASTERN
SOUTH EASTERN
WESTERN

FIRE SERVICE AREAS

NORTHERN
NORTH EASTERN
ANGUS
FIFE
PERTH and KINROSS
CENTRAL
LANARK
WESTERN
SOUTH EASTERN
SOUTH WESTERN
1 GLASGOW

REGIONAL WATER BOARD AREAS

NORTH
ROSS and CROMARTY
NORTH-EAST
INVERNESS
EAST
FIFE and KINROSS
ARGYLL
LANARK
SOUTH EAST
AYR and BUTE
SOUTH-WEST
1 MID-SCOTLAND
2 LOWER CLYDE

PLANNING REGIONS:
by Administrative Areas

HIGHLANDS AND ISLANDS
NORTH-EAST
TAYSIDE
EAST-CENTRAL
BORDERS
WEST CENTRAL
SOUTH-WEST
1 FALKIRK & STIRLING

POLICE FORCE AREAS

ZETLAND
ORKNEY
CAITHNESS
ROSS AND SUTHERLAND
NORTH-EAST
INVERNESS
ANGUS
FIFE
PERTH and KINROSS
ARGYLL
LANARK
BERWICK
ROXBURGH and SELKIRK
DUMFRIES AND GALLOWAY
AYR
A Aberdeen
D Dundee
E Edinburgh
G Glasgow
1 LOTHIANS & PEEBLES
2 STIRLING & CLACKM
3 DUNBARTON
4 RENFREW & BUTE

Planning but there is no machinery for their doing so. . . .[8]

A feature of the Scottish local authority system was the comparative ease with which a town could gain political independence. Any town of 700 people (raised in the Local Government (Scotland) Act 1947 to 2,000) could apply to the sheriff of the county to be formed into a small burgh. Few towns availed themselves of this opportunity for since 1945 only Pitlochry, Stevenston, Bearsden and the new towns of East Kilbride and Cumbernauld have gained burgh status. Apart from creation by royal charter or special legislation there was nothing in England similar to this machinery for the formation of new boroughs.

The rapidly increasing ownership of the car has made the old local authority boundaries obsolete, especially around the cities. The car has brought greater flexibility. Individuals can penetrate every corner of the region and business responds to the opportunity — supermarkets, cash-and-carry stores, garden centres and car showrooms migrate to the city periphery. Yet the centre remains an important place of employment, shopping and recreation. This is not a simple rearrangement of functions, with the city as the workplace and the countryside as the dormitory, for many city people go out on their Sunday run to enjoy rural tranquility. Rural councils found themselves coping with an influx of young couples, often with small children. Extra demands were made on water and sewage services, schools which had been shrinking began to fill up again. At the same time, however, the generation of income and much of the spending of it still took place in the city. On the other hand the cities were faced with the demand from this daytime population to relieve the road congestion that they themselves were causing. The city ratepayer did not relish spending money on urban motorways, with the resultant disruption of his environment, so that the urban deserter could have an easy getaway. This fragile pyramid rested upon cheap fuel, and collapsed the moment the Egyptians crossed the Suez Canal on 6 October 1973.

Society has gone to great lengths to change political structures to meet the challenge of the growth of the city region. The review of local government in Scotland was started in 1963 with the publication of a White Paper.[9] In 1966 a Royal Commission was set up under the chairmanship of the Rt Hon. Lord Wheatley to enquire into the weaknesses in local government. At the root of the trouble was the structure of local government, which had remained basically the same for forty years while everything around it had changed. The recommendations of the *Wheatley Report*, published in 1969, formed the basis of the reforms that came into operation on 16 May 1975.[10] The Commission centred its enquiries on the question of the *functions* to be exercised over suitable *areas* by appropriate *authorities*. Functions seemed to fall naturally into two groups, one being impersonal services like planning, roads, water and industrial development, the other group consisting of personal services such as education, social work, health and eventually housing. Most controversy arose over the question of areas. From the onset the Commission had insisted that local government services should be provided over areas corresponding to genuine communities, and decided that a community could best be defined in terms of an area focusing on the town which formed its main centre and to which the inhabitants of the area travelled for business, shopping and recreation.

Throughout the enquiry the Commission subscribed to the city region concept, 'the distinction between town and country cannot be maintained'. The criteria selected for the identification of 'areas of community of interest' were: journey to work patterns, circulation of local weekly and some daily newspapers, postal areas, telephone exchange areas, and the location of head post offices, electricity and gas showrooms. Without exception these were already located within the city or large town. Seven regions were identified, of which four were city regions. Of the other three, the Highlands and Islands represents a special case which has been met in part by the Highlands and Islands Development Board; the South West is a rich agricultural region with small towns, and the Central Region lacks not only an obvious urban core but is also vulnerable to the influence of nearby city regions.

Wheatley's proposals were not accepted in their entirety. Edinburgh's city region lost the Borders and then southern Fife, and northern Fife was taken away from Dundee's city region so that the Kingdom of Fife retained its identity. No verdict can be pronounced on Wheatley's proposals for they need time to be tested, and pressure for devolution, which was unforeseen when the Commission sat, will lead to further changes.

The definition of areas capable of providing unity of purpose, and consequently suitable local government units, has provided the basis for both major local government reforms in this century. Unfortunately institutional inertia is so great that one could postulate that local government reform is always one reform too late and consequently today's problems are usually subjected to yesterday's answers. The structure of local government after the 1929 reform was ideal for the rapid pace of nineteenth-century urbanization, and similarly the 1975 regionalization will be ideal to accommodate the introduction of the car and the increase of personal mobility. Yet Scotland is in the midst of a national upheaval that reduces previous regional strengths and weaknesses to insignificance. The desire by the Scottish people for a National Assembly is due in part to their awareness of the urgency for a political institution (as compared to a bureaucracy like the Scottish Office) to bear the *responsibility* and *accountability* of arbitrating between the east of Scotland, emerging as the premier growth point, and the old declining industrial areas in the west. The urban communities being generated by North Sea oil exploitation require a housing strategy on a *national* level. It is not accidental that central government is increasingly assuming responsibility for housing. Strategic planning, such as that undertaken by the Scottish Development Department, is far more responsive to rapidly changing economic conditions than the tiered regional approach. Central government financial support to local government is around 70 per cent and makes a mockery of independence. Political devolution certainly will rob the regional units of some of their power, or kill them off completely. The districts, however, will come out of this devolution strengthened, for in many ways they are in harmony with the emergence of a society based on low growth rate and high energy cost. When one examines the boundaries of these new districts, some very ancient marks are revealed. As the period of unfettered growth has yielded to a more prudent use of resources, a regional identity will be harder to create and we may yet witness the renaissance of the medieval shire.

Notes

1. A. E. Smailes, *The Geography of Towns* (Hutchinsons University Library, London, 1953).

2. Patrick Geddes, *Cities in Evolution* (London, 1915), pp. 41-3. For a detailed discussion on conurbations see T. W. Freeman, *The Conurbations of Great Britain* (Manchester University Press, 1959), with a chapter on the Scottish conurbations by Catherine P. Snodgrass.

3. *Rail News*, November 1970.

4. Charles Boot, *A Scheme for the Abolition of Large Slum Areas*, n.d. (SRO BR (lib)); E. W. Chalmers Kearney, *Rapid Transit in the Future*, 2nd ed. (London, *c.* 1912).

5. Papers relating to Royal Commission on Local Government 1924-7 (SRO DD5/1143); Scottish Office, *Proposals for Reform in Local Government in Scotland and in the Financial Relations between the Exchequer and Local Authorities,* Cmnd.3135 (HMSO London, 1928).

6. Report by the Small Burgh's Committee of the Convention of Royal Burghs on matters affecting the interests of the small burghs, with reference to the effects of the Local Government (Scotland) Act 1929 (SRO DD5/731).

7. Local Government (Scotland) Act 1929. Request for appointment of Royal Commission 1938 (SRO DD5/756).

8. Memorandum by F. P. Tindall, County Planning Officer for East Lothian, to the Wheatley Commission, *Written Evidence*, V, p. 45.

9. *Modernisation of Local Government in Scotland*, Cmnd.2067 (HMSO, Edinburgh, 1963).

10. *Report of the Royal Commission on Local Government in Scotland (Wheatley Report)*, Cmnd.4150 (HMSO, Edinburgh, 1969) (short version Cmnd.4150-1); *Reform of Local Government in Scotland*, Cmnd.4583 (Edinburgh, 1971).

14

The towns and cities in which we live are a legacy from the past and a bequest to the future. Each generation has the responsibility for moulding the future townscape and upon their decisions depends the quality of urban living. To what extent do we need or can we afford to preserve the past? Can we preserve a sense of community and, at the same time, preserve buildings? Do we have an adequate housing stock, of the right kind in the right place? Can the cost of public housing be supported even at present levels? It has been estimated that Britain's accumulated public housing debt will have risen to £30,000 million by 1980 — *'the annual interest charges on which would alone be sufficient to wipe out the whole of the government's expected revenue from North Sea oil at peak production'.*[1] Is owner-occupation the alternative and, if so, are Scots willing to buy their homes? Are there adequate services in our towns and cities for young and old, healthy and sick, rich and poor? There can be no simple answers, for circumstances differ within the varied urban geography of Scotland. Furthermore, any attempts that were being made to answer these questions by this generation have been profoundly affected by three phenomena: the discovery of North Sea oil, the emergence of interest in conservation and the rise of Scottish nationalism with its insistence on devolution.

The discovery in 1959 of the Slochteren gas field in the Netherlands stimulated geological exploration and ultimately brought the realization that 2 per cent of the world's oil reserves lie in the strata off Scotland's east coast.[2] The geographical implications of this are profound, for it has reinforced a movement back to the population and settlement distribution that prevailed before the Industrial Revolution. This trend has relieved pressure of population in some of the older industrial areas, but while society has been trying desparately to eradicate old sores, new industrial communities like Invergordon have emerged. As a result of the build-up in the offshore exploration and development programme, there are at least four categories of related onshore industrial activity which affect population and settlement — exploration, fabrication, extraction and processing.[3] Exploration requires good existing harbours and facilities for the vessels supplying offshore rigs, and almost every east coast port is benefiting from this phase as the oil companies dominate the larger centres and force the fishing industry into smaller ports.

Aberdeen, more than any other town, has borne the brunt of this phase and provides a case study of the disruptions caused in an urban area under pressure from a massive oil boom. Aberdeen's

problems cannot all be laid directly at the door of the oil boom —
for many years the city has suffered shortages of water and land,
and of reasonably priced private houses — but oil discoveries have
given another twist to the inflationary spiral. Those not enjoying oil-
related wages, such as teachers and local government workers, have
been priced out of the housing market and pressures are building up
on the city's essential services. Development in settlements around
Aberdeen has increased sharply, due partly to land shortage within
the city. Since the end of the 1960s industrial sites have been sought
at an accelerating rate: Aberdeen County Planning Officer received
over four times as many enquiries for suburban sites in 1972 as in
1971.

Government strategy for North Sea oil development has been
made clear: it should be urban-orientated and, as far as possible,
sited in the Central Belt.[4] The ability of towns to ride the oil boom
successfully will vary enormously, as will the resilience of the landward areas from which skilled labour is being drawn for short-term
projects. The benefits being brought to urban communities, such as
Aberdeen and Peterhead, could prove illusory, and already doubts
are being voiced. Great effort will be necessary to control 'Scotland's
Oil' and prevent its transformation into 'Scotland's Curse'. Doubts
about the future may even be expressed in places apparently rescued
from oblivion by oil-related employment. The burgh of Buckhaven
and Methil, a predominantly mining community that was faced with
closures in the 1960s, has now achieved a shaky prosperity. Many
former miners are among the 800 men building platform jackets in
the construction yard on the site of the former Wellesley Colliery.
But even here they live with insecurity, always waiting for the next
contract, and the population has continued to drop, from 21,318 in
1961 to 17,859 in 1974.

The extraction of oil will engender little urban development, for
it will flow directly to the refineries with only a few jobs created at
the terminals, Cruden Bay and St Fergus near Peterhead. Only the
remote Sullum Voe in the Shetland Islands will see major developments, from a simple landfall and storage area into a full petro-chemical complex with housing for 1,200 people nearby.

The processing of oil will affect future generations most severely.
Already the petro-chemical complex at Grangemouth occupies 300
hectares and output is almost equal to Scottish demand.[5] Much of its
specialized output is exported to England and Northern Ireland for
use in manufacturing industries and the proportion is bound to rise
with the advent of North Sea oil. As yet no one knows how much
regional growth will ensue from the expansion of oil refining at
Grangemouth, but output will certainly double within a decade and
the effects must be significant. Whilst other proposals for refinery
sites have been scrutinized by public inquiries, the change in the
planned use of large areas to allow for this expansion has been

passed unopposed. However, although one would have expected the population of Grangemouth to have grown in the years 1971 to 1974, in fact 327 people had left the town during these boom years.

A crucial question is the extent to which the benefits of oil will spread into West Central Scotland. Latest estimates suggest that the maximum number of jobs likely to be created in this way is only a small part (10 to 15 per cent) of the long-term needs of the area. As the projected requirement to maintain a reasonable economy in the region is 150,000-240,000 new jobs, oil may offer only a modest contribution of 20,000 jobs.[6] Underlying these statistics is the disquieting fact that despite unemployment there is a shortage of skilled men on Clydeside. The flood of emigration over the years has left a labour force without the skills to enjoy the transitory benefits of oil.

The prosperity brought by oil will throw additional burdens upon those making decisions for Scotland's future. Time and again growth and the protection of national heritage will conflict. Recent dogma that everything old is 'feudal' and that a utopian future can only be built upon totally cleared sites has destroyed much of the historic fabric of Scottish towns (End map 4).[7] Medieval Dundee exists no more, and G.G. Simpson suggests that there are few burghs where there is not danger of their old centres being demolished. Controversy over the survival of Rossend Castle in Burntisland and the centre of Kirriemuir are but examples of a continuous process of attrition. The attitudes of the 1960s were summed up in this report: 'city motorists joining the weekend trek down the East Lothian coast have long been conscious of the formidable task facing Prestonpans folk in the rehabilitation of a little town *burdened* by a heavy proportion of ancient properties'. Many high-quality historic properties were demolished, 'showing to the passing world how Prestonpans has triumphed over the problems posed by antiquity'.[8]

Conservation is not about the past but about the future. What in our cities and towns should we preserve and protect for future generations? Buildings are usually created for current use, rarely for posterity. Some are easily adapted for changing times but all too often obsolescence presents a dilemma between preservation and destruction. Ironically, the best preserver of urban fabric has been economic decline. Much of late seventeenth and early eighteenth century Bo'ness survives because of this. The delights of Culross are an inheritance of its economic failure. In contrast Grangemouth is a successful town where not a building remains from its creation barely two hundred years ago. The centre of Dundee had until recently all the hallmarks of a successful town fallen on hard times, but now it looks like the central redevelopment of Coventry, Southampton, Exeter or any other city built after the German blitz.

For a long time conservation meant the preservation of the fabric of a building, without regard to its context or its role in the community. Recently, under Section 1 of the Civic Amenities Act (1967), it has become the duty of every local planning authority to determine 'areas of special architectural or historic interest, the character or appearance of which it is desirable to preserve or enhance', and the Act provides for their formal designation as Conservation Areas. Government gave a lead in this Act. Now it is for district councils and the community to decide, not just whether historic buildings are to be saved but whether a traditional way of urban life is wanted.[9] Whilst there has been much effort to create Conservation Areas for environmental reasons, economic circumstances will reinforce the trend towards conservation. The restoration of older fabric can be cheaper than large-scale clearance and rebuilding. Furthermore, recent major civic schemes, especially for roads, have been abandoned and the older fabric retained. Suddenly it pays to conserve. The next question is, what to conserve?

Only a minute proportion, 0.7 per cent, of Scotland's houses were built before 1851.[10] Two-thirds have been built since 1919, the majority being local authority houses (Table 13). The other third consists mainly of poorly maintained tenements with low internal standards, built between 1871 and 1914. If most older working-class dwellings must be abandoned to the demolition gang, is there a future for older middle-class houses? These are substantially built, though often without a damp course which may have led to dry rot or other severe problems. Maintenance is expensive, and plumbing, electric wiring and other features may need renewal. Size is also a problem, for these houses were designed for large families with resident servants. Conservation can also include business premises, as in the New Town of Edinburgh. Many developers are now building modern office blocks behind original facades, but surely a building is the whole structure and not merely the external stonework? The problems of conservation also spill over into industry. Should important examples of industrial architecture be retained when they have lost their function?

Table 13. Scotland's stock of dwellings by age. Estimated percentage distribution

	Pre-1851	1851-1870	1871-1890	1891-1918	1919-1944	Post-1944
Scotland	0.7	4.2	11.0	18.3	19.5	46.3
Great Britain	4.1	4.9	10.3	15.5	23.4	41.8

Source: *Housing and Construction Statistics* (HMSO No.5, 1973).

Conflicts of interests may create dilemmas for local authorities. Recently there was a strong move to designate as a Conservation Area the village of Torry, south of the River Dee at Aberdeen. Then North Sea oil was discovered and the site became valuable for the extension of oil facilities. What was the right decision in those circumstances? Previous arguments for conservation gave way to economic expediency.

Edinburgh has embarked on a major programme of conservation. A great deal of effort has been expended by the town council, but so far the majority of Conservation Areas have been designated, not in the old town, but in peripheral residential areas. Articulate residents' associations in middle-class village communities in Cramond, Swanston, Duddingston and Blacket have been the catalyst for conservation area status. The Blacket area in the Newington district of the city exemplifies the forces at work in the creation of a Conservation Area.[11] Planned as an exclusive suburb enclosed by substantial walls and gates, it is a well-defined group of houses and gardens of distinctive character. The houses are of two styles; those built before about 1855 are austerely elegant in the tradition of classical proportions and detail, and those of the later nineteenth century display the exuberance of prosperous Victoriana. However, this description could apply to large areas of middle-class Edinburgh. What made Blacket so special that it became Edinburgh's first Conservation Area? The key lies in the nature of the community, for the proportion of professional people, especially medical and academic, is remarkably high. Their Association offered full co-operation to the Corporation and its planning department and achieved their aim of stopping the attrition of the residential nature of the area, whilst in its turn the Corporation entered the Conservation Area league. It was cynically suggested that Blacket was designated only because 'its nobby occupants kept it in such good repair that it could not possibly cost anything to conserve it'.[12]

Meantime Glasgow is restoring several splendid Victorian terraces in the Park and Glasgow West Conservation Areas, and Aberdeen's High Street will become a pedestrian precinct. Dumfries is restoring the ancient Devorgilla's Bridge over the Nith; Inverness is restoring its Market Arcade, now unique in Scotland; Kirkcaldy is to restore part of Fitzroy Street in Dysart, while Thurso is to improve buildings in Traill Street. A boost was given to conservation by the European Architectural Heritage Year 1975 which focused attention on the rich variety of Scotland's urban fabric and reinforced the need for its preservation. Two of the four United Kingdom pilot projects for Heritage Year were in Scotland. The 'Little Houses' improvement scheme run by the National Trust for Scotland resulted in the rehabilitation of more than 120 houses, most of them in small burghs. The restoration of the New Town of Edinburgh, a large project indeed, will take many years to complete.

Scotland will contrast markedly with the rest of the world in its future pattern of urban living. Whilst urban centres in most under-developed countries will rocket into multi-million cities, the Scottish cities will stabilize or continue to decline, quite dramatically in the case of Glasgow. Glasgow's population of 1,057,000 in 1961 had fallen to 897,000 within a decade and to an estimated 816,000 in 1974, and is expected to be between 700,000 and 750,000 by 1981. The result could well be a sad city with an ageing, underskilled workforce, an obsolete industrial structure, a housing stock unattractive to incomers, much of the inner city lying as urban fallow, and human problems such as vandalism, all fostered by the crash programmes of the 1950s and '60s. How can we rescue the spirit that made Glasgow great? It will take imagination to achieve a balanced community in a pleasing environment which can attract industry and government departments. Will private housing be encouraged within the city boundary? Will riverside areas such as the obsolete Broomielaw Quays and Princes Dock be redeveloped with imagination? The interrelationship of people and environment is poorly understood but experience shows that a contented community is not ensured merely by providing houses with the statutory number of fitments. The sheer scale and impersonality of new housing developments have brought the realization of the need for personal identity. Oscar Newman has identified some of the problems and has suggested the term 'defensible space' to describe those immediate surroundings which can be regarded as one's own. Until the individual has a defensible space and a resulting sense of responsibility the rates of vandalism and crime will continue to rise.[13]

In contrast to Glasgow, Edinburgh continues on her complacent way. Architectural scale in the city centre remains from an earlier age; only the shadow of the Appleton and Hume Towers of the University and the blank facade of the new St James Centre rob man of dignity. The townscape is so rich that at times the citizens have been less than careful about the attrition of their heritage. Yet the wounds that so scar the face of Glasgow can be found hidden throughout the city. In Leith a lively community has been allowed to decay and only now are slow steps being taken towards revival. The South Side of the city sports the gaps of half-finished comprehensive redevelopment. Massive council estates like Pilton, Oxgangs and Moredun lie isolated on the periphery.

Our nineteenth-century industrial towns are undergoing a crisis of identity; to face the future they need not only better houses and shops but also a new economic base. Located mainly on exhausted coalfields far from oil-based industry, they require greater economic success than they have enjoyed from regional policies during the last thirty years. Who has the imagination, capital and skill for this task?

Not all in urban Scotland is depressing, however. As we have seen, post-war new towns are successful and are developing that sense of community found in more ancient burghs. Small town revival has begun to reverse a long drift from country to city. If this trend continues, then city domination would be broken and a new urban future would have begun.

Although the urban fabric has been accumulated during eight hundred years of history, most of what we see is relatively modern. Every stone, brick or stretch of asphalt speaks of the past. It has to be remembered that the story of the Scottish burgh is a lowland one, for even burghs in the Highlands are outposts of the lowland way of life. The average Scot lives in a town far from heather and glen and, if we are to shape Scotland's future, the town is the place to start.

Notes

1. *The Observer*, 11 May 1975.

2. Royal Scottish Geographical Society, *Scotland and Oil* (Teachers Bulletin No.5, 1973).

3. J. Francis and N. Swan, *Scotland in Turmoil: A Social and Environmental Assessment of the Impact of North Sea Oil and Gas on Communities in the North of Scotland* (Saint Andrew Press, Edinburgh, 1973), see chap. 12 for the impact of oil on Peterhead, Montrose, etc.

4. *North Sea Oil and the Environment: A Report to the Oil Development Council for Scotland* (HMSO, Edinburgh, 1974).

5. K. Chapman, 'The Structure and Development of the Oil-Based Industrial Complex at Grangemouth', *Scottish Geographical Magazine*, vol. 90 (1974), pp. 98-109.

6. J. Francis and N. Swan, *Scottish Oil Shakedown: An Assessment of Some Future Prospects for Oil-Related Industry in the West of Scotland* (Church of Scotland Home Board, February 1975), pp. 33, 64, quoting *The West Central Scotland Plan*, Supplementary Report I, *The Regional Economy* (1974), p. 174.

7. G.G. Simpson (ed.), *Scotland's Medieval Burghs: An Architectural Heritage in Danger,* Report by the Council of the Society of Antiquaries of Scotland (Edinburgh, 1972).

8. *Edinburgh Evening News*, 5 December 1961.

9. *Housing Act 1974: Renewal Strategies*, Circular 13/75 (HMSO London, 1975).

10. Kathleen M. Riley, 'An Estimate of the Age Distribution of the Dwelling Stock in Great Britain', *Urban Studies*, vol. 10 (1973), pp. 373-9.

11. Town Planning Department Edinburgh Corporation, *Blacket Potential Conservation Area* (February 1971).

12. *New Statesman*, 18 August 1972.

13. Oscar Newman, 'Defensible Space: Crime Prevention Through Urban Design', *Ekistics* 36, 216 (1973), pp. 325-32; and *Defensible Space* (Architectural Press, London, 1973).

APPENDIX: THE FOUNDATION OF SCOTTISH BURGHS

Dates of foundation taken from G.S. Pryde, *The Burghs of Scotland: A Critical List* (Oxford University Press, 1965).

ROYAL BURGHS

Aberdeen 1124-53
Airth *c*.1195-1203
Annan 1532
Anstruther Easter 1583
Anstruther Wester 1587
Arbroath 1599
Auchterarder 1246
Auchermuchty 1517
Auldearn (Earn) 1179-82
Ayr 1203-06
Banff 1189-98
Berwick 1119-24
Brechin 1641
Burntisland 1541
Campbeltown 1700
Clackmannan 1153-64
Crail 1150-52
Cromarty 1264
Cullen (Invercullen) 1189-98
Culross 1592
Cupar 1327
Dingwall 1227
Dornoch 1628
Dumbarton 1222
Dumfries 1186
Dunbar 1445
Dundee 1191-95
Dunfermline 1124-27
Dunkeld 1704 [an inoperative
    promotion]
Dysart 1594
Earlsferry 1589
Edinburgh 1124-27
Elgin 1136-53
Falkland 1458
Forfar 1184
Forres 1130-53
Fortrose 1590
Fyvie 1264
Glasgow 1611
Haddington 1124-53
Hamilton 1549
Inveraray 1648
Inverbervie 1341
Inverkeithing 1153-62
Inverness 1153-65
Inverurie 1195
Irvine 1372

Jedburgh 1124-53
Kilrenny 1592
Kinghorn 1165-72
Kintore 1187-1200
Kirkcaldy 1644
Kirkcudbright 1330
Kirkwall 1486
Lanark 1124-53
Lauder 1298-1328
Linlithgow *c*.1138
Lochmaben 1440
Montrose 1124-53
Nairn (Invernairn) *c*.1190
New Galloway 1630
Newburgh (Fife) 1631
North Berwick 1425
Peebles 1124-53
Perth 1124-27
Pittenweem 1541
Queensferry 1636
Rattray 1564
Renfrew 1124-47
Rosemarkie 1590
Rothesay 1401
Roxburgh 1119-24
Rutherglen 1124-53
St Andrews 1620
Sanquhar 1598
Selkirk 1328
Stirling 1124-27
Stranraer 1617
Tain 1439
Tarbert 1329
Whithorn 1511
Wick 1589
Wigtown 1292

ECCLESIASTICAL BURGHS

(R = Royal burgh)

Arbroath (R) 1178-82
Brechin (R) 1165-71
Canongate 1128-53
Crawford 1242-49
Dunfermline (R) 1303
Earlsferry (R) 1541
Glasgow (R) 1175-78
Kelso 1237

Kirkcaldy (R) 1315-28
Musselburgh 1315-28
Newburgh (Fife) (R) 1266
Queensferry (R) 1315-28
Rosemarkie 1455
St Andrews 1124-44
Whithorn 1325

BURGHS OF BARONY AND REGALITY

Aberdeenshire

1   Aboyne, Charleston of 1676
2   Alford 1594/5
3   Balgownie 1707
4   Clatt 1501
5   Dalgattie or Meikletoun of Slains 1699
6   Echt 1698
7   Ellon 1707
8   Fintray, Hatton of 1625
9   Forgue 1599
10 Fraserburgh or Fathlie 1546
11 Huntley or Milton of Strathbogie or Tirrisoule 1488
12 Insch 1677
13 Kildrummy 1509
14 Kincardine O'Neill 1511
15 Leslie or Old Leslie 1649
16 Marywell 1740
17 Monymusk 1588/9
18 Newburgh 1261
19 Old Aberdeen 1489
20 Old Meldrum 1671
21 Peterhead or Keithinch 1587
22 Rayne 1492/3
23 Redford 1683
24 Rhynie 1684
25 Rosehearty 1681
26 Strathdon 1677
27 Tarland 1683
28 Tarves 1673
29 Turriff 1511/12
30 Woodhead of Fetterletter 1685

Angus

31 Auchry 1666
32 Auchterhouse 1497
33 Balgavies or Greenmyre 1587
34 Dudhope 1707
35 East Haven of Panmure 1540
36 Edzell 1588
37 Glamis 1491
38 Kirriemuir 1458/9
39 Newtyle 1682
40 Rottenrow or Hilltown of Dundee 1672

Argyll

41 Campbeltown 1667
42 Inveraray 1474
43 Kilmun 1490

44 Laggan or Islay 1614
45 Melfort 1688
46 Oban 1811

Ayrshire

47 Ardrossan 1846
48 Auchinleck 1507
49 Ballantrae 1541
50 Citadel of Ayr or Montgomeries-Toun 1663
51 Cumnock 1509
52 Dalmellington or Castlemerk of Dalmellington 1607
53 Dundonald, Kirkton of 1638
54 Fairlie 1601
55 Fullarton 1707
56 Girvan 1668
57 Kilbirnie 1642
58 Kilmarnock 1591/2
59 Kilmaurs 1527
60 Largs 1629
61 Mauchline 1510
62 Maybole 1516
63 Newmilns 1490/1
64 Newton of Gogo 1595
65 Newton-upon-Ayr c1314-1371
66 Prestwick 1165-1174
67 Saltcoats 1528/9
68 Tarbolton 1671

Banff

69 Aberlour, or Charleston of Aberlour 1814
70 Balveny, Milton of 1615
71 Deskford 1698
72 Down or Doune 1528
73 Fordyce 1499
74 Macduff 1783
75 Newmill of Strathisla 1673
76 Ordiquhill, Kirkton of 1617
77 Portsoy 1550
78 Rothiemay, Kirkton of 1617

Berwickshire

79 Cockburnspath 1612
80 Coldingham 1638
81 Dryburgh 1526/7
82 Duns 1489/90
83 Earlston 1489
84 Eyemouth 1597/8
85 Hyndlawhill 1635
86 Langton 1394
87 Old Greenlaw 1596
88 Preston 1602
89 Thirlestane 1661

Bute

90 Kilbride in Arran 1668
91 Mount Stuart 1703

Caithness

92 Hemprigs 1705

93	Magnusburgh or Inver of Dunbeath 1624
94	Reay 1628
95	Scrabster 1526/7
96	Thurso 1633
97	Wick c.1393

Clackmannan

98	Alloa 1497
99	Dollar 1702
100	Tillicoultry 1634

Dumfrieshire

101	Amisfield 1613
102	Dalgarnock 1636
103	Langholm 1621
104	Meikle Dalton 1755
105	Moffat 1648
106	Moniaive 1636
107	New Delgarno or Thornhill 1664
108	Ruthwell 1507/8
109	Sanquhar 1484
110	Staplegorton 1320
111	Torthorwald 1473

Dunbartonshire

112	Helensburgh 1802
113	Kilpatrick 1672
114	Kirkintilloch 1211-1214
115	Luss 1642
116	Portkill 1667

East Lothian

117	Cockenzie 1591
118	Dirleton 1631
119	Drem 1616
120	Dunbar 13cent.
121	Dunglass 1489
122	Innerwick 1630
123	North Berwick 1381-88
124	Pencaitland 1505
125	Preston(Pans) 1552
126	Seton 1321
127	Tranent 1541/2
128	Tynninghame 1591

Fife

129	Aberdour (West) 1500/1
130	Anstruther Easter 1571/2
131	Anstruther Wester 1540/1
132	Auchtertool, Milton of 1617
133	Ceres 1620
134	Colinsburgh 1707
135	Corshill-over-Inchgall 1511
136	Culross 1490
137	Drummochy 1540
138	Dunbog 1687
139	Dysart 1510
140	Elie 1598/9
141	Ferryport-on-Craig or South-ferry or Tayport 1598/9

142	Fifeness 1707
143	Innergelly 1623
144	Kennoway 1663
145	Kilrenny 1578
146	Largo 1513
147	Leslie Green 1457/8
148	Leven 1609
149	Linktown 1663
150	Markinch 1673
151	Methil 1662
152	Newbigging 1541
153	Pitlessie 1540
154	Pittenweem 1526
155	St Monans 1596
156	Strathmiglo 1509/10
157	Valleyfield 1663
158	Wemyss or Wester Wemyss 1511

Inverness-shire

159	Beauly or Fraserdale or Lovat 1704
160	Campbelltown 1623
161	Dunachton 1690
162	Grantown-on-Spey or Grant, formerly Castleton of Freuchie 1694
163	Inverness, Citadel of or Kingsburgh 1666
164	Kingussie 1464
165	Petty or Fishertoun of Petty 1611
166	Ruthven or St George burgh 1684

Kincardine

167	Arbuthnot 1543
168	Cowie 1540/1
169	Drumlithie 1602
170	Durris 1540/1
171	Fettercairn 1504
172	Fordoun 1554
173	Halkerton 1612
174	Inglismaldie or Egglismaldie 1682
175	Kincardine 1531/2
176	Laurencekirk 1779
177	Miltonhaven 1695
178	Stonehaven 1587
179	Torry 1495

Kinross

180	Crook of Devon 1615
181	Kinross 1540/1

Kirkcudbrightshire

182	Buittle 1325
183	Cardoness or Clachan of Anwoth 1702
184	Carpshairn, Kirkton of, or Tantallocholme 1635
185	Castle Douglas 1791

186 Creetown 1791
187 Gatehouse of Fleet 1795
188 Heron 1698
189 Kelton 1705
190 Maxwelltown 1810
191 Minnigaff 1619
192 Preston 1663
193 Terregles or Herries 1510
194 Troquhen 1688
195 Urr 1262

Lanarkshire

196 Airdrie 1821
197 Anderston 1824
198 Biggar 1451
199 Blantyre 1598/9
200 Bothwell 1602
201 Calton 1817
202 Carluke or Kirkstile 1662
203 Carnwath 1451
204 Carstairs 1765
205 Cartland 1607
206 Crawford 1510/1
207 Crawfordjohn 1668
208 Douglas 1458/9
209 Hamilton 1475
210 Leadhills or Hopetoun 1661
211 Lesmahagow 1668
212 Roberton 1631
213 Stonehouse 1667
214 Strathaven 1450

Midlothian

215 Canongate 1587
216 Carrington or Primrose 1664
217 Crichton 1706
218 Citadel of Leith 1662
219 Clerkington or Nicolson,
    later Rosebery or Ancrum
    1669
220 Cranston 1662
221 Dalkeith 1401
222 Leith 1636
223 Musselburgh 1562
224 Newbattle or Easthouses and
    Westhouses 1634
225 Portsburgh 1649
226 Preston 1663
227 Restalrig and Calton or
    Easter and Wester
    Restalrig 1673
228 Roslin 1456
229 Wester Duddingston 1673
230 Woodhouselee or Fulford
    1664

Moray

231 Belliehill 1499/1500
232 Covesea 1698
233 Cromdale 1609
234 Darnaway 1611
235 Findhorn or Seatoun of

     Kinloss 1532
236 Fochabers 1598/9
237 Garmouth 1587
238 Kinloss 1497
239 Muirtown 1674
240 Spynie 1451

Nairn

241 Geddes or Chapelton of
    Easter Geddes 1600
242 Lochloy 1608

Orkney

243 Carrick 1632
244 Stromness 1817

Peebleshire

245 Eddleston 1607
246 Kilbucho c. 1650
247 Skirling 1592
248 West Linton 1306

Perthshire

249 Abernethy 1458/9
250 Auchtergaven 1681
251 Balnakilly 1511
252 Balnald 1511
253 Blackford 1706
254 Blairgowrie or Blair 1634
255 Coupar Angus 1607
256 Craig 1626
257 Crieff 1672
258 Dalnagairn 1510
259 Doune-(Campsie) 1611
260 Dunblane 13th or 14th
    cent.
261 Dunkeld 1511/2
262 Dunning 1511
263 Errol 1648
264 Forgandenny or Forgound
    1630
265 Inveruchill 1682
266 Keithick 1492
267 Kenmore 1694
268 Killin 1694
269 Kincardine-on-Forth 1663
270 Kinnoull or Bridgend of
    Tay 1706
271 Kirkmichael or Kirkhill or
    Kirkton or Tomlachan 1511
272 Lacock of Abercairney 1706
273 Logierait 1671
274 Longforgan 1672
275 Meigle 1608
276 Meikleour 1665
277 Port of Menteith 1466/7

Renfrewshire

278 Ardgowan 1634
279 Cartsdyke or
    Craufordsdyke 1669
280 Gourock 1694

281	Greenock 1635		

281 Greenock 1635
282 Houston 1671
283 Kilbarchan 1704
284 Newton Mearns 1621
285 Paisley 1488
286 Pollockshaws 1813
287 Port Glasgow 1668

Ross and Cromarty

288 Auchmartin and Easter
Balbair 1677
289 Bonarness or Ardgay 1686
290 Castlehaven or Portmahomack
1678
291 Coul or Contin 1681
292 Culbockie or Findon 1678
293 Foulis 1699
294 Gairloch or Clive 1619
295 Gordonsburgh later
Maryburgh 1618
296 Keppoch 1690
297 Obsdale or Alness 1690
Pluckton 1808
298 Redcastle 1680
299 Stornoway 1607
300 Tarbat 1678

Roxburghshire

301 Hawick 1511
302 Kelso 1614
303 Longnewton 1634
304 Maxton 1587/8
305 Melrose 1605
306 Minto 1695
307 Nether Ancrum 1639
308 Rutherford formerly Cape-
hope, later Hunthill 1666
309 Smailholm 1687
310 Town Yetholm 1665

Selkirk

311 Galashiels 1599

Shetland

312 Lerwick 1818

Stirlingshire

313 Buchlyvie 1672
314 Elphinstone 1673
315 Falkirk 1600
316 Gargunnock 1677
317 Kilsyth 1620
318 Mugdock 1680
319 Polmont 1611
320 West Kerse 1643

Sutherland

321 Inverbrora 1601

West Lothian

322 Abercorn or Newton of
Abercorn 1603
323 Bathgate 1663
324 Borrowstouness 1668
325 Bridgeness 1750
326 Dalmeny 1616
327 Grange(pans) 1643
328 Kirkliston 1621
329 Livingston 1604

Wigtownshire

330 Ballinclach 1496/7
331 Glenluce 1705
332 Innermessan 1426
333 Knockreavie 1642
334 Lochryan formerly
Cladahouse 1701
335 Merton 1504
336 Myreton 1477
337 Newton Stewart 1677
338 Portpatrick or
Montgomerie 1620
339 Stewarton or Stuarton 1623

GLOSSARY

Bailie. A farm steward; a city magistrate.

Bastide. A medieval walled town.

Booth. A stall at a market.

Breve. A pope's letter.

Burgage. An urban plot held by a burgess. It consisted of a house
with a long narrow strip of land behind.

Burgh. A settlement given privileges in trade, land-holding and self-
government by means of a charter from either the king or a
lord.

Burgh muir. A town moor.

Burgh of barony. A late medieval burgh, holding from a subject of
the Crown, having limited privileges of manufactures, markets
and fairs.

Burgh of regality. A post-Reformation burgh, holding from a subject
of the Crown. It was similar to a burgh of barony, but exercised certain extra rights of Justice.

Burgh roods. Arable land belonging to the burgesses (also called
burgh acres or croft lands).

Butts. Open land at the edge of a burgh used for archery practice
and for the holding of wapinschaws.

Caput. The stronghold of a barony, although by the fifteenth
century the caput was identified with the jurisdiction rather
than the lands of the barony, for the lands could be transferred separately to another person.

Cess. A land tax.

Chairmen. Carriers of sedan chairs.

Cloig. A piece of wood tied to a hen's leg to stop it flying away.

Close. A narrow alley.

Conservator. A guardian, custodian.

Coquet. The distinctive seal of a custom house.

Cordwainer. A shoemaker.

Cot-houses. The dwellings of the poorest country people, the
cottars.

Cottager. A tradesman, weaver, ditcher, thatcher, shoemaker, tailor,
etc. who earned day wages.

County of a city. One of the four burghs (Edinburgh, Glasgow,
Dundee and Aberdeen) designated by the Local Government
(Scotland) Act 1929, and responsible for all local services.

Crag-and-tail site. A hill-form with a steep declivity at one end and
a gentle slope at the other.

Croft lands. Arable lands.

Cruive. Various meanings, but in this case a sty or small building.

Customs. Tolls.

Customs, trone and three-port. Dues levied on eggs, butter, cheese, etc. at the town gate.

Dean of guild court. A guild court which had charge of weights and measures and dealt with all internal trade disputes and the interests of the incorporated trades.

Ecclesiastical burgh. A modern term to distinguish a burgh holding from an ecclesiastical subject of the Crown, and having the usual privileges of a burgh of barony.

Fermtoun. A small farming community of six to eight families of joint-tenants who farmed in runrig.

Feu-ferme. The burgh mails or rents accruing to the Crown were leased out to an individual for a fixed sum in perpetuity.

Head court. A burgh court at which were elected the bailies and other burgh officers such as the liners (who inspected boundaries), ale-tasters, apprisers of flesh, kirk-master and treasurer. Its criminal jurisdiction was strictly limited.

Headroom, heidroom. The end of the toft (also known as the tail of the toft).

Hinterland. The area which supplies a town and receives support from the same centre.

Indweller. One who dwells in a burgh.

Kirset. A period of from one to ten years during which a newcomer to a burgh might build his house and pay no rent.

Large burgh. One of twenty burghs so designated by the Local Government (Scotland) Act 1929, each having a population over 29,000. The large burgh was responsible for all local authority functions except education and rating valutions, which were administered by the county council.

Loan. A road leading to the common grazing lands.

Manbote. Payment to the king for breach of the peace, or for a crime committed in his precinct.

Market colonization. The erection of permanent buildings in the open market street, often leading to the erection of two narrower streets.

Michaelmas. A quarter day, 24 September, on which rent or interest is payable; it was a customary date for entry or removal from property.

Muir. A moss.

Pie powder court. A court set up for the duration of a fair under the steward of the lord of the manor or ecclesiastic who held the franchise. The court delivered summary justice to itinerant traders. Derived from Old French *pieds poudreux* (dusty-footed pedlar).

Planning blight. The accelerated decline of urban fabric brought about by planning proposals that shorten the life of the buildings prior to land use change.

Police burgh. A town after 1850 which had provision for popularly elected commissioners to choose magistrates from their own number, to set up a police force and elementary improvement services and to levy rates to meet the costs.

Pontage. A toll for crossing a bridge.

Port. Originally it meant a walled or market town, later a point at which tolls were collected, or a gate or gateway of a walled town.

Repletion. The gradual filling-up of burgages with secondary building development in the gardens at the rear.

Roup. An auction.

Runrig. The intermixture of rigs (strips) occupied by different proprietors and/or tenants in the infield and sometimes in the outfield.

Sasine. The act of giving legal possession of feudal property; infeftment.

Small burgh. One of 174 burghs exercising powers under the Local Government (Scotland) Act 1929, being responsible only for housing, water, sewerage, lighting and cleansing. Any community with a population over 700 could become a small burgh until 1975.

Stallenger. A stall holder at a weekly market.

Stent. A valuation of property.

Stentmasters. Those appointed to fix the quota on any duty payable by the inhabitants of a burgh.

Stent-roll. Valuation roll.

Strath. A broad valley.

Tenement. The land held by a tenant in a community, i.e. his land in the fields of the township and the common rights attached to it.

Toft. Originally applied to a house, but later it came to be applied to a house site rather than a building.

Tolbooth. The building used for the burgh court, council and jail.

Tron. A weighing machine, but came to mean the market place.

Villein. An inhabitant of a manor to which he was bound as a
chattel to his lord.

Wapinschaw. A periodical muster or review of the men under arms
within a particular lordship or district.
Wynd. A narrow alley or street.

INDEX

Dalton, Meikle, 280
Damnonii 13
Darnaway 281
Darvel, population loss 257
daubing 58
David I, King of Scots (1124-53):
    burghs 21, 22; feudal policy 14;
    coinage 41
David II, King of Scots (1329-71)
    20, 21
Dean of Guild Court 152; origins of
    45
death-rates see population
deeds, register of 27
defensible space, concept of 276
depression, economic: 1877 onwards
    156; 1900s, 167, 194; interwar
    171, 195, 209, 234; 1950s 237,
    239
Deskford 279
development areas 238, 239, see also
    special areas
development plans 224-5, 260, 265
Dickson, James, MP 68
Dingwall 235, 278
Dirleton 280
disease, control of 137-41
distilleries 55, 77
district heating schemes 178, 213
ditcher 59
dog power 89
Dollar 280
Dornoch 256; councillors 129;
    foundation of 278; service centre
    255
Douglas, origins of 26, 281
Doune (Banff) 279
Doune (Perthshire) 251, 281
Dounreay nuclear plant 255
Down see Doune
Drem 280
drink, problem of 69, 88, 152, 156
Drumlithie 280
Drummochy, 280
Drummond, George, Provost of
    Edinburgh 74
Dryburgh 27, 279
Dublin 14
Duddingston, Wester 281
Dudhope 279
Dufftown 254, 257
Dumbarton 21, 193; corruption 128;
    early stronghold 13; foundation
    of 278; sacking of 13
Dumfries: castle 16; conservation
    275; crosses 36; dairies 99;
    Fish Cross 36; foundation of 280;
    gates 37; industries 249; markets
    39-40; population 246; royal
    burgh 278; walls 37
Dumfriesshire, Vikings in 14
Dunbar: corruption in 128; founda-
    tion of 278

Dunbeath, Inver of 280
Dunblane 252, 281
Dunbog 280
Dundas of Kerse, Sir Lawrence 109
Dundee: Beechwood 182; compre-
    hensive redevelopment areas 180,
    273; council housing 177-8;
    Craigiebank 178; death rates 140;
    development plan 178; district
    heating scheme 178; Fleming
    Gardens 178; Georgian expansion
    81-3; High School 82; Hilltown
    of 279; Hospital Park 178;
    housing stock 177-80; Improve-
    ment Act (1825) 82; Improve-
    ment Scheme 159; Kingsway 178;
    linen industry 92-3; Logie 178;
    origins 20, 278; overcrowding
    176; parks 148; public lighting
    in stairs 152; railways 113;
    Reform Street 82; roads 260;
    Rottenrow of 279; sewage 136;
    Stirling Park 178; Suburban
    Railway 118; Taybank 178;
    tramways 125; walls 37; water
    supply 136
Dundonald 279
Dunfermline: abbey 24; charter 22,
    278; development plan 206-7;
    ecclesiastical burgh 278; fortifica-
    tions 37; royal burgh 24, 278;
    trade of 24
Dunglass 27, 280
Dunkeld 14, 278, 281
Dunning 281
Dunoon 255-6; council housing 184;
    growth of 117; population loss
    257
Duns: administrative centre 249;
    bus services 249; foundation of
    279; population 247
Durris, failure of 27, 280
Dyos, H.J. 113
Dysart 45; burgh of barony 280;
    royal burgh 278
Earlsferry 24, 278; ecclesiastical
    burgh 278
Earlston 90, 279
East Kilbride 211-2; building research
    station 235; industrial growth
    239; neighbourhood units 212;
    opposition by Glasgow 227;
    proposed new town 210, 226;
    small burgh 267; target popula-
    tion 218, 219
East Linton 257
ecclesiastical burghs 24
Echt 279
Eddleston 281
Edinburgh: Abbeyhill 192; Advisory
    Committee on City Development
    211; archaeology 29; Atholl
    Crescent 76; Barnton Park 119;

293

Stobo 14
Stonehaven 252-3, 280
Stonehouse: burgh of barony 281;
 new town 218, 240
Stornoway: foundation 26, 56, 282;
 growth 256
Stranraer 250; dairies 99, 250; ferry
 terminal 250; origins 26, 278
Strathavon 33, 281
Strathclyde, kingdom of 13, 14
Strathdon 279
Strathisla 279
Strathmiglo 280
Strathmore 13
Strathyre 65
street manure 132
street pattern 31; convergent 33;
 medieval 33; parallel 33
Stromness: burgh of barony 281;
 population 256; water supply 137
Stuarton 282
Sutherland, Countess of 58
Swan, Joseph, inventor 145
swordmaker 43

Taba 13
tailor 59
Tain 236 255; foundation of 278
tallow and fat melter 132
Tarbat 282
Tarbert 278
Tarbolton 97, 279
Tarland 53, 279
Tava 13
Tayport 257, 280
Telford, Thomas, engineer 76, 135
tenements (buildings) 156-7; collapse
 of 74; investment in 166-7; model
 84
tenement (urban plot) 20, 21
Terregles 281
territorial theory 21
thatcher 59
Third Garden City Ltd 209
Thirlestane 279
Thomson, J. and G., shipbuilders 96,
 117
Thornhill 280
Thurso 255; atomic plant 246, 255;
 conservation 275; foundation of
 280; planning powers 223; popu-
 lation 257
Tillicoultry 280
tobacco trade 106; loss of 108; mer-
 chants 77, 108
Tobermory 256, 257
toft 20, 25, 33; tail of 37
Tolbooth 35, 42, 79
Toothill Report 239-40
Torphichen 51
Torry 26, 280
Torthorwald 280
town atlas 31

town council minutes 27
town definition of 11, 12
Town and Country Planning Associ-
 ation 209, 221
Town and Country Planning, mini-
 stry of 223
town house 35
Town Yetholm 282
Trades' Maiden Hospital, lands of
 188
tramways 119-25, 207; cable 122
Tranent 280
transportation, criminal 141
Trimontium 13
Tron 24, 35, 37
Troon 208
Troquhen 281
tuberculosis 140-1
Turriff 279
Tynninghame 280
typhoid 136

Uddingston 118
underground railway 119
Union, the 46, 51, 74, 106
Unwin, Raymond: Gretna 170;
 Letchworth 203; pamphlet 203;
 Westerton 207
urban aid programmes 231
urban archaeology 29
urban field 259
urban history, sources of 27
Urr 281
Uthwatt Committee 223
utopian settlements 203

Vale of Leven 240
Valleyfield 280
Victoria, town of 203
Vikings 13, 14
villa burghs 150
villages: coal-mining 55, 97; farm
 57-8; industrial 53
Votadini 12, 13

wages 156
Walkerburn 90
walls, town 36-7, 43
Wapinschaws 37, 43, 286
war, impact of: American 108;
 Crimean 93; French 141; World
 War I 169-70, 209; World War II
 31, 97, 105, 119, 176, 221, 223-4
watch and ward 21, 42
water supplies, 134-7
water power 42, 44, 58; cotton
 industry 88
Watherston, John & Sons, builders 77
Watt, James, engineer 88, 89
Waulk mill 68
weavers 44
weaving 53
weights and measures 41-2; courts for
 regulating 45